Typical and Atypical Child and Adolescent Development 7

Social Relations, Self-awareness and Identity

This concise guide offers an accessible introduction to social development, social relations, identity development and self-awareness from childhood to adolescence. It integrates insights from both typical and atypical development to reveal the fundamental aspects of human growth and development, and common developmental disorders.

The topic books in this series draw on international research in the field and are informed by biological, social and cultural perspectives, offering explanations of developmental phenomena with a focus on how children and adolescents at different ages actually think, feel and act. In this volume, Stephen von Tetzchner explains key topics including: attachment; sibling and peer relations; self and identity; gender development; play; media and understanding of society; and the transition toward adulthood.

Together with a companion website that offers topic-based quizzes, lecturer PowerPoint slides and sample essay questions, *Typical and Atypical Child and Adolescent Development 7: Social Relations, Self-awareness and Identity* is an essential text for all students of developmental psychology, as well as those working in the fields of child development, developmental disabilities and special education.

Stephen von Tetzchner is Professor of Developmental Psychology at the Department of Psychology, University of Oslo, Norway.

T0347491

The content of this topic book is taken from Stephen von Tetzchner's core textbook *Child and Adolescent Psychology: Typical and Atypical Development.* The comprehensive volume offers a complete overview of child and adolescent development – for more information visit www.routledge.com/9781138823396

Topics from Child and Adolescent Psychology Series
Stephen von Tetzchner

The **Topics from Child and Adolescent Psychology Series** offers concise guides on key aspects of child and adolescent development. They are formed from selected chapters from Stephen von Tetzchner's comprehensive textbook *Child and Adolescent Psychology: Typical and Atypical Development* and are intended to be accessible introductions for students of relevant modules on developmental psychology courses, as well as for professionals working in the fields of child development, developmental disabilities and special education. The topic books explain the key aspects of human development by integrating insights from typical and atypical development to cement understanding of the processes involved and the work with children who have developmental disorders. They examine sensory, physical and cognitive disabilities and the main emotional and behavioral disorders of childhood and adolescence, as well as the developmental consequences of these disabilities and disorders.

Topics books in the series

Typical and Atypical Child and Adolescent Development 1
Theory and Methodology

Typical and Atypical Child and Adolescent Development 2
Genes, Fetal Development and Early Neurological Development

Typical and Atypical Child and Adolescent Development 3
Perceptual and Motor Development

Typical and Atypical Child and Adolescent Development 4
Cognition, Intelligence and Learning

Typical and Atypical Child and Adolescent Development 5
Communication and Language Development

Typical and Atypical Child and Adolescent Development 6
Emotions, Temperament, Personality, Moral, Prosocial and Antisocial Development

Typical and Atypical Child and Adolescent Development 7
Social Relations, Self-awareness and Identity

For more information on individual topic books visit www.routledge.com/Topics-from-Child-and-Adolescent-Psychology/book-series/TFCAAP

Typical and Atypical Child and Adolescent Development 7

Social Relations, Self-awareness and Identity

Stephen von Tetzchner

Routledge
Taylor & Francis Group
LONDON AND NEW YORK

Cover image: © Getty Images

First published 2023
by Routledge
4 Park Square, Milton Park, Abingdon, Oxon OX14 4RN

and by Routledge
605 Third Avenue, New York, NY 10158

Routledge is an imprint of the Taylor & Francis Group, an informa business

© 2023 Stephen von Tetzchner

British Library Cataloguing-in-Publication Data
A catalogue record for this book is available from the British Library

Library of Congress Cataloging-in-Publication Data
A catalog record has been requested for this book

ISBN: 978-1-032-27409-6 (hbk)
ISBN: 978-1-032-26782-1 (pbk)
ISBN: 978-1-003-29257-9 (ebk)

DOI: 10.4324/9781003292579

Typeset in Bembo
by Apex CoVantage, LLC

Access the companion website: www.routledge.com/cw/vonTetzchner

Contents

Introduction

Human development to maturity stretches over about 20 years. It is an age-related process involving changes in structures and functions. Social relations are the essence of human life, and participation in social and societal activities promotes social development and enculturation. Infants are attentive to social stimulation from birth, and their first social relationships are usually within the family. Children and adolescents form social relationships and find their place in society. Changes in social relations are thus an integrated part of development, from the early family relations to the development of identity and fulfilling of various roles in society. In the first years of life, children are dependent on caregivers for physical and emotional protection and survival. Peer relations gradually become more important through childhood and adolescence. The six parts of this book present core issues related to the development of social and societal relations, the formation of self and identity and becoming a citizen, building on the models of development and the developmental way of thinking presented in Book 1, *Theory and Methodology*.

Most individual differences in personal traits and abilities emerge not directly from a particular biological or environmental factor but rather as a result of *interaction effects*, where biological and environmental factors are moderated by one or several other factors. Moreover, development is never a one-way process: it is a *transactional process*, characterized by reciprocal influences between the child and the environment over time. Readers may find it useful to consult the part about developmental models in Book 1, *Theory and Methodology*, or the corresponding chapters in the complete book before reading the present book.

The present book includes both typical social and societal development, which is the most common course with unimpaired functions and ordinary individual differences between children, and atypical development, which represents various degrees of unusual or irregular development, including the development of children and adolescents who have difficulties establishing social relations or adapting to their roles in society. The issues presented in this book are particularly relevant for teachers, special educators and other staff in preschool and school. Their task is to support development and learning, and insight into the processes underlying children's and adolescents' relations with adults and peers is necessary for adapting educational strategies to each student's needs, as well as the social environment in kindergarten and school.

Infants are dependent on others for care, protection and survival, as well as for exploring and learning about the world. They are equipped to ensure social closeness. *Part I Attachment* is about children's development of early social relations and the establishment of emotional bonds between children and their caregivers. Children will usually seek proximity to the caregiver when they perceive a situation as uncertain or stressful, and caregivers will typically react by giving comfort and care and functioning as a secure basis for young children's exploration in new situations. The basic assumption of attachment theory is that attachment gives the child a feeling of security when the caregiver is available and one of insecurity if the caregiver is away and unavailable when the child is in situations they perceive as uncertain or stressful. Children's experiences with exploration and caregivers' sensitivity and availability in unknown or uncertain situations will influence the attachment process and how children perceive the social world and cope in uncertain social situations. It is assumed that children's early interaction patterns with exploration and attachment contribute to individual differences in social understanding and how children meet people and establish social relations later in life. Most children develop secure attachment and positive social relations, but some experience many situations with poor availability of caregivers. A small group of children grow up with abusing or unpredictable caregivers, and they may develop attachment disorders (see also Book 1, *Theory and Methodology*, Part IV).

Siblings and peers are central in children's and adolescents' social life. *Part II Sibling and Peer Relations* is about the development of horizontal relations and the influence of siblings and peers on children's and adolescents' development. Sibling relations are unique, because siblings usually share all kinds of events, spend much time together and have close emotional bonds. They show both care for each other and competitiveness and learn from their many collaborations and disagreements. This relationship may be even more significant when one of the siblings has a disability. Sibling relationships often last a lifetime.

Peer relations represent the beginning of a wider social network and are important from an early age. Infants and toddlers tend to be more attentive to peers than to adults. Older children and adolescents may spend more time with peers than with their parents. Popularity and acceptance from peers are very important for most children and adolescents, and popularity status can have significant positive or negative influences on their development, academic achievement and social adaptation. It is a reciprocal influence: peer acceptance may reflect children's social adaptation, and children's social adaptation may reflect how they are accepted by peers.

Friendships are pivotal relationships. Children start to have special relationships early; there are some children they like more than others, and, although friends may change, friendships remain essential throughout development. Children's perception of friends changes with age, from somebody they play and do things together with to a person with whom they share emotional closeness and engage in long conversations. Contact on social media has become an important aspect of friendship among older children and adolescents (see Chapter 38, this volume).

Friendships constitute a positive social force in the lives of children and adolescents, but peer relationships also include enemies. Hostile relations are a negative social force that may be as stable as friendships.

The awareness of being a unique person together with many other unique persons in the world distinguishes humans from other species. *Part III Self and Identity* is about the emergence of self-understanding and identity and the age-related changes in how children and adolescents perceive themselves, establish social affiliations and find their place in society. Self-perception emerges gradually, a sense of being and acting in a multifaceted world, and children and adolescents present increasingly differentiated and complex self-descriptions. Identity formation represent a continuation of self-perception, involving the experience of being similar to some and different from other groups in society. Identity implies finding one's place in society and managing the relevant roles. Self-understanding and identity both connect the individual with others and set them apart. It is a complex developmental process leading to individual differences in how children and adolescents perceive and evaluate themselves. Self-perception and identity are closely related to personality (see Book 6, *Emotions, Temperament, Personality, Moral, Prosocial and Antisocial Development*, Part II). The importance of self-development is also reflected in the relation between low self-esteem and depression, and between atypical development of self-image and eating disorders and narcissism.

Gender is a major factor in developmental psychology, and studies routinely report separate results for boys and girls. *Part IV Gender Development* is about the emerging identity as a girl or a boy and the development of sex-typed behaviors. Boys and girls develop somewhat differently in some areas, show differences in activity preferences and have somewhat different ways of meeting challenges, both in childhood and later in life. The developmental psychological issue is how these differences may arise and how they differ between cultures. Boys and girls are treated somewhat differently by parents, other adults and peers and are typically portrayed in line with the society's gender roles in literature and film. Studies tend to focus on differences between boys and girls, but, from a developmental perspective and way of thinking, equality and lack of differences are as important as differences. Moreover, in most areas, there is considerable variation among girls and among boys. These variations are often much larger than the average group difference between boys and girls. Some children and adolescents show atypical development of gender identity. They may feel that they are born into the wrong body or have difficulties living the role as boy or girl. It affects their basic understanding of themselves and their role in society, and many in these groups experience severe mental health problems.

Human societies include large and small shared activities. The content of the activities varies with cultural background and age, and in most societies play is a leading activity in childhood. *Part V Play* is about the development of different forms of play throughout childhood and the functions developmental theories attribute to play. Play may take many forms, from building small block towers to assembling complex Lego buildings or from moving a toy train in circles to integrating the train in an interesting travel story, and may involve real or imaginary places, people and animals. Symbolic play is often a way for children to investigate the adult world in their own way and thereby gain insight into how their society works. Play is thus a part of the enculturation process and contributes to children's learning and adaptation, both within and outside home and school. Children's earliest play depends on adult involvement and support, but, as they get older, children play more with peers and become increasingly independent of adult support.

How children play reflects their general development, and play is sometimes used to assess children's development. Some children have difficulties engaging in play. For example, children with motor impairments may have difficulties performing the physical actions needed in the play, and children with autism spectrum disorders may struggle to understand pretend play. However, play is equally important for children with disabilities and for children with typical development. It is often an important goal of intervention to guide children with disabilities to take part in play activities.

Part VI Media and Understanding of Society is about media use among children and adolescents and their development of societal knowledge. The social media are used for organizing peer interaction and are a major force in shaping the social interaction patterns of modern societies. Children are exposed to media from an early age, and the majority spends much of their free time attending to entertainment, gaming, chatting or having distance conversations on the internet. The developmental question is how the internet and social media impact the development and learning of children and adolescents, and especially their attitudes to society and events that take place. The internet and social media have become important influences on social development and interaction among children and adolescents, and the consequences are not yet known.

Modern societies are complex, and children are quite old before they begin to understand the social organization and the processes involved in the economic system. *Part VI* also addresses children's emergent understanding of society and how children and adolescents understand the social, economic and political processes of the society in which they live, including the causes and implications of economic and social inequality. This knowledge is important for their development of autonomy in society and coping in adult life.

Some of the terminology used in developmental psychology may be unfamiliar to some readers. Many of these terms can be found in the Glossary.

Part I

Attachment

1

Early Social Relations

From birth throughout the life span, human beings are oriented toward social stimulation and participation, making social relations a core area of developmental psychology. This chapter is about children's early social relations and the influence they may have on the child's social functioning and **development**. According to **attachment** theories, early close relationships provide children with knowledge about social relations that forms the basis for how they meet other people and contributes to forming their later reactions and behaviors.

Attachment behavior is defined as "any behavior that results in a person attaining or maintaining proximity to some other clearly identified individual who is conceived as better able to cope with the world" (Bowlby, 1982, p. 669). Thus, the function of attachment behaviors is to ensure a feeling of safety by reducing the physical distance to specific individuals, *attachment figures*. If a child's attachment system is to perform its function, attachment figures must respond to the child's attachment behavior. Adults react to signaling behavior by reducing the distance to the child when necessary, calling the child or moving closer when the distance exceeds a certain limit, for example when the child has wandered off (Bowlby, 1969).

DOI: 10.4324/9781003292579-2

2

Theoretical Perspectives on Attachment

Views differ with regard to the basis of attachment and the possible outcomes of different types of attachment. John Bowlby presented the first comprehensive theory of attachment and laid the foundation for all later theories (Hinde, 2005). Bowlby's ethological theory will therefore be presented first and in particular detail, although some other views predated his.

Seeking security by the mother.

DOI: 10.4324/9781003292579-3

Ethological Theory

Attachment has to do with relationships, the biological basis of which, according to Bowlby (1969), is survival. From an evolutionary perspective, the survival value of attachment behavior lies in the fact that human infants would be unable to survive without a caregiver. The same applies to infant monkeys, although their development is somewhat faster (Suomi, 2008). The **imprinting** behavior of ducks and other birds seems to fulfill a similar function as attachment behavior in humans (see Figure 2.1), with the difference that imprinting in birds must occur within a short **critical period** to be functional as birds mature quickly. Also, birds show distress at separation from their mother after being imprinted. In humans, the attachment process moves far more slowly, and attachment relations can only change over longer periods (Ainsworth & Bowlby, 1991; Bowlby, 1982).

According to Bowlby (1969, 1973, 1980), attachment is an innate **behavioral system** with the task of ensuring **protection** through proximity to an attachment figure. The need for security is an independent drive in line with nutritional needs and sexual behavior.

Figure 2.1 Imprinting in birds.

The imprinting of ducklings relies on the fact that they follow the first moving object or living being they see within a period of **48** hours and will seek out the imprinting object in situations that elicit attachment behavior. Konrad Lorenz (1935) was able to imprint ducklings to any moving object within the critical period, regardless of whether it was a human being or a rolling ball, providing the eggs were hatched in an incubator. When the mother duck sits on her eggs, she will usually exchange sounds with the unhatched ducklings toward the end of the incubation period. This exchange allows the ducklings and the mother to recognize each other, helping to ensure that imprinting between mother and offspring takes place and reducing the likelihood that the ducklings will be "malimprinted" (Hess, 1972).

John Bowlby.

Attachment behavior is regulated by a *control system* comparable to the autonomous parts of the nervous system that regulate blood pressure and body temperature. The function of this control system is to keep the attachment figure within certain boundaries of distance and availability, depending on the child's state and the situation. To achieve this, children use increasingly sophisticated ways of communicating, making the development of **communication** and language an important element in attachment. Attachment is an active process rather than passive dependence (Ainsworth & Bowlby, 1991).

The theory is based on the premise that attachment behavior must be reciprocated by someone who provides the necessary care. Bowlby proposes that adults have a *caregiving behavioral system* that is activated by the child's attachment behavior. Parents (and other adults) are thus biologically predisposed to react in certain ways to children's attachment behavior. Given a normal development, parents will experience a strong urge to hold their child, give comfort when the child cries, keep the child warm and protect and feed the child. As the **caregiving**

system, too, has evolved through evolution, parental behavior will to some extent follow a predetermined pattern, but the parents' social and cultural experiences determine how this behavior manifests itself.

At the core of the theory lies the notion that children form "working models" for their later relationships with other people (Bowlby, 1969). A **working model** is a "map" based on past experiences that includes information about the interactions with another person in a relationship, and particularly the person's availability and responsiveness to the child. These working models form the basis for children's perceptions and expectations of others and themselves and determine how children meet their social environment and new relational partners. Feelings toward others are an integral part of the working models, and children's feelings, as well as the quality of the relationship, are the result of attachment experiences. By and large, they lead to security and love, but can also give rise to anger and rejection.

Experiences from early relationships are thus preserved in the form of working models. As children have a particular need for protection during the first 3–4 years of life, these years can be seen as a primary period in the development of relationships. The formation of working models affects children's security and explorative behavior in the years to come. Although later experiences can lead to changes in working models, change is usually limited and occurs slowly over time, according to Bowlby. Despite any such changes, early working models set a strong precedent for how children relate to other people later in life.

Primary Needs

The earliest explanations of attachment behavior suggested that children become attached to the people who fulfill their primary needs. **Psychoanalytic theory** viewed attachment behavior as an expression of dependency resulting from the fulfillment of primary needs and oral stimulation (Levert-Levitt & Sagi-Schwartz, 2015). **Behaviorism** placed attachment on equal terms with all other behavior, learned through **conditioning** and reinforced by satisfying primary needs (Dollard & Miller, 1950).

Monkey studies have been used to gain insight into the importance of feeding and nursing in establishing attachment relationships. In a classic study, eight infant monkeys were separated from their mothers 12 hours after birth and grew up in a cage with two "mother figures" – one made of wire, the other of soft cloth (Harlow, 1959; Box 2.1).

Box 2.1   The Role of Primary Needs in the Development of Attachment (Harlow, 1959)

Infant monkeys were separated from their mothers 12 hours after birth and placed alone in a cage with two "surrogate mothers" – one made of wire, the other made of soft cloth. Four of the infant monkeys could suck milk from the teat of the wire figure, while the other four could suck milk from the cloth figure. In the first 6 months of their lives, the monkeys spent 14–18 hours a day with the cloth figures and far less time with the wire figures. Even when the wire surrogate dispensed milk, the monkeys spent less than 2 hours a day with it. When an unfamiliar mechanical "spider" with blinking lights was placed in the cage, an event that normally would elicit attachment behavior, all the monkeys kept near the soft cloth surrogate. (Photographs courtesy of Harlow Primate Laboratory)

The infant monkeys spent far less time with the wire mother than with the cloth mother, regardless of where they got the milk, and, in situations that normally would elicit attachment behavior, all the monkeys kept near the soft cloth surrogate. This suggests that the cloth "mothers" provided better external comfort and help for the monkeys' ability to regulate their emotional insecurity than the steel wire figures that dispensed milk. The results indicate that attachment behavior is not related to fulfillment of basic needs and thus refute the views of early behavioral and psychoanalytic theories.

Separation Theory

Margaret Mahler represents object-relation theory in the psychodynamic tradition. In **psychodynamic theory**, a mental "**object**" is an internal representation of a person or a thing targeted by a drive, or the means by which the drive can achieve its goal (see Book 1, *Theory and Methodology*, Chapter 11). One of the key features of Mahler's theory is newborns' inability to distinguish between internal and external regulation, such as experienced restlessness due to hunger and nourishment provided by the caregiver (Mahler et al., 1975). Mahler believes infants establish their first mental **representations** of the environment together with their mother and only slowly learn to distinguish between her and themselves through what she calls a "psychological birth." Although infants incorporate a representation of themselves as well as one of the maternal object, they are unable to fully distinguish between them until the age of 12–18 months. Therefore, no clear relationship exists between the two objects early in children's lives. The **self** as an object is gradually distilled through a process of *separation-individuation* that leads children to form a distinct and independent representation of themselves. In Mahler's theory, relationships are not formed as the result of common experiences between caregiver and child, such as Bowlby's theory proposes. Instead, the relationship emerges as a link between self-object and maternal object once children are able to distinguish between mental representations of themselves and of their mother. As the separation and individuation process, according to Mahler, is affected by maternal sensitivity, it is the mother who shapes the child's attachment.

Mahler's description of development and her assumption that children are unable to mentally distinguish between themselves and their mother have met with considerable criticism, also within the psychodynamic tradition. According to Daniel Stern (1998), there is no empirical basis for such an assumption. He maintains that newborns begin by forming a **perception** of themselves that furnishes the basis for the maternal relationship as well as relationships with other caregivers (see Chapter 20, this volume). Additionally, the results of attachment research are clearly at odds with Mahler's assumption that a child's first relationship exclusively revolves around the biological mother (see Chapter 3, this volume).

Peter Fonagy represents a radical deviation from the common conception of attachment. He builds on Mahler's theory but considers that the function of early relationships and attachment is to pave the way for **mentalizing** and **mind understanding** (see Book 4, *Cognition, Intelligence and Learning*, Part IV; Fonagy et al., 2002, 2007). In Fonagy's theory of self-reflection and mentalizing, the experiences in the attachment relationship lead to an understanding of self and others. This has limited relevance for attachment as a relational and emotional system, as it is understood by Bowlby and most others. Moreover, studies have found little direct connection between attachment and mind understanding (Ontai & Thompson, 2008).

3

The Development of Attachment

Around the age of 2 months, children begin to show selective **recognition** of familiar persons, but distinct attachment behavior involving *positive selection* of other people does not occur until about 7 months. Children at this age also begin to show *negative selection* in the form of reticence toward strangers (see Book 6, *Emotions, Temperament, Personality, Moral, Prosocial and Antisocial Development*, Chapter 6). However, there are significant individual differences, and the age at which children begin to show clear selectivity can vary from 3½ to 15 months.

There are two main classes of attachment behavior: *signaling behavior* includes facial expressions, smiling, crying, and **gestures** or postures that cause others to approach; *approach behavior* includes crawling, walking and other forms of locomotion that bring the child closer to the attachment figure. Once children are capable of independent locomotion, their approach behavior increases. Tension is reduced when proximity is achieved, whereas failing to achieve proximity results in separation anxiety (Table 3.1).

Attachment behavior is activated when a child is at some distance from the attachment figure *and* experiences emotional arousal such as pain, fear, stress, insecurity or anxiety (Bowlby, 1969, 1982). In most such situations, there is no actual danger, but the child is feeling insecure. In younger children, the absence of an attachment figure in insecure situations leads to anxiousness and attachment behavior. Unfamiliar people, places and routines are always alarming to children, especially when they meet them on their own. Illness, fatigue and the like will additionally lower children's threshold for seeking an attachment figure, as they make children more vulnerable and increase their need for protection. It is the combination of the child's condition and the distance from the attachment figure that activates attachment

DOI: 10.4324/9781003292579-4

Table 3.1 Characteristics of attachment behavior (based on Bowlby, 1982)

- Attachment behavior is selective and directed toward specific figures who elicit attachment behavior in a way and to an extent not found in interaction with other people
- Attachment behavior involves seeking and trying to maintain physical proximity with the attachment figure
- Attachment behavior is most readily elicited when children are ill or otherwise in a vulnerable state
- Attachment behavior creates a sense of comfort and safety as a result of having attained proximity to the attachment figure
- Attachment behavior leads to separation anxiety when the bond to the attachment figure is severed, and proximity cannot be achieved

behavior. Children's reaction to the absence of an attachment figure can be mitigated, however, by the presence of a familiar person such as a sibling or a friend, and even an object such as a favorite teddy bear can have a mitigating effect.

What causes attachment behavior to *cease* is determined by its emotional intensity. If it is low, sight or the voice of the child's mother or other attachment figure will be sufficient. At higher intensities, it will only cease when the child can touch or cling to the attachment figure. When children are very upset and frightened, prolonged comfort may be necessary. An important consequence of attachment behavior is that the attachment figure helps the child understand and master situations involving insecurity and fear. Children with secure attachment (see the following) associate negative **emotions** with help and support from an attachment figure and therefore do not become emotionally overwhelmed by such emotions. They seek help and receive emotional support in directing their attention and resources at evaluating the situation and discovering appropriate coping strategies, while adults represent a *safe base* for exploring objects and places that potentially elicit fear. The attachment process thus forms part of the foundation for the development of **emotion regulation** in general (Zimmer-Gembeck et al., 2017).

As infants usually spend most of their time together with the mother, attachment behavior is often directed at her, especially when intensity is high. However, as early as 18 months of age, the majority of children show attachment to several persons (Schaffer & Emerson, 1964), and the loss of a nanny "can be almost as tragic as the loss of a mother" (Bowlby, 1958, p. 7).

Studies of children who were adopted after growing up in poor orphanages with limited access to adults suggest that the first 2 years constitute a **sensitive period** for establishing primary attachment relations (see Book 6, *Emotions, Temperament, Personality, Moral, Prosocial and Antisocial Development*, Chapter 16). Attachment behavior is most apparent in the second and third years of life. Around 4 years of age, the basic attachment period is over, and children's physical and social world greatly expands. From this age on, children no longer react to physical separation from an attachment figure in the same way as during early **childhood**, as they *know* that the person will be available. Four-year-olds show less anxiety at being separated from their mother than 3-year-olds when the mother's temporary absence has been agreed on in advance. They also begin to feel more secure with people other than attachment figures, providing the person is familiar, such as a teacher or a schoolmate. This also assumes that the child is not ill or distressed about something and knows that the person will be available in the foreseeable future. In preschool-age children, attachment behavior, including crying and expressions of despair, is particularly common in situations with little overview, for example when a child is separated from the parents in a busy shopping mall. Although children's attachment behavior becomes less pronounced as they approach **school age**, they continue to seek out their parents or other close individuals when they feel afraid or insecure, and attachment behavior is as important in early school age as in **infancy** (Marvin et al., 2016). This can also include peers, but friendship and attachment are two different things. Interview studies have found that children like to spend time with their friends, but seek out their parents for security (Seibert & Kerns, 2009).

In the course of childhood, both security and insecurity manifest themselves in new ways. Things that caused children to react with fear or anxiety in **preschool age** are no longer perceived as threatening. Availability of attachment figures entails that they are receptive and open to communicate about emotional issues. In school age, psychological proximity becomes more important than physical proximity; knowledge about future availability, that an attachment figure will return, takes precedence. Children are now able to be apart from their mother and other attachment figures for longer periods and do not need to make direct contact to restore a sense of security – a phone call can be enough (Kerns & Brumariu, 2016; Mayseless, 2005).

In **adolescence**, attachment becomes less distinct and the behavior more varied. The need for security via others not only diminishes but runs counter to adolescents' need for independence and the growing **autonomy** typical of this age (Ammaniti et al., 2000). Adolescents more often use their friends when they feel a need for security, and, although they begin to develop emotional ties in romantic relationships, these are activated and terminated under different conditions and therefore do not replace the attachment relationship with parents. Romantic relationships are more reciprocal than attachment relationships, in which an older generation protects a younger one.

Still, even in adulthood, attachment to parents and other important persons does not disappear. According to Bowlby, attachment fulfills the same function throughout life: to seek and maintain proximity. Adult relations, too, can be described as either secure or insecure. Signs of insecure attachment in adulthood include lack of openness or undiscriminating intimacy, excessive jealousy, feelings of loneliness in relationships, a reluctance to commit oneself, and excessive demands for attention by the other person (Hazan & Shaver, 1994; Morrison et al., 1997). The unavailability of an attachment figure in difficult situations – either physical or mental – can lead to problems with emotion regulation and occasionally result in a deactivation of the attachment system (Marvin & Britner, 2008; Mikulincer & Shaver, 2008).

Exploration

The attachment system provides children with knowledge about the availability of people who can ensure their safety and whereabouts, but they also need to learn what is safe and what is dangerous in their surroundings, knowledge they acquire through **exploration** (Bowlby, 1982). **Exploratory behavior** consists of three basic elements: an **orienting response**, movement in the direction of the object and physical investigation of the object by manipulating it or experimenting with it in other ways. Exploration is activated by unfamiliar and/or complex objects and locations. Once an object has been investigated and becomes familiar to the child, exploration ceases.

Attachment and exploration are activated under almost identical conditions, but, whereas attachment behavior leads to proximity, exploratory behavior creates more distance to the attachment figure. Attachment behavior is elicited by fear and insecurity, whereas exploration takes place when something catches children's interest and they feel relatively secure. When the attachment figure moves further away from the child, attachment behavior is activated, whereas exploratory behavior is more easily activated when the attachment figure approaches, for example in situations involving fascinating objects such as toys or animals. By means of attachment, familiar adults become a **secure base** for controlled exploration of objects and locations that otherwise can elicit insecurity or fear, a base the child alternately leaves and returns to (Ainsworth, 1963). Young children typically show rapid shifts between attachment and exploratory behavior, skepticism and interest, most often with an initially skeptical attitude.

Thus, attachment and exploration are to some extent complementary ways of meeting new situations, meaning that exploratory behavior is inhibited in situations in which children show attachment behavior. When the two systems come into conflict with each other, children may obtain emotional information by watching others (**social referencing**; see Book 6, *Emotions, Temperament, Personality, Moral, Prosocial and Antisocial Development*, Chapter 6), which then determines what system is activated. If the child sees the attachment figure smile, tension is reduced, and the exploratory system is activated. If the attachment figure looks worried or frightened, tension increases, and the attachment system is activated.

4

Individual Differences in Attachment

According to Bowlby (1969, 1982), **individual differences** in attachment behavior are the result of children's experiences in connection with separation from or loss of an attachment figure. The attachment figure provides the child with information about the environment, alerts the child to danger and safety, and helps the child understand what takes place in the surrounding world, knowledge children eventually seek out themselves through social referencing. When children first seek physical closeness, they do not know what this closeness entails, but the physical proximity fundamental to attachment behavior simultaneously forms the basis for the emotional relationship between child and attachment figure. By being sensitive to children's gradual coping with such situations, caregivers ensure children's cooperation and give them the security to explore the world (Ainsworth, 1983).

Children can show many different reactions in situations that activate attachment behavior, and no other type of behavior is accompanied by stronger emotions. Children's experiences when they seek physical proximity to an attachment figure determine the kinds of feelings they develop for this person. Joy and devotion are the most common. When 4-month-old infants see their mother or another caregiver after a brief separation, their most likely reaction is a smile of recognition, which often leads the caregiver to respond by smiling, chitchatting and similar. Also, later in children's lives, a reunion that leads to the termination of attachment behavior will usually involve expressions of joy.

Most children are met with warmth and care, but some children experience being rejected or even beaten when they approach an attachment figure. Under such conditions, children can associate the relationship with emotions such as anger, hatred and insecurity. These

DOI: 10.4324/9781003292579-5

emotional reactions are not the result of defunct love, but rather of children's past experiences with situations that activate attachment behavior, telling them that the relationship includes these types of emotions. It is children's way of adapting their emotions to the environment. Although positive feelings are most common, the emotional outcome depends on the availability of attachment figures and the way in which the relationships between children and their attachment figures develop.

How children themselves react to reunion also depends on their state of health and mind. After a brief separation without unfamiliar things or illness in the child's life, the most likely reaction is a smile. If the separation has lasted for a longer period without regular routines, the child will often cry and cling to the attachment figure or become quiet and less responsive. After prolonged separation, attachment behavior can assume more unusual forms by either increasing in intensity or being absent altogether. Anger can be a reaction to the unavailability of an attachment figure. In connection with temporary separations, which represent the majority of instances, anger has two functions: first, to empower the child to overcome the obstacles on the way to reunion, and, second, to try to ensure that the attachment figure does not disappear again. This type of anger does not destroy the emotional bond between child and attachment figure but strengthens it. The attachment figure, too, can show anger, for example when a child suddenly runs across the street or otherwise exposes herself to danger.

Thus, both anger and physical approach are behavioral strategies rooted in the attachment system. Children may react to insecurity by wanting to establish maximal access to the attachment figure and by showing anger at feelings or potential threats of abandonment. It is an emotional balancing act. Children can be furious at the attachment figure, only to seek confirmation and consolation from the same person the next moment. Paradoxically, children who have been abused by their parents show strong signs of attachment. Children who have been adopted away from a neglectful or abusive attachment figure can show anger and rejection for some time before becoming attached to caring adoptive or foster parents (Raby et al., 2017). As fear and anger are activated under the same conditions, they often occur simultaneously, and an increase in the intensity of one emotion can at times strengthen the other.

Occasionally, anger can become so intense as to damage the emotional bond between child and caregiver. This happens when children are exposed to many separations and threats of abandonment, threats they perceive as real and plausible. Under such circumstances, children can experience tremendous conflict. They meet the threat of separation with anger, but dare not show their anger for fear of being abandoned, or express it toward other people or in other contexts. They can show a strong sense of ownership, deep insecurity and intense anger toward their attachment figures, sometimes resulting in a vicious circle: their fear of losing the attachment figure creates anger and in turn increases their fear of separation, and so on. They show anxiety, ownership and concern for the other person's welfare, afraid that something might happen to the attachment figure. There is a thin line between love and hate in an attachment relationship.

Measures of Attachment

Several ways for measuring attachment have been developed (Solomon & George, 2016). However, the **Strange Situation** is regarded as the "gold standard" for measuring attachment in 1–3-year-olds by observing how they react to separation from and subsequent reunion with their mother or another attachment figure in unfamiliar surroundings (Ainsworth & Wittig, 1969). It consists of seven 3-minute episodes in which the child is either together with the mother and/ or a stranger, or left alone (see Table 4.1). Particular emphasis is on the different ways 1-year-olds react to episodes 4 and 7 in which the mother comes back after having left the room and the child has been alone with a stranger.

An observer records the child's level of activity, play, crying and other signs of uneasiness, distance to the mother (or other familiar person), attempts to get her attention, distance to the stranger and willingness to interact with her or him. Apart from the 30-second introduction (episode 0), each episode lasts for 3 minutes, for a total of 21 minutes.

Children's reactions in the Strange Situation are commonly classified into three main groups: *A – insecure-avoidant*, *B – secure* and *C – insecure-resistant* (Ainsworth et al., 1978). Later research has led to an additional category, D – *insecure-disorganized* (Main & Weston, 1981). The behaviors that characterize each of these four types are described in Table 4.2. Secure attachment (B) can be observed when the child shows signs of missing the attachment figure at the time of separation, greets her and shows joy over the reunion and once again returns to

Table 4.1 The Strange Situation (Ainsworth et al., 1978, p. 34)

Episode	Persons	Event
0	Mother, child	The observer leads the mother (or another person familiar to the child) and child into the experiment room
1	Mother, child	The mother places the child on the floor among a collection of toys and leaves to sit down in a chair at the other end of the room. The child observes without the mother's participation. If necessary, the mother encourages the child to play during the last minute
2	Mother, child, stranger	The stranger enters, remains quiet for 1 minute and speaks to the mother for 1 minute. Then he or she tries to get the child to play with a toy
3	Child, stranger	The mother leaves the room inconspicuously. The stranger's behavior depends on the child. If the child neither cries nor shows other signs of uneasiness, the stranger quietly sits down next to the child. If the child cries or seems upset, the stranger tries to comfort the child
4	Mother, child	The mother returns, greets or comforts the child and tries to get the child to play while the stranger leaves
5	Child	The mother leaves, and the child is left completely alone
6	Child, stranger	The stranger enters, his or her behavior depending on the child as in episode 3
7	Mother, child	The mother returns, and the stranger leaves

Note: An observer records the child's level of **activity**, play, crying and other signs of uneasiness, distance to the mother (or other familiar person), attempts to get her attention, distance to the stranger and willingness to interact with her or him. Apart from the 30-second introduction (episode 0), each episode lasts for 3 minutes, for a total of 21 minutes.

play with toys. Categories A and C do not represent disorders but alternative strategies for dealing with separation. There is disagreement about whether the behavior in category D actually reflects an attachment relationship or the fact that the child has not formed such a relationship. It is lack of, rather than a quality of, attachment. As children in this category often develop **mental disorders**, their behavior is of major clinical importance (Bernier & Meins, 2008; Rutter et al.,

Table 4.2 Types of attachment

A Insecure-avoidant	Children pay little attention to their mother while she is in the room and often show no signs of distress when she leaves. They turn or look away when their mother returns, rather than seeking closeness and comfort. Some children reject their mother, while others show mixed attempts at interaction and avoiding interaction. They are as easily comforted by the stranger as by the mother
B Secure	Some children do not care that their mother is leaving, whereas others become quite upset. When the mother returns after the separation, the child approaches her, is easily quieted if upset and quickly begins to play again. Some children notice their mother returning and immediately continue to play, whereas others go up to her
C Insecure-resistant	Children in this category are often upset simply because they are in a foreign environment, even when they are together with their mother. They get quite agitated when she leaves, seeking both proximity and resisting contact when she returns. They can cry in order to be picked up and comforted, and fight to be let go of when they are picked up
D Insecure-disorganized	These children typically show contradictory behavior, for example by approaching their mother without looking at her. Some children can appear disorganized, unemotional and depressed

2009). In addition, the classification is not absolute: some children show behaviors that do not clearly fall into any of the four categories.

The purpose behind these categories is not to specify children's general characteristics, such as descriptions of **personality traits**, but to characterize the quality of the specific relationship between the child and the adult in the Strange Situation. Usually, it is the child's mother or father, but can also include other people with whom the child has a relationship. Additionally, it is important to emphasize that the differences between children lie in the *quality* of the attachment relationship; its strength or intensity is irrelevant as long as the relationship is intact (Rutter et al., 2009; Sroufe et al., 2005).

Main and Weston (1981) compared children's attachment behavior when they were together with each of the parents. Some children showed secure attachment to the mother and insecure attachment to the father. For others, the reverse was true. Although children often relate in similar ways to both parents in situations that activate attachment, a significant percentage of children show different types of attachment behavior with each parent (Fox et al., 1991). Children's attachment behavior does not always form a consistent pattern, but depends on the individual relationship. The close relationships children engage in, however different they may be, together form the basis for how the children meet other people.

The Strange Situation can provide valuable insights into children's early relationships and has been used extensively in research. Kagan (1998a), on the other hand, maintains that it is unreasonable to assume that a 21-minute observation would be able to capture important qualities of children's relationships that have taken shape over thousands of hours of time spent in the company of others. Besides, most studies use only a few of the standard 21 minutes. Cultural differences in the statistical distribution of attachment behaviors give reason to question what children's reactions in the Strange Situation actually reveal (see Chapter 6, this volume). The Strange Situation should furthermore be used with caution in clinical practice, as its use is limited to the age of 2–3 years, and research has found relatively little **correspondence** between early insecure attachment and later disorders (Rutter et al., 2009).

Another way of measuring attachment is the *Attachment Q-set* (Waters, 1995). It is an observation form that consists of 90 behavioral types that provide information about the child's behavior in natural situations involving attachment reactions, and it is considerably more time-consuming than the Strange Situation. In addition, there are a growing number of questionnaires and interviews to measure various aspects of attachment relationships from infancy to adulthood (Crowell et al., 2008; Fairchild, 2006; Kerns & Brumariu, 2016).

Attachment and Adult Sensitivity

For a relationship to be secure, the attachment figure must be available, reliable and predictable, characteristics Ainsworth, in line with Bowlby's theory, refers to as "**sensitivity**." In a study of 21 children, she found a high **correlation** (0.78) between the children's attachment behavior and the mothers' sensitivity, meaning how frequently, quickly and adequately they reacted to their child. Mothers of children who showed secure attachment in this situation reacted quickly when the child cried, consistent with what they believed to be the cause of the crying. Mothers of children who showed insecure attachment responded more rarely and inconsistently to the child's crying. Children with insecure-resistant attachment had mothers who seemed little concerned, whereas mothers of children with insecure-avoidant attachment tended to feed and look after their children based on rules and routines rather than in response to signs indicating that the child had specific needs (Ainsworth et al., 1972).

Other studies have found significantly lower correspondences between maternal sensitivity and children's attachment (correlations of about 0.24). Although this suggests a certain connection between maternal sensitivity and children's attachment behavior, it is fairly modest. Other characteristics of maternal behavior show nearly the same correlation with children's attachment types, such as stimulation strategies, reciprocity and emotional support (Goldsmith & Alansky, 1987; Nievar & Becker, 2008; de Wolff & van IJzendoorn, 1997). One reason may be that maternal sensitivity is not related to attachment alone, but influences many aspects of development. Moreover, within a **transactional model**, the child may influence the mother's sensitivity (see Book 1, *Theory and Methodology*, Chapter 6).

Some parents show very little sensitivity and may instead evoke fear in their child. In particular, children with insecure-disorganized attachment (category D) may have been subjected to abuse, maltreatment or frightening experiences. This form of attachment behavior may be the result of inconsistent parental behavior, with conflicting **signals** and a mixture of approval and rejection the children are unable to decode and therefore cannot develop strategies to deal with (Crockenberg & Leerkes, 2000).

Mobile Phones and Parent Availability

The mobile phone has become a tool of remote parenting from pre-school age to adolescence, and parents often buy the first mobile phone for their child to ensure safety and regulate the child's independence outside the home (Ling & Haddon, 2008; Rudi et al., 2015). Research on mobile phone use and child development is still sparse (Yan, 2018), but the parental availability provided by mobile phones is likely to influence children's attachment behavior and exploration.

It may provide a feeling of security by keeping caregivers informed and available and, in addition, allow older children to take advantage of several attachment figures, including a divorced parent they are not living with (Ribak, 2009; Ling & Haddon, 2008). Parents tell that they strive to be available to their children when they are at work, and many parents are almost constantly available, in order to make their children more secure in situations away from them (Strandell, 2014). Such availability may even imply parenting across borders when mothers have to go to another country to find work (Chib et al., 2014). Some parents use surveillance apps to keep track of their child's whereabouts. This may increase the child's exploration of unfamiliar spaces, but many older children and adolescents react negatively to being surveilled (Barron, 2014; Ribak, 2009). However, the mobile phone also represents a disturbing element that may interfere with child–parent interactions, make a parent less emotionally available and create an "absent presence" (Gergen, 2002; Kildare & Middlemiss, 2017; McDaniel & Radesky, 2018).

Temperament

Some theorists suggest that attachment behaviors have their origins in children's **temperament**, rather than in the way children have been treated by their caregivers (Kagan, 1982). However, it has proved difficult to formulate alternative descriptions of the four attachment types in Table 4.2 with categories based on temperament traits (see Book 6, *Emotions, Temperament, Personality, Moral, Prosocial and Antisocial Development*, Chapter 12), and only a limited correspondence has been found between children's temperament and the four attachment categories (Thompson, 1998; Vaughn et al., 2008). The fact that there is a moderate correspondence in attachment behavior toward mother and father also supports the assumption that attachment behavior reflects the child's relationship with the person rather than a general disposition, as in the case of temperament.

Despite these theoretical contradictions, temperament and attachment are often seen in context. In the *unified theory of attachment*, temperament is a contributing factor in determining how infants interpret other people and themselves, and how they respond to separation. Children's temperament thus affects their behavior as well as the reactions of attachment figures (Groh et al., 2017; Stevenson-Hinde, 2005). For example, the temperamental trait *negative* **emotionality** has been viewed as an important precursor to insecure attachment (van dem Boom, 1989). Mangelsdorf and colleagues (1990) found little direct connection between children's temperament at 9 months and Strange Situation attachment behavior toward the mother at 13 months, or between maternal **personality** and children's attachment behavior. However, they found a connection with attachment behavior when the child's temperament was seen in the context of the mother's personality: children with an irritable temperament who had mothers with a reserved personality showed a tendency toward insecure attachment behavior at 13 months of age. Another study found that children with irritable temperament tended to show insecure attachment, but only when the mother received little social support from her surroundings (Crockenberg, 1981). Together, these results support the assumption that children's temperaments affect the development of their attachment relationships. Although there is no direct relation between temperament and attachment category, **interaction effects** between temperament and characteristics of the attachment figure have an impact on the child's attachment behavior. This emphasizes the transactional nature of the attachment process.

Attachment in Atypical Development

Disabilities can affect the development of attachment behavior and attachment relationships, but the attachment process is robust, and children with disabilities essentially show the same development as children without them. Blind children can show similar attachment behavior as sighted children, although delayed and with later reactions to strangers (Dale & Edwards, 2015). Deaf children with deaf parents show the same patterns as hearing children with hearing parents, while a slightly larger proportion of deaf children with hearing parents show insecure attachment (A and C), probably reflecting the hearing parents' limited competence in signing and insecurity in caring for a deaf child (Dale & Edwards, 2015). Mothers of children with **cerebral palsy** often report strong separation reactions in their children and having to be together with them all the time (Quinn & Gordon, 2011). This is probably related to these children's motor impairments, which inhibit their development of self-propelled and independent approach behavior.

Memory and other aspects of cognitive development are of importance to the attachment process. For example, *person permanence*, the understanding that persons exist also when they are not perceived by the child (analogue to **object permanence**; see Book 4, *Cognition, Intelligence and Learning*, Chapter 3), is a cognitive basis of the working model (Bowlby, 1969; Sherman et al., 2015). Children with **intellectual disability** develop attachment relationships with their parents and other adults such as kindergarten personnel just like other children, but development is delayed, and behavior patterns can differ somewhat (De Schipper et al., 2006). In a Strange Situation study of 26-month-olds with **Down syndrome**, many of the children showed behaviors that could not be categorized, but this proportion was lower at 42 months (Atkinson et al., 1999). Children with **autism spectrum disorder** are impaired in their social interaction, and approximately half show secure early attachment behavior in Strange Situation studies. In one study, 8–12-year-old high-functioning children with autism spectrum disorders and typically developing children and their mothers completed the Kerns Security Scales (Kerns et al., 2001), designed to measure attachment security. There were no significant differences between the two groups, either in the parents' or the children's own assessments of the scale's statements related to attachment security (Chandler & Dissanayake, 2014). However, among children with autism spectrum disorder, those who also have intellectual disability are more likely to show insecure attachment behavior (Rutgers et al., 2004). In addition, more unclear attachment behavior and a demanding caregiving situation may increase the likelihood that parents with children with autism spectrum disorder do not respond to their child's approach behavior in situations the child experiences as insecure (Rutgers et al., 2007).

Some adolescents and adults with severe intellectual disability continue to show approach behavior in new and insecure situations without access to an attachment figure. Often, their behavior is not understood by others as an attempt to seek security and is therefore rejected, increasing the risk of self-injury and other forms of challenging behavior (Janssen et al., 2002; Perry & Flood, 2016; von Tetzchner, 2004).

5

Continuity of Attachment

Attachment can change over time, but, once children's working models are established, a high degree of **stability** is expected. However, observations of attachment behavior toward the same person at different ages show varying results. Studies of children at ages 12 and 18 months showed stability ranging from 42 to 96 percent. Despite the fact that two-thirds of all children belong to category B, secure attachment, 40 percent typically change category in the course of these 6 months (Thompson, 2006). This may be related to the increasing mobility that characterizes this age and leads to changes in the repertoire of children's attachment behavior (see Campos et al., 2000). Additionally, specific events can cause relatively major changes in attachment behavior. For example, a sibling represents a potential threat to the mother's availability, and, after the birth of a younger sister or brother, many firstborns show less secure attachment to their mother in the Strange Situation. The greatest difference can be seen in children whose mothers are depressed or have trouble with their relationship around the time of birth. When mothers feel happy and show affection toward their firstborn, attachment behaviors tend to remain secure (Teti et al., 1996).

At the same time, stability does not seem to increase with age: attachment interviews at quite small intervals in adolescence show only correlations of around 0.5–0.6 or lower. Over longer periods, stability is modest, for example from **toddlerhood** to middle childhood and adolescence. One study found correlations of around 0.15 between early attachment behavior in the Strange Situation and attachment measured by interview in adulthood (Raby et al., 2013). This may partly be caused by changes in attachment over time, but also by the widely differing

DOI: 10.4324/9781003292579-6

methods of measuring attachment at different ages (Allen & Tan, 2016; Kerns & Brumariu, 2016; Solomon & George, 2016).

Attachment theory is based on the assumption of a certain continuity across generations: the attachment figures' own attachment history affects their sensitivity and reactions when children feel afraid or insecure (Bretherton, 1990). Parental reactions to attachment behavior are based on the parents' own working models as well as the experiences with their child, which leads to individual differences in availability (George & Solomon, 2008). However, just as in the case of early and later measures of attachment, only modest correlations have been found between mothers' attachment in their own childhood and the attachment type of their children. The one exception is mothers with early insecure-disorganized attachment (category D) – more than half had children who fell into category D (Raby et al., 2015), suggesting that it was the mothers' own highly deviant development that most clearly affected the children in this group. The attachment relationships of children with more conventional attachment histories can be affected by many factors. However, attachment behavior is thought to be mainly a result of experience, and genes do not seem to have a significant impact on the development of attachment relationships (Raby et al., 2013).

6

Cultural Differences

Ainsworth (1967) did her first studies of attachment in Uganda, and studies indicate that children's behavior in the Strange Situation can be classified according to the same categories in all **cultures**. However, cultural differences in caregiving patterns are mirrored in the distribution of attachment types. Infants among the Aka people in the Central African Republic, for example, have more than 20 different caregivers every day. One-year-olds of the Nso tribe in the Northwest Region of Cameroon do not react to being picked up by a stranger and will readily follow the stranger's initiative (Otto et al., 2014). Israeli kibbutzim practice communal child rearing, and children sleep away from their parents (Sagi-Schwartz & Aviezer, 2005). Italian 1-year-olds are more accustomed to being separated from their mother daily for shorter periods, for example in day care centers or with grandparents or babysitters, and normally do not pay particular attention to their mother when she returns. They are therefore likely to relate in ways that are classified as insecure-avoidant attachment (category A), although half of them show secure attachment (Simonelli et al., 2014). Conversely, Japanese infants are rarely separated from their mother, and many of them react strongly to separation in the Strange Situation. They are difficult to comfort at reunion, and more of them therefore end up in category C (Takahashi, 1990).

These findings do not contradict the assumption that attachment behavior is universal, but do raise questions about the suitability of the Strange Situation as a universal method of measuring reactions to security and stress. Attachment behavior is found among children of all cultures, but the conditions that elicit such behavior vary. This is also demonstrated by cultural variations in the proportion of children who cry when their mother leaves them in an unfamiliar situation

DOI: 10.4324/9781003292579-7

(see Box 6.1), variations that do not reflect cultural differences in children's affection. How much children cry is not related to the quality of caregiving, but to how accustomed children are to separation from their mother.

Box 6.1   Children from Different Cultures React Differently When the Mother Leaves the Room in a Strange Situation (based on Kagan et al., 1978, p. 107)

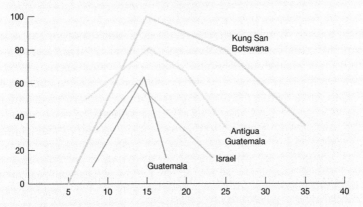

In a Strange Situation study, children aged 4–40 months from different cultures were observed when their mother left the room. The children were from the Kung San tribe in Botswana, a village in Guatemala, the City of Antigua in Guatemala, and a kibbutz in Israel. The figure shows that the percentage of 1-year-olds who cried when their mother left the room ranged from 60 percent of the children in an Israeli kibbutz to nearly 100 percent of the Kung San children in Botswana. These differences lasted until the age of about 3 and reflect the children's experience with their mother's absence. Among the Kung San, young children spend nearly all their time together with the mother, whereas kibbutz children from early on are cared for by adults other than the parents during daytime.

7

Attachment and Later Functioning

According to Bowlby's theory, children's inner working models form the basis for their expectations of social relations and contribute to social **adaptation** and competence (Sroufe et al., 1999). Some studies have found a moderate connection between children's attachment to parents and their peer relations; others have found little statistical relationship between **assessments** of early attachment to each parent and social competence and friendships at school age (Elicker et al., 1992; Sroufe et al., 2005; Thompson, 2016). Nonetheless, secure attachment to both parents over time seems to increase the likelihood of positive social development and relationships in later childhood and adolescence, whereas children with insecure attachment to both parents often show poorer peer relations and are more likely to develop **behavioral disorders** (Boldt et al., 2014; Kerns & Brumariu, 2014).

It is commonly assumed that secure attachment leads to protection, whereas insecure attachment may contribute to **internalizing disorders**, and disorganized attachment to **externalizing disorders**, but results have been inconsistent (Brumariu & Kerns, 2010; Lowell et al., 2014). Egeland and colleagues (1993) found low correspondences between 18-month-olds' attachment behavior in the Strange Situation and teachers' assessments of children's externalizing or inhibited behavior during the first few years of school. However, when the same children were assessed at a summer camp, a situation in which children usually form many new relationships, staff evaluations showed that children with secure maternal attachment had somewhat better social skills and self-esteem, were less dependent and had more friends than children with insecure attachment at 18 months of age.

DOI: 10.4324/9781003292579-8

No relation was found between attachment behavior at 12 months and later functioning (Sroufe et al., 2005).

Other studies have found a clear relation between early disorganized attachment behavior and later behavioral disorders and oppositional behavior (Theule et al., 2016), as well as between measures of attachment and social competence, and behavioral disorders at school age (Boldt et al., 2016). When children have insecure attachment to the mother, their attachment to the father is of particular importance (Boldt et al., 2014; Kochanska & Kim, 2013).

Although studies generally show that children with early insecure attachment develop anxiety and depression somewhat more often than children with secure attachment, the differences are small. This highlights the fact that attachment is only one of the factors that can contribute to the development of such disorders (Kerns & Brumariu, 2014; Madigan et al., 2013; Sroufe et al., 2005). Attachment behavior is one of several *markers* that to a greater or lesser extent predict later functioning depending on the changes that occur in the child's life. As most environments have a high degree of **continuity**, developmental markers in childhood predict the environment as well as later relationships (Clarke & Clarke, 2000). At the same time, it is possible to influence children's caregiving environment, attachment behavior and parental coping by counseling with a focus on parental sensitivity and responsiveness, both in cases of typical and **atypical development** (Barlow et al., 2016; Kerr & Cossar, 2014; Letourneau et al., 2015).

On the whole, studies suggest that secure attachment provides the best basis for development, at least in Western middle-class children (Belsky, 2005). Nonetheless, a given type of attachment behavior will not necessarily be equally successful under all social conditions. All forms of attachment entail social **learning** and adaptation. Children's working models represent a preparedness to meet the social world they have come to know through their attachment relationships. A child with relatively insensitive and unpredictable caregivers may show a tendency to become aggressive and competitive, traits that may well prepare the child to cope with a stressed and unpredictable environment. Parenting may be influenced by stress in times of war, and the development of insecure attachment patterns may be functional (Belsky, 2008). In this perspective, aggressive and competitive relational behavior does not represent a deviation from optimal development, but rather an adequate adaptation to the world as it appears to the child (Belsky, 2005; Hinde, 1992). Besides, in line with the low correlations, an aggressive and competitive behavior pattern is not merely the result of the mother's relational style or that of other attachment figures. From a transactional point of view, the characteristics of the child as well as other people in the environment contribute to the development of these types of behavior patterns.

8

Attachment-Related Disorders

Attachment gives a sense of security when an available and responsive attachment figure is present, and insecurity when the attachment figure is absent. Some children experience prolonged separation from caregivers, such as unaccompanied refugee children and adolescents (Bowlby, 1951; Derluyn & Broekaert, 2007; Smith, 2010). Robertson and Bowlby (1952) describe a sequence of reactions to the absence of an attachment figure, from protest via despair to **detachment** in the case of prolonged or permanent separation – the loss of an attachment figure. The protest phase might begin immediately or after some time, lasting from a few hours to weeks and months. In this phase, children often search for the attachment figure and cry. During the despair phase, they continue to focus on the absent attachment figure but are not as preoccupied with finding her. Crying becomes monotonous or ceases altogether. Children become passive, lose their appetite and make no demands on their surroundings. Gradually, they start to show more interest in the people around them and begin to eat once again. This is a process of detachment whereby attachment behavior is no longer activated in relation to the attachment figures the child has been separated from. For children fleeing from war or catastrophe, this can include all former attachment figures. When an attachment figure comes to visit an orphanage or other place where the child is living, the child will not exhibit the attachment behavior typical of such reunions, but remains passive and shows no initiative or interest. The system can be reactivated, however, if child and attachment figure are fully reunited. When children repeatedly lose an attachment figure, they will gradually invest less and less in potential new attachment figures (Foster et al., 2003; Kobak & Madsen, 2008; Newman & Steel, 2008).

DOI: 10.4324/9781003292579-9

Some children grow up under social conditions that do not offer the necessary qualities to form normal attachment relationships. Two disorders are clearly linked to the caregiving environment: "reactive attachment disorder" and "disinhibited social engagement disorder." Both diagnoses require that the child has been subjected to serious neglect or abuse (see Book 1, *Theory and Methodology*, Chapter 34), and, although some children exhibit characteristics of both inhibited and indiscriminate attachment behavior, the two disorders seem to have a different basis (Zeanah et al., 2004).

Children with *reactive attachment disorder* show inadequate or deviant attachment behavior in situations that usually elicit attachment behavior. In a study of children with this diagnosis, approximately half the children showed early insecure-disorganized attachment behavior (category D), nearly a quarter were so withdrawn as to allow no classification, and the remainder showed secure attachment behavior. Almost none of the children showed other forms of insecure attachment behavior, which could have indicated that they had found strategies to cope with stress and separation. The lower the quality of the caregiving environment, the more distinct the symptoms of reactive attachment disorder. There was clear evidence, in other words, that these disorders had been caused by rearing environments in which children had not developed attachment relationships owing to a lack of sufficiently available and consistent attachment figures. However, these disorders disappeared quickly once the children came to a better caregiving environment, such as adoptive care or a foster home (Zeanah & Gleason, 2015). Similarly, symptoms of reactive attachment disorder quickly disappeared in a group of children from Romanian orphanages after they had been placed in good foster homes, whereas children who remained in the orphanage showed the same symptoms 6 years later. One of the decisive factors, however, was whether the children came to a good caregiving environment before or after the age of 2 years, suggesting that the earliest years may represent a sensitive period for primary attachment (Smyke et al., 2010).

Children with *disinhibited social engagement disorder* show little restraint toward strangers and are "indiscriminately friendly" in situations that elicit attachment behavior. Many children growing up in orphanages develop this disorder, which previously was thought to be caused by inadequate access to permanent attachment figures (Lawler et al., 2014; Zeanah & Gleason, 2015). Studies, however, have only been able to find a moderate link between early attachment type and disinhibited social engagement, suggesting that indiscriminate attachment behavior in new and stressful situations is rather part of a general pattern of poorly adapted social behavior. Whereas children with reactive attachment disorder show a lack of attachment behavior, children with disinhibited social engagement show too much. As they approach strangers without seeking security or comfort, their behavior is not attachment-related but a general social impairment involving physical approach behavior with strangers, both in situations that elicit attachment behavior and situations that do not. It is not a matter of establishing indiscriminate attachment relationships, but of indiscriminate social behavior in interaction with strangers, of showing attachment behavior in social situations in which such behavior is inappropriate (Dozier & Rutter, 2008; Zeanah & Gleason, 2015). Adolescents who have been subjected to severe early neglect and placed in different foster homes may also show signs of disinhibited social engagement (Kay & Green, 2013).

The developmental trajectories described in these studies clearly indicate that different disorders are involved. Whereas the symptoms of reactive attachment disorder quickly disappeared once the children had been adopted and established new attachment relationships, the symptoms of children with disinhibited social engagement only showed a slow reduction. Many of the children continued to show signs of disinhibited social engagement in later childhood, also with their peers (Zeanah & Smyke, 2015).

Not all children who grow up under extremely poor caregiving conditions develop reactive attachment or uninhibited social engagement disorder (Zeanah et al., 2004). A poor environment is not enough. Development can be related to differences in genetic **vulnerability**, **resilience** and temperament, and even negative environments can include protective elements in the form of persons who are partially available and reduce the environment's negative impact (Soares et al., 2013).

Some children with atypical development show a behavioral pattern similar to attachment-related disorders. Both reactive attachment disorder and autism spectrum disorder (see Book 1, *Theory and Methodology*, Chapter 32) involve social impairment, and it can be difficult to distinguish between them. However, children with reactive attachment disorder show greater social reciprocity and, unlike children with autism spectrum disorder, are positively affected by moving to a better caregiving environment (Davidson et al., 2015).

Similarly, children with **Williams syndrome** are exuberant, friendly and socially uninhibited (see Book 2, *Genes, Fetal Development and Early Neurological Development*, Chapter 3), and these are traits that may be confounded with disinhibited social engagement disorder (Soares et al., 2013).

9

Attachment Theory and Social Work in Practice

Bowlby's theory was initially based on observations of children in orphanages with little social contact and staff with little stability, or children who otherwise had lost a stable attachment person (Bowlby, 1951). It is therefore only natural that attachment theory has had a major impact on child welfare practice and similar social services. Large orphanages have been closed down in many countries and replaced with foster homes and smaller institutions, with greater emphasis on promoting stable relationships between children and adults. Attachment theory has influenced the way foster care and adoption are organized (Byrne et al., 2005; Dozier & Rutter, 2008; Rutter, 2008) and is used to lend professional support to why it is important for children to maintain ties to both parents after a divorce, spend enough time together with each of them and stay overnight at each parent's home (Kelly & Lamb, 2000).

Attachment theory has also been used to argue that an early start in kindergarten can be harmful to children (Belsky, 2001; Vandell, 2004). Studies, however, do not support such a claim (Borge et al., 2004; Côté et al., 2007). It is the quality of caregiving at home and in kindergarten that determines whether they contribute to the child's positive development (Rutter, 2008).

DOI: 10.4324/9781003292579-10

Summary of Part I

1   *Attachment* is about developing relationships and feelings for other people. The function of attachment behaviors is to ensure a feeling of safety by reducing the physical distance to specific individuals, *attachment figures*.

2   In Bowlby's *ethological* theory, attachment is an innate *behavioral system* the aim of which is to provide security. Inner *working models* carry information from interaction with important persons, their availability and responsiveness, and form the basis for how children meet their social environment. Adults have a *caregiving behavioral system*. Traditional *psychoanalysis* and *behaviorism* view attachment behavior as a means of satisfying primary needs. According to Mahler's *psychodynamic theory*, attachment relationships are formed as a relation between *self-object* and *maternal object* once children begin to distinguish between mental representations of themselves and their mother.

3   At 2 months of age, children begin to show *selective attention* for familiar people, and positive and negative selection by 7 months. Attachment behavior includes *signaling behavior* and *approach behavior*, activated when children are at a physical distance from the attachment figure and experience pain, anxiety, insecurity or stress. Proximity to an attachment figure provides security and ceases the attachment behavior.

4   Attachment behavior is most pronounced in the second and third year of life, and, by around 3–4 years of age, the basic attachment period is over. Children are now able to be apart from their attachment figures for longer periods and do not need to make direct contact to restore a sense of security. With age, attachment reactions become rarer and less intense, and knowledge of

future availability becomes more important than physical proximity. Adolescence is characterized by increasing autonomy, but the attachment system remains functional throughout life.

5 *Explorative behavior* is activated when children are interested in something new and do not experience too much insecurity. The attachment figure represents a *secure base* for exploration of new objects and places.

6 Children's experiences in connection with separation or loss lead to *individual differences* in attachment behavior. The *Strange Situation* is based on the fact that separation from an attachment figure in unfamiliar surroundings elicits attachment behavior. Behavior is categorized as *insecure-avoidant* (A), *secure* (B), *insecure-resistant* (C) and *insecure-disorganized* (D). Most children show secure attachment. A secure relationship depends on the availability, reliability and predictability of the attachment figure. Prolonged separation and absence or loss of an attachment figure can lead to protest, with crying and despair. As children form attachments with different people, their behavior toward them can vary.

7 According to Bowlby and Ainsworth, the attachment figure's *availability* and *sensitivity* are essential prerequisites for secure attachment, but studies have found a low correspondence between maternal sensitivity and children's attachment. The mobile phone influences the availability of parents and other attachment figures. Parents seek to be easily available, but mobile telephones can also create "absent presence." A difficult life situation may increase parental stress and contribute to insecure attachment in the child.

8 Some theorists believe differences in attachment are caused by *temperament* rather than how the child is treated by the caregiver. In a *unified theory*, temperament forms part of the basis for infants' interpretations of other people and themselves and their reaction to separation.

9 Attachment is a robust system, and children with intellectual disability, autism spectrum disorders and other disabilities largely show the same distribution of attachment types as children with typical development, even if their behavior may be delayed and somewhat different, and some continue to exhibit physical approach behavior at a much later age than others.

10 A high degree of stability in attachment behavior is expected, but observations of attachment behavior toward the same person at different ages show varying results. Correlations are usually

modest or low. This may partly be owing to different measures. Stability in parental sensitivity in childhood is modest.

11 Attachment is found in all cultures, but cultural caregiving patterns result in differences in the proportion of children who show a given attachment type.

12 Secure attachment to both parents increases the likelihood of positive social development and relationships. Disorders are somewhat more common in children with early insecure attachment than children with secure attachment, but the differences are minor. Insecure-disorganized attachment carries the greatest *risk* of developing emotional and behavioral disorders.

13 Robertson and Bowlby describe reactions related to prolonged or permanent separation from an attachment figure. Children with *reactive attachment disorder* have grown up with relatively unavailable and inconsistent attachment figures and show inadequate or deviant attachment behavior. Children with *disinhibited social engagement disorder* show little restraint toward strangers and behave indiscriminately in situations that elicit attachment behavior. This social disorder commonly occurs in children who have lived in orphanages. Children who are adopted relatively late usually establish attachment relationships with their adoptive parents. Some children are resilient in negative environments.

14 All forms of attachment involve social learning and adaptation. The actions and behaviors of attachment figures are incorporated into working models that provide children with clues to the type of environment they can expect. Insecure attachment behavior is not necessarily a deviation from "healthy" development, but rather an adequate adaptation to the world as experienced by the child.

15 Attachment theory has had a major impact on child welfare practice and similar social services. Large orphanages have been closed down in many countries and replaced with foster homes and smaller institutions, with greater emphasis on promoting stable relationships between children and adults.

Core Issues

- The biological bases of attachment behavior.
- The role of temperament in attachment relations.
- The relationship between adult sensitivity and attachment.

Suggestions for Further Reading

Ainsworth, M. D. S., & Bowlby, J. (1991). An ethological approach to personality development. *American Psychologist, 46*, 433–441.

Jin, M. K., et al. (2012). Maternal sensitivity and infant attachment security in Korea: Cross-cultural validation of the Strange Situation. *Attachment and Human Development, 14*, 33–44.

Main, M., & Weston, D. R. (1981). The quality of the toddler's relationship to mother and father: Relation to conflict behavior and readiness to establish new relationships. *Child Development, 52*, 932–940.

Mangelsdorf, S., et al. (1990). Infant proneness-to-distress temperament, maternal personality, and mother–infant attachment: Associations and goodness of fit. *Child Development, 61*, 820–831.

Raby, K. L. (2017). Attachment states of mind among internationally adoptive and foster parents. *Development and Psychopathology, 29*, 365–378.

Rutter, M., et al. (2009). Emanuel Miller Lecture: Attachment insecurity, disinhibited attachment, and attachment disorders: Where do research findings leave the concepts? *Journal of Child Psychology and Psychiatry, 50*, 529–543.

Seibert, A. C., & Kerns, K. A. (2009). Attachment figures in middle childhood. *International Journal of Behavioral Development, 33*, 347–355.

Suomi, S. J. (2005). Mother–infant attachment, peer relationships, and the development of social networks in rhesus monkeys. *Human Development, 48*, 67–79.

Part II

Sibling and Peer Relations

10

A Growing Social Network

Peer relations refer to a broad set of direct and indirect experiences with non-familial age mates (Rubin et al., 2015). They constitute a social setting that exerts immediate and proximal influence on the child (Chen et al., 2006). Interactions with siblings and peers are qualitatively different from those with adults and have a prominent place in children's social lives from an early age. Siblings are part of the child's immediate environment, whereas peers gain a gradually greater role as the child's social world expands.

Peer relations are usually horizontal, whereas relationships between children and adults are vertical (Hartup, 1992). In **vertical relations**, one part has more knowledge and social power than the other, and the relationship is asymmetrical and complementary. Adults have control, and children are given protection and security. Children seek knowledge and help, and adults provide it. In peer relationships, social power is more equally distributed, although children may have different roles when interacting. One of them throws the ball, the other catches. One dresses the doll, the other pushes the cart. **Horizontal relationships** offer experiences and learning that vertical relationships cannot provide, including both competition and cooperation. Peer relations can moderate the effects of other positive and negative influences (Bukowski & Adams, 2005).

Friendship is a horizontal reciprocal relationship characterized by a strong emotional bond and is based on equality and symmetry. *Popularity* is about being accepted and liked within a particular group or more generally, whereas friendship (and being enemies) is a special relationship between two children.

DOI: 10.4324/9781003292579-12

Key developmental issues in this part are the nature of sibling relationships, when and how children establish friendships, what factors contribute to some children being more popular and accepted than others, and the importance of sibling and peer relations for children's social and cultural adaptation.

11

Sibling Relationships

Children spend much time together with their siblings, often more than with their parents (Howe & Recchia, 2014). Sibling relationships represent both social resources and challenges, and the family's emotional climate affects the relationship between siblings (McHale et al., 2012). During times of parental conflict or divorce, siblings can support each other, but animosity between siblings can also increase in connection with a divorce (Gass et al., 2007; McGuire & Shanahan, 2010). Observations of children's behavior toward their siblings in the Strange Situation as well as in the everyday environment suggest that they often feel attached to their older siblings (Gass et al., 2007; Stewart, 1983). Siblings who have been abused often have a close bond, and siblings who come into foster care together usually show a better development than siblings placed separately (Fraley & Tancredy, 2012; Washington, 2007).

Positive sibling interactions involving play and mutual help occur early on, as do competition and conflict. As early as 16–18 months of age, children can purposely destroy an object their sibling is particularly fond of. In the course of their second year, most children have begun to tease their siblings, and, before the age of 3, they have called their mother's attention to something wrong an older sibling has done (Dunn, 1988, 1993).

Parents and older siblings represent different **domains** of authority. During play, toddlers usually follow their older siblings' guidance and instruction and are usually more obedient toward their siblings than their parents. In other activities, they are less willing to do what their older siblings tell them. Nonetheless, Dunn (1988) found a high correlation (0.90) between younger and older siblings' cooperative actions outside the play situation, indicating

DOI: 10.4324/9781003292579-13

Peer relations are important in childhood.

that children can have a major influence on how their younger siblings meet their surroundings. Siblings imitate each other, especially younger siblings, but older siblings also imitate the younger (Howe et al., 2017). Older siblings engage in "teaching" their younger siblings (Howe et al., 2016).

Children aged 5–10 years are more collaborative as well as conflictual when talking to siblings than when talking to friends (Cutting & Dunn, 2006). Siblings share positive experiences, play together and jointly create fantasies and stories (Kramer, 2014). At the same time, sibling conflicts are more frequent and intense than quarrels in other relationships. The siblings' temperaments affect their relationships, and children with an active temperament experience more sibling conflicts than those who are less active (Brody, 1998). Children with aggressive and uncongenial older siblings are at greater risk of problems in their later relationships than children with siblings who have been warm and loving toward them (Dunn, 1996; Pike et al., 2005).

At school age, sibling conflicts typically have to do with what is fair and reasonable in relation to the siblings' age, sharing of personal belongings, physical aggression and general irritation over something a sibling says or does. Although sibling conflicts decrease in number, physical fights are common around the age of 10–11 and more frequent than when siblings are together with other children. Eventually, fighting is replaced by teasing and other indirect forms of **aggression**. However, even in later school age, many sibling conflicts are resolved when parents intervene or are dragged into the dispute. In interview studies, children themselves tell that negotiation and compromise rarely resolve the conflicts with their siblings. In step with their development of social cognitive skills, siblings nonetheless solve conflicts increasingly on their own, usually by withdrawing from the situation (McGuire et al., 2000). Moreover, despite spending much time together, children are more like their friends than their siblings when it comes to emotional style and conflict resolution (Lecce et al., 2009). This is not particularly surprising, however, considering that children typically both choose friends who resemble them in important ways and influence each other (see p. 62).

As siblings approach adolescence, their relationship becomes more equal, but they also spend increasingly less time together. This is probably the result of more time spent with friends outside the family, especially among boys (Buhrmester & Furman, 1990; Noller, 2005). An important aspect of the sibling relationship is also the fact that siblings speak differently with each other than with their parents. Girls are generally warmer toward their younger siblings and confide more often in them than boys do (Brown & Dunn, 1992; Dunn, 1996). Sisters tend to talk more about close relationships than brothers, and the closeness between same-sex siblings shows little change throughout childhood and adolescence. In adolescence, the relationship between different-sex siblings increases considerably in closeness, as girls and boys generally spend more time together (Kim et al., 2006).

Sibling relationships thus include cooperation and care as well as disagreement and conflict. It is this combination of warmth and conflict that uniquely contributes to the social learning and development among siblings (Kramer, 2014; McGuire et al., 1996). And it is a special relationship with lasting impact. For example, although the competitive mentality that may have dominated the siblings in childhood decreases, it does not completely disappear. Brothers tend to maintain competition the most, different-sex siblings the least. Siblings who have established their own families tend to experience a strong emotional bond and often confide in each other. It is rare for siblings to lose contact entirely, and about 50 percent of adult siblings

Siblings usually have a close relationship.

talk with each other once a month or more (Cicirelli, 1996). For many people, sibling relationships are the most enduring of all: from childhood to old age.

Siblings with Atypical Development

Sibling relationships are usually based on some sense of being equals, even though age differences can lead to a number of differences in status and physical strength. When one sibling has a **disability**, this may change the relationship in some ways (Meltzer & Kramer, 2016). Children with severe disabilities often become "younger siblings," regardless of their actual age rank among the others. In many areas, the relationship is the same as for siblings without disabilities but characterized by more warmth and care than other sibling relationships. When high-functioning adolescents with autism spectrum disorder were asked about their siblings, the feelings and attitudes they expressed were similar to other sibling relationships (Petalas et al., 2015).

A **longitudinal study** of children with disabled siblings found that they developed an early awareness of the uncommon characteristics

The sibling relationship is special when one sibling has a disability.

of the disabled sibling, and the younger children usually began to comment on their sibling not long after beginning to speak. Around the age of 2, they started to use their parents as a model for how to relate to the disabled sibling and, around the age of 4, began to ask their parents about the future – whether the sibling's disability will change, and whether they will be going to the same school as their sibling. However, younger children do not fully understand disability and find it difficult to tell their peers about it. Once they enter school age, they become more aware of their sibling's need for care, worry about how things will go and often say they want to take better care of their sibling in the future. By early adolescence, they usually have gained a good understanding of the cause of the disability and are able to explain the extra **chromosome** in children with Down syndrome, for example (Dew et al., 2008; Hames, 2008). However, even younger adolescents may still have misconceptions about the condition of a sibling with a rare disease, such as stating that a chromosome is a kind of nerve and that the signals are weak (Vatne et al., 2015).

Siblings with and without disabilities generally spend less time together and therefore experience both less conflict and less shared **prosocial behavior** (Cuskelly & Gunn, 2003; Dallas et al., 1993a, b; Seligman & Darling, 2007). Still, for severely disabled children, who may have difficulties engaging in ordinary peer relations, siblings may have a very special role (Petalas et al., 2015).

12

Peer Relations

Observations show that children have an early interest in other children. Three-month-olds look longer at other infants than at adults (Fogel, 1979). Vandell and associates (1980) observed simple interactions between 6-month-olds every 4 minutes, and every 3 minutes between 9-month-olds. They mostly consisted of one-way actions in which one child did something without a reciprocal action by the other. Genuine interactions involving looking, vocalizing and smiling did not occur until the end of the first year (Figure 12.1).

In their second year, children show an even greater interest in their peers. A study of 12–18-month-olds sitting together with their

Figure 12.1 Four 1-year-olds engaged in interaction without adult guidance (photograph courtesy of Ben S. Bradley).

DOI: 10.4324/9781003292579-14

mother showed that they looked more than twice as long at a child of the same age than at another female adult (Lewis et al., 1975). When 11- and 23-month-old children in another study were paired and engaged in interaction with an adult, they too looked more at the other child than at the adult. When the adult deliberately excluded one of the children from interaction, the excluded child tried to establish contact with the other child far more often than with the adult (Tremblay-Leveau & Nadel, 1996). Although most early interaction is dyadic, meaning that one child interacts with another child or adult, 2-year-olds are able to engage in triadic interaction. Occasionally, this involves interaction between all three children, but more often two children interact while the third child watches (Ishikawa & Hay, 2006; Selby & Bradley, 2003).

In the course of early childhood, children spend increasingly more time together. In modern Western societies, children spend much time in organized and unorganized activities with other children, while children in many other cultures are more integrated into adult activities from early on (Lam & McHale, 2015; Rogoff, 2014). As early as 2–3 years of age, children in Western societies spend more of their time outside kindergarten in the company of other children than adults, and, as school age approaches, less and less of their leisure time is spent with adults (Ellis et al., 1981).

The relationships between children change with age (Box 12.1). Children of preschool age essentially represent a collection of separate individuals. Over time, they increasingly form into groups with norms and internal organization and have to harmonize the competing demands of the groups they belong to. Some of these norms are related to relationships with the opposite **sex**, norms that are strictly adhered to in order to maintain gender boundaries (Sroufe et al., 1999).

Box 12.1   Topics in Peer Relations of Children and Adolescents (after Sroufe et al., 1999)

Preschool Age: Positive Attention to Peers

- Choosing specific partners
- Maintaining turns in interactions

o   Negotiating conflicts in interactions
o   Maintaining organization when excited
o   Finding joy in the interaction process

- Participation in groups

School Age: Investing in a World of Peers

- Establishing loyal friendships
- Maintaining relations

o   Negotiating conflicts in interactions
o   Tolerating many emotional experiences
o   Promoting self in relations

- Functioning in stable, organized groups

o   Following group norms
o   Maintaining gender borders

- Coordinating friendship and group functioning

Adolescence: Integrating Self and Peer Relations

- Establishing intimate relations

o   Self-disclosure in same gender peer relations
o   Cross-gender relations
o   Sexual relationships

- Commitment in relations

o   Negotiating conflicts relevant for self
o   Emotional vulnerability
o   Self-disclosure and identity

- Functioning in a network of relations

o   Mastering systems with multiple rules
o   Establishing flexible borders

- Coordinating multiple relations of same and different gender

o   Intimate relations and functioning in the group

As many peer relations originate in school, children who attend the same class may become lifelong friends. School is an important factor in whom children spend their time with, such as children from different social backgrounds as well as children with typical and atypical progress at school (Crosnoe & Benner, 2015).

Emotional involvement and vulnerability increase during adolescence, and peer relationships become an important part of young people's identities (see Chapter 24, this volume). Friendships and group relations between the sexes increase in number, as do intimate relationships with friends and sexual partners. All these relationships have to be reconciled with the norms and requirements of each group, and it can be difficult to maintain established relationships in case of misunderstandings and conflicts (Sroufe et al., 1999).

13

The Development of Friendship

Friendships have an important role in children's development: Friends develop social skills and understanding together, talk about themselves and others and gain insight into moral values, conflict resolution and social and cultural rules (Bagwell & Schmidt, 2011; Dunn, 2004).

As early as children's second year, parents tell about special relationships with other children and how their children miss the playmates when they are away from kindergarten or play at home. Children start to talk about whom they like or dislike in kindergarten and other places early on (Dunn, 2004). Interaction between children increases around the age of 2, but, as they still lack adequate independent social skills, the development of their play interactions and emotional relationships would run into problems without adults to facilitate play and offer emotional support (Howes, 1996). It is uncertain whether these early relationships have the necessary qualities to be called friendships, but cooperation is typical for this age nonetheless. Two-year-olds more often offer toys to others than take a toy someone else is playing with.

By around 4 years of age, children have firmly established preferences and friendship relations. One study found that about 50 percent of a group of 4-year-olds in kindergarten had a special relationship with another child they spent over 30 percent of their time with (Hinde et al., 1985). About 75 percent of all preschool children say they have friends, while 80–90 percent of adolescents say they do (Hay et al., 2009). About 15 percent of all children and adolescents do not have a reciprocal friendship for 6 months or longer (Rubin et al., 2013).

Preschoolers have on average 1–2 friends, whereas school-age children typically mention 3–5 friends, depending on whether the

DOI: 10.4324/9781003292579-15

friendship is reciprocal or not. This figure remains stable throughout adolescence. In childhood, girls have a slightly smaller network of friends than boys, but, in adolescence, the trend reverses. Both children and adolescents spend much time together with their friends. In adolescence, this amounts to nearly one-third of all their time (Hartup & Stevens, 1997).

Children are more cooperative and positive toward their friends than toward other peers. Friends have more fun together, often engage in more advanced forms of play and solve school assignments better together than nonfriends. They spend more time talking about the assignment and less time beating about the bush. This probably has to do with their shared interests and the fact that friends are familiar with each other's behavior, strengths and weaknesses. In addition, spending time with friends offers important opportunities to learn how to resolve conflicts. Conflicts arise as often between friends as between nonfriends, and most conflicts in childhood actually occur within the family or between friends. What distinguishes conflicts between friends is the way in which they are resolved. Friends negotiate conflicts, whereas children who are not friends insist more on their own point of view. Friends more often work out compromises and solutions that do not ruin the friendship, instead of trying to out-trump or defeat each other. Both children and adolescents argue, but adolescents are more concerned with the relationship itself than younger children, who focus more on competition (Bukowski et al., 2009; Hartup & Stevens, 1997; Laursen & Pursell, 2009).

Most childhood friendships are between children of the same sex. As early as the age of 3, children show a distinct preference for playmates of the same sex among mixed groups of children. In a study of fifth–sixth-graders, 94 percent of reciprocal friendships were between children of the same sex (George & Hartmann, 1996). Part of the reason is that many childhood friendships are established through participation in social activities that tend to differ between boys and girls (see Part IV, this volume). Boys more often participate in group activities with a certain age spread and spend much of their time on competitive team sports with a focus on cooperation and leadership. Girls more often collect in smaller groups and are more preoccupied with intimacy and who is in and outside the clique. Girls also prefer to play with other girls because they dislike the rough play of boys (Maccoby, 1990).

In adolescence, friendships are characterized by intimacy and personal issues. In conversations with friends, adolescents "disclose" themselves in an entirely different way than in conversations with their parents, especially girls (see p. 104). At the same time, friendships are the most fragile relationships: many adolescents worry about their friendships and about not being accepted (Coleman, 1980; Dolgin & Kim, 1994). Friendships with the opposite sex and romantic relationships become more common during adolescence, and those with early physical maturity and a high status among the group often lead the way. Others gradually follow suit, and, eventually, mixed-gender groups become common. Many adolescents are unsure of themselves and the social relations they engage in. Learning to interact with the opposite sex is an important step in the social development of this phase, and friends play an important part in the process (Dunn, 2004).

Social media are important for young people to stay in touch with their friends, and digital communication with real friends is far more common than with other so-called "friends" on the internet; it is among "real-life" friends that social media can contribute to the quality of friendship (Furman & Rose, 2015).

Developing Perceptions of Friendship

When preschoolers are asked about their friends, they answer based on whom they do things together with, that they are friends because they play together. Adults, too, tend to perceive and describe younger children's relationships in this way. Joint activities are an important criterion for friendship among older children and adolescents as well, especially among boys. With age, however, perceptions of friendship increasingly involve feelings of perceived closeness and shared emotions. Friends are understanding, loyal and can be trusted. Older children associate friendship to a greater extent with similar attitudes and values. They are friends because they enjoy the same activities and the same music. In adolescence, descriptions of friendships additionally begin to include shared secrets and feelings and opportunities for emotional support. It is with friends one can talk about one's innermost thoughts. Adolescents who are anxious and withdrawn look at their friends as a source of help and comfort (Bukowski et al., 2009; Mathur & Berndt, 2006; Schneider & Tessier, 2007). At the same time, adolescents are more selective than younger children in whom they consider to be their friends (Poulin & Chan, 2010).

Changes in children's perception of friendship partly reflect their developing mind understanding and the growing realization that not everyone thinks the same way they do (Fink et al., 2015). This creates a need to learn more about others as well as to tell others about oneself. Friendship opens up important opportunities to talk about private issues, including personal likes and dislikes. Children and adolescents tend to gossip more about others with their friends than those who are not friends generally do (Gottman & Mettetal, 1986).

Children's understanding of friendship also varies along cultural lines. Supporting a friend's **self-image**, for example, is considered a more important friendship quality among children and adolescents in Western, **individualistic cultures** than in more collectively oriented cultures such as China or Indonesia. Although Chinese and Indonesian children place somewhat greater emphasis on the utility of friendship, they attach equal importance to intimacy and emotional closeness as Canadian children (Chen et al., 2006).

Some children show an atypical understanding of friendship. For example, children with autism spectrum disorder may refer to barely familiar children and hired adult assistants as their friends (Petrina et al., 2014). Children with severe motor impairment who lack speech and use communication aids may perceive other children as friends but are not always considered a friend by them (Østvik et al., 2017). There are friendships between children with and without a disability, but the **prevalence** of true reciprocal friendship involving children with severe disabilities is much lower than friendships among typically developing children. They may depend on adult intervention, and, typically, developing "friends" may sometimes act as helpers rather than as friends (Guralnick et al., 2007; Rossetti & Keenan, 2018; Sterrett et al., 2017).

Stability of Friendships

Children's earliest friendships are quite stable, typically lasting for more than a year, and, by the age of 4, friendships have often lasted for 2 years. Their stability is probably related to the limited choices offered by the kindergarten, the neighborhood and the playmates introduced by parents. Relationships become more variable, with a typical duration of 6–12 months, during the preschool period (Dunn, 1993; Howes, 1996, 2009).

Children's radius of action expands, and previous groups split up once children start in school, and school-age children regularly change best friends (see Box 13.1). One study found that nearly one-third of

Box 13.1   Best Friends (adapted from Gulbrandsen, 1998, pp. 15–17)

Robert (R) is participating in a longitudinal study where he is interviewed regularly by the researcher (G).

Second Grade, September

G: *Do you have a best friend?*
R: *Yes, Tom is my best friend.*

Second Grade, February

G: *Did you walk to school today?*
R: *Yes, and I bicycled some of the way. My friend and I bicycled together.*
G: *Was it Tom?*
R: *No, it was Magnus. Tom and Martin were driving.*
G: *So only you and Magnus bicycled?*
R: *Hm.*
G: *Did you not want to drive?*
R: *No. because Tom is so stupid. He teased Magnus and said he was slow and such. Magnus is my best friend, and then I don't go with Tom.*

Second Grade, May

G: *When you went home from school yesterday, did you go together with somebody?*
R: *Tom.*
G: *Last time I talked with you, Tom and you were a little unfriendly.*
R: *Yes, but we are not anymore.*
G: *You are not unfriendly any more.*
R: *Now we are best friends.*

Third Grade, December

G: *Do you see Tom much now?*
R: *No, not much. He plays horse so much and I am tired of that. And at home, then they only play with the computer.*

children in fourth and eighth grade had replaced all their best friends in the course of 6 months (Berndt et al., 1986). Shifting friendships are typical for early adolescence, but, in the years to come, friendships become more stable again (Poulin & Chan, 2010). Although children change friends, the status of having or not having friends has a high degree of stability. Children with friends at one age level usually also have friends at a later age (Elicker et al., 1992). Friendships lasting for shorter periods can reflect the quality of the friendship. For example, children with **ADHD** have shorter and less stable friendships (Chupetlovska-Anastasova, 2014). Also, children with **antisocial behavior** often have unsatisfactory and shorter-lasting friendships (Dishion et al., 1995).

Similarities between Friends

Friends tend to resemble each other in terms of social background and behavior, and two mechanisms seem to contribute to this (Howes, 2009; McDonald et al., 2013). **Social selection** means that children choose their friends based on similarities in age, gender, **socioeconomic** and ethnic backgrounds, as well as temperament, interests and values. In an **experiment** with 7–8-year-olds who had never met and were gathered in groups on several occasions, the very first meeting revealed who liked and disliked each other, and children who liked each other played more alike than children who did not like each other (Rubin et al., 1994). *Social deselection* means that children choose not to become friends with others who differ from themselves in these areas, or end the friendship once they realize that they and their friend develop in different ways (Brown et al., 2008). Social deselection can also include children with intellectual disability, autism spectrum disorder or other disabilities (Schneider, 2016).

There seem to be greater similarities in antisocial behavior, such as fighting and **bullying**, than in prosocial behavior, such as cooperation and helpfulness (Haselager et al., 1998). One study found that boys (but not girls) who chose a friend with a relatively high level of antisocial behavior themselves had a tendency for such behavior. Neither boys nor girls with low levels of antisocial behavior chose friends with this type of behavior. Children with high levels of prosocial behavior chose friends with the same behavior (Eivers et al., 2012). When children with antisocial behavior select friends with the same type of behavior, it may mean that they accept this behavior, but this may be because they have been deselected by more prosocial children and thus have few to choose from. Their friendships may originate not in mutual attraction but in the children's inability to find other friends (Killen et al., 2009; Haselager et al., 1998).

Similarities are also promoted by the fact that friends consolidate their attitudes and behavior patterns when they are together. In this context, *social influence* is a transactional process in which children actively cooperate to construct, support and reject beliefs and attitudes through conversations about people, events, movies, books and so on. The older or more popular part in a friendship usually has somewhat greater influence than the younger or less accepted part (Furman & Rose, 2015), but it is rare that one of them is either "good" or "bad" as such and the other simply has gotten a good or a bad friend. Friendship relations usually involve active *mutual* influence after an initial period of selecting and deselecting potential friends. Some children have friendships with conflicting influences, something that is not uncommon among children from minority backgrounds with friends belonging to both the majority and the minority culture (Berndt & Murphy, 2002; Brown et al., 2008). The degree of similarity between friends also tends to affect whether a friendship is maintained (Hafen et al., 2011; Poulin & Chan, 2010).

Boys who are friends tend to be more similar in terms of physical activity than nonfriends. Girls who are friends are more alike in physical attractiveness and the size of their social network than girls who are not friends. Female friends also share more similarities in prosocial and antisocial behavior than male friends. The opposite is true of shyness, which is a less problematic trait for girls than for boys (Cairns et al., 1995; Haselager et al., 1998).

14

Enemies

Being enemies involves a *relationship of mutual antipathy*. Just as in the case of friendships, there are corresponding degrees of hostile relationships: best friends and worst enemies. Children can be enemies for shorter periods in connection with conflicts among playmates, or have more prolonged hostile relationships that are equally stable as friendships (Casper & Card, 2010). About 35 percent of all children and adolescents report having one or more enemies, with a slight increase during early school age and a decrease in adolescence. More boys than girls report having enemies. Enemies often share a unique negative background (Card, 2010; Rodkin et al., 2003), while friendship can be maintained by having a common enemy (Rambaran et al., 2015).

Having enemies is not related to general social competence and adaptability, but, when a child has many enemies, it usually indicates a problem with social interaction. Adolescents with many enemies are less accepted and bullied more often, and some enemy relationships are founded on bullying and mutual antipathy (Hafen et al., 2013; see also Book 6, *Emotions, Temperament, Personality, Moral, Prosocial and Antisocial Development*, Chapter 27). Some adolescents with many enemies, particularly boys, show a lot of aggressive behavior. Others tend to be more socially withdrawn than those with few or no enemies, but, unlike **unpopular children**, do not report feeling lonely (see p. 72). Consequently, having enemies can in a certain sense fulfill a socially "protective" role. Girls who are generally disliked often feel sad. Girls who have enemies, but are not disliked, rarely feel sad. This underlines the role of mutual antipathy as an active relationship and integral part of the social network, even if its

DOI: 10.4324/9781003292579-16

dynamic is negative. Additionally, it requires a certain social competence to establish a negative relationship to which both parts must contribute to maintain their antagonism. Although adolescents with many enemies show somewhat more antisocial and aggressive behavior than those without enemies, adolescents with prosocial behavior have enemies as well, and the differences are minor (Abecassis et al., 2002; Pope, 2003).

15

Popular and Rejected Children

Some children are popular. Everyone wants to spend time with them, and they get to participate in anything they like. Others are largely excluded from joint play unless organized and supervised by adults (Cillessen & Rose, 2005). Popularity and rejection can be measured by observing which children in a group spend little or much time together with other children. Another method is to ask children whether they want to spend time with a particular child, or to name the three children they would like to be together with the most, and the three they would rather not be together with. One should be careful, however, when asking children to classify their peers in negative ways (Martinsen et al., 2010; Schneider, 2016).

Children's sociometric status is commonly divided into five major groups: popular, rejected, neglected, controversial and neutral (Rubin et al., 2006). Importantly, peer popularity or rejection is not a characteristic that resides in the child. It represents the feelings of others toward the child and only makes sense in the context of a peer group (Bagwell & Schmidt, 2011).

Popular children are actively accepted. Often they are physically strong, with an attractive appearance, but their willingness to share, their ability to cooperate and other social skills are equally important for their popularity among peers (Parker & Asher, 1993; Asher & McDonald, 2009).

Rejected, or *unpopular*, children are actively excluded by other children. Although aggression may be regarded as the primary reason for rejection (Rubin et al., 2015), only 40–50 percent of rejected children actually show particular signs of aggression, while others appear more submissive. Socially withdrawn children make up 10–20 percent

DOI: 10.4324/9781003292579-17

of the rejected group, and 25 percent of withdrawn children are rejected (Rubin et al., 2013). This group also includes children who are immature and childish compared with their peers (Berndt, 2002). Nonetheless, aggressive behavior does not necessarily lead to rejection – it depends on how the behavior is expressed. In many situations, **popular children** are as assertive and aggressive as rejected aggressive children. One study found that only half the children who were considered extremely aggressive had rejected status. Aggressive actions in response to threats from others were seen as positive (Cillessen et al., 1992). Tough children who are able to "speak out" and at times even use their fists, but who rarely show the socially disruptive and aggressive behavior typical of unpopular rejected children, can be quite popular among their peers (Rodkin et al., 2006). Children who behave aggressively while at the same time being able to establish a social network rarely end up in the unpopular group; they have positive qualities that outweigh their aggressive behavior (Cairns et al., 1988; Pedersen et al., 2007).

Neglected children are neither accepted nor rejected but interact less with their peers than children in the neutral group. They are quite similar to other children, usually show little aggressive behavior and try to avoid aggression somewhat more than other children, but nonetheless do not appear anxious or withdrawn. Children with the latter characteristics typically end up in the withdrawn rejected group.

Controversial children are both accepted and rejected and have traits in common with popular as well as rejected children. At times they can appear active, aggressive, destructive and angry, or socially withdrawn; at other times they can show cooperation, leadership, helpfulness and social sensitivity. Their behavior varies depending on the situation and whom they are with. Other children tend to perceive their behavior as contradictory as their positive traits do not represent enough of a counterweight to place them in the popular or neutral category, while their negative traits are not dominant enough to make them unpopular.

Neutral children fall in between the other groups. They are neither particularly popular, rejected or controversial, but are not neglected either.

When children are asked whom they like and dislike, their answers are always affected by recent events and changes in mood. Not all children remain in the sociometric category they first start out in, but rejection from peers is more stable than acceptance during childhood (Hardy et al., 2002; Pedersen et al., 2007).

Social Strategies and Popularity

Initiating contact with other children is a natural start of peer relationships. Some of the differences between popular, rejected and neglected children clearly show up in the social strategies they use, for example when joining a game already in progress. Popular children usually first observe the situation for a moment before gradually joining the play themselves. Pushy unpopular children tend to throw themselves into play, often in a way that interrupts the activity. They do not understand the rules and therefore are unable to fit in naturally. Their attempts to join play are an expression of wanting social contact, but their clumsy way of interfering makes them disliked by their peers. As they are excluded from participating in the activity, they never get a chance to learn the rules. Aggressive unpopular children are usually not aware of their own lack of social skills and are therefore bewildered and frustrated when other children reject them (Dodge et al., 1983; Martinsen & Nærland, 2009).

Unpopular submissive children are often directly rejected when they seek contact with their peers and typically ask adults for help in resolving conflicts with other children. They perceive social conflicts and can identify possible solutions, but are often unable to carry them out. They have insight into their own social problems and express feelings of perceived loneliness to a greater degree than aggressive rejected children (Hymel et al., 1993). Neglected children stand on the sidelines and look on without making an active effort to join in. They are not included in play by other children, but merely observe and do not disturb the others' play. Therefore, they gain a better understanding of the rules of play than children in the aggressive rejected group. Unlike unpopular submissive children, neglected children do not give the impression of experiencing loneliness (Howes, 2009).

In the course of childhood, many factors can affect whether children are accepted by their peers. Toddlers depend on adults to establish interaction and play, and several studies have found a relation between the way parents monitor and intervene in their child's activities and the child's relationships with other children. Children with mothers who indirectly manage the child's activities are better liked than children whose mothers are more direct. For boys, maternal over and under involvement both seem to entail a lower social status among peers. Girls with a high social status among their peers typically have under-involved mothers, and their own efforts to make contact with other children considerably exceed those of the mother. Mothers of popular children interfere less with play than mothers of unpopular, rejected children and tend to address the entire group when explaining something or intervening in children's play activities (Ladd & Hart, 1992). All these differences are not merely the result of maternal characteristics; maternal strategies are equally influenced by the characteristics of the child and the child's friends (Furman & Rose, 2015).

Temperament and the ability to self-regulate influence how children try to establish relationships with other children (Eisenberg et al., 2009). Children with an early inhibited temperament are often socially reticent in the company of their peers when they grow older (Rubin et al., 2002). Children with a **difficult temperament** tend to be more impulsive and aggressive than other children, increasing the likelihood of rejection by their peers. A study found that 5–10-year-olds who scored high on **sociability** were more popular and had more positive relationships than children who scored lower on this temperament trait. The children who scored high on the emotionality trait had poorer relationships with their peers than children who were less emotional (Stocker & Dunn, 1990). Similarly, sociable children with poor emotion regulation tend to exhibit aggressive and destructive behaviors that make them unpopular. They would rather join in than be destructive, but are unable to cope with the situation. Sociable children with good emotion regulation tend to be socially competent. Socially wary children with good **self-regulation** easily blend into play with others, while socially wary children with poor self-regulation appear anxious and cautious (Rubin et al., 1995).

At every age level, children carry with them the expectations and strategies they have developed through earlier peer interactions. Not only do popular and unpopular children act in different ways, they also have a different understanding of other people's perspectives and intentions and may have quite different expectations of companionship. Aggressive unpopular children often mention rivalry as a motive to spend time with other children, whereas popular children express interest and pleasure in companionship as such. Some unpopular children put the blame on others when they get into a quarrel. They have a more hostile attitude to solving conflicts and fewer suggestions for prosocial solutions. Other unpopular children believe their social success is the result of external circumstances while blaming social failure on their own personal characteristics (Crick & Dodge, 1994; Dunn, 1999). These types of differences in children's perception of the social environment and themselves can be seen in light of their own experiences with being rejected, but they can also become self-fulfilling prophecies which impact on their later development (Bierman, 2004; Rubin et al., 2006). Thus, the social *life space* (Lewin, 1935) of popular and unpopular children can be quite different.

Cultural Differences

The studies referred to here were conducted in Europe and North America. As cultural norms and characteristics regarded as positive and socially competent vary from one culture to another, the characteristics of popular and unpopular children also show some variation between different countries. Aggression in any form, for example, is frowned upon in China and many other Asian countries, whereas sensitive, careful and controlled behavior is considered an expression of social maturity and competence. Accordingly, this type of behavior is relatively more prominent in popular children in Asian than in Western countries. In most cultures, popular children and adolescents show cooperation, prosocial behavior, friendliness and sociability, while social withdrawal leads to rejection in many cultures (Rubin et al., 2010, 2013).

Friends, Popularity and Adaptation

Throughout childhood and adolescence, peer relations play an important role in learning how to adapt. Peer relations help younger children learn to collaborate, resolve conflicts and other social skills. Among older children and adolescents, they contribute to the development of **identity** and a broader understanding of other people, but can lead to both positive and negative outcomes: when friends show positive social behavior, cooperation and good solutions, they protect against a negative social development. Friends who are cooperative to begin with become more cooperative over time. Similarly, friends with poor social adaptation and conflict resolution skills will increase the likelihood of a negative social development (Berndt, 2002; Hartup & Stevens, 1997). Well-functioning friendships in which one or both parts show deviant behavior increase the risk of negative development (Dishion & Piehler, 2009).

Some children do not have friends their own age and miss out on the social and relational skills brought about by emotionally close, reciprocal friendships. For some, this is owing to specific social impairments such as autism spectrum disorder (Attwood, 1998; Petrina et al., 2014), but there are also children without such impairments who do not gain the necessary experience with common social interaction. This increases their likelihood of poor social adaptation and emotional disorders.

Studies show that children who have friends generally are less dominating, controlled and tense, and more independent, emotionally supportive and sensitive to other people's feelings than children without reciprocal friendships. They have better social skills, are more sociable and unselfish and show better adaptation and performance at school. At school age, play between friends is more reciprocal, cooperative and positive-affective than play between children with few or no friends. Children without friends show poorer interaction with their peers and a reduced ability to take the perspective of others. They are perceived negatively by others as well as themselves. Children without friends are more vulnerable to internalizing than externalizing disorders (Furman & Rose, 2015; Rubin et al., 2013).

Poor social skills can be the result of lack of social experiences, but lack of social experiences can also be the result of poor social skills. Children who have suffered neglect or abuse are socially less competent, less prosocial and more aggressive toward their peers than children who have not been subjected to such harm. They can be withdrawn, although this is more common in children who have suffered neglect than those who have been subjected to physical abuse. Even if their peers take positive initiatives, they may respond with aggression (see Book 6, *Emotions, Temperament, Personality, Moral, Prosocial and Antisocial Development*, Chapter 27). They can either show a complete lack of trust in other people or appear excessively confident. Both forms of behavior make interaction with other children difficult. These children are often disliked by their peers and have difficulty establishing friendship relations. In one study, children who had never met before were divided into eight play groups, each with one child who had suffered neglect and three children who had received normal care. After 4 weeks, nine of the 24 children who had not been subjected to neglect formed reciprocal friendships. Only one of the eight children who had suffered neglect established this type of friendship in the course of the same period (Price, 1996). This shows that neglect from significant adults may impact children's development of social skills and confidence to establish social relationships with their peers. However, some children who have suffered gross neglect and physical abuse develop resilience and form positive relationships and friendships that, to a certain extent, mitigate the consequences of their abuse (Dubowitz et al., 2016; Houshyar et al., 2013).

Friendship and popularity status may have both similar and different consequences. In one study, children in fifth and sixth grade reported having approximately the same number of friends, but the unpopular children had only half as many *reciprocal* friendships as the neutral children, and only one-third as many as the popular children. Additionally, the popular group had the greatest number of popular children as reciprocal friends. Most reciprocal friendships among unpopular children were with neutral children, in addition to a relatively larger proportion of unpopular friends, compared with popular children (George & Hartmann, 1996). The unpopular group in this study also had more reciprocal friendships exclusively outside school, most likely because rejection at school led the unpopular children to seek social recognition and friendship elsewhere. Consequently, peer relations in the long-term stable environment of school were of relatively less importance for these children than for others. This might have contributed to contact with extreme or antisocial groups in adolescence.

Friendships are important for children's self-image, and children without friends generally have a less positive perception of themselves than children with friends. Submissive rejected children in particular have a poor self-image (Rubin et al., 2006). Harter (1987) describes a vicious circle in the development of friendship relations and self-image: children with a low sense of self-worth feel they receive little support from their classmates and friends, adding further to their low self-evaluation, and so on. Relatively speaking, children without best friends are lonelier than children with best friends, no matter how popular they are (Parker & Asher, 1993). Unpopular children are at risk of social isolation, particularly when they have no friends. Most unpopular children say they have friends, in which case their low popularity generally has less severe consequences for their ability to adapt. Friendship thus provides protection against perceived loneliness in both popular and unpopular children. It is the combination of not having friends *and* being unpopular that negatively affects the development process.

It is rare for children to either have or not have friends throughout their entire childhood. Children constantly establish new relationships and sometimes change best friends many times before reaching adolescence. It is not each individual friendship that is essential, but their positive or negative sum total. Nonetheless, from a transactional perspective on development, it is the quality of former friendships that forms the foundation for new ones and for the expectations children have of friendships and their own contribution to the relationship.

16

Adolescent Groups

A group is a social network within which individuals interact and relationships are embedded (Rubin et al., 2015). As part of the emancipation process, adolescents seek out smaller and larger groups outside the home. Some are "skaters," some are "nerds," others are involved in politics or sports or have an ethnic affiliation outside mainstream society. Some groups have values that differ radically from those of society, but most groups reflect society at large, with typical attitudes and values that generally characterize young people in society. They may function as **reference groups** for the individual, meaning that the groups' rules, values and norms largely determine adolescents' attitudes and behaviors, whether they are prosocial or antisocial. These groups have little stability, however, and change when adolescents switch school or take up other interests, in addition to developments within the group itself and society in general. The individual relationships and attitudes within groups of close friends in particular change in line with development (Faircloth & Hamm, 2011).

Adolescents are particularly vulnerable to rejection from their peers. Many are worried about not being accepted by their peers, and a high degree of conformity with friends and reference groups is typical of adolescence. **Conformity** means to adopt the attitudes and behaviors of others owing to actual or perceived pressure from them. In many contexts, it is the attitudes of friends that become decisive, rather than the norms and values of the family or society in general (Berndt, 1979). Adolescents do many things because "everyone else does it." In relation to society, the attitudes and norms of a group can be conformist (comply with society), non-conformist (act independently of society) or anti-conformist (act contrary to society's norms). They might start to smoke, drink or shoplift because their friends tell

DOI: 10.4324/9781003292579-18

them they are gutless or childish if they do not participate. Also, the negative consequences of placing adolescents with deviant behaviors together with other deviant peers demonstrate adolescents' influence on each other (Prinstein & Dodge, 2008; see also Book 6, *Emotions, Temperament, Personality, Moral, Prosocial and Antisocial Development*, Chapter 27). However, following the norms of a group is not the same as submitting to the group altogether. Adolescents may seem conformist because they seek out groups whose values they accept and that accept them in return, influencing the groups they are part of as well as being influenced by them.

17

Peer Relations and Later Disorders

Peers are a core element of children's social environment, and this is reflected in the **associations** between early social acceptance and later disorders. Children who start school together with friends, for example, are more positive about school and adapt better in first grade than children who do not have friends when they start school – the school environment becomes less alien to children who have friends with them (Dunn, 2004; Ladd, 1990). In later childhood and adolescence, affiliation with different groups can contribute to a strengthened self-image and protect against the development of mental disorders (Newman et al., 2007).

Children who have been rejected by their peers before starting school show poorer adaptation at school (Wentzel, 2009). Those in the aggressive rejected group are at risk of behavioral problems, poor impulse control and aggression regulation, hostility and antisocial behavior, even in adolescence. One study found that a higher proportion of 11-year-olds classified as rejected had dropped out of school 7 years later. Compared with popular or neglected children, three times as many had been in contact with the police (Kupersmidt & Coie, 1990). Submissive rejected children are more vulnerable to developing anxiety, depression and low self-esteem (Rubin et al., 2013; Hymel et al., 1990). Chronic rejection represents a negative developmental spiral, and children who experience chronic rather than intermittent rejection have the greatest risk of later disorders (Bierman, 2004; DeRosier et al., 1994).

If friendship is to have a positive social impact, it must have positive qualities. Some friendships are distinguished by little equality and high levels of conflict. When interaction is not based on the relational equality a friendship requires, children's expectations of friendship

DOI: 10.4324/9781003292579-19

and their peer interaction strategies can become dominated by negative qualities (Berndt, 1996; Dishion et al., 1995; Newcomb & Bagwell, 1996). Although some friendships are characterized by positive inner qualities such as equality, emotional support and a high degree of loyalty and intimacy, they can still contribute to the development of aggressive and antisocial behavior when friends support and encourage each other in such behavior (Hartup, 1999; Kupersmidt et al., 1995). This type of friendship thus represents a form of negative social capital.

The studies referred to in this chapter provide a complex picture of children's relationships with other children. Many factors are at play when children engage in friendships and other peer relationships: children's own characteristics such as temperament, emotion regulation and social cognitive skills, as well as their accumulated experiences from interaction with other children and adults. It is the totality of all these factors that leads each child to form unique expectations of social relationships and strategies, and that colors their further development. Nonetheless, vulnerability to internalizing and externalizing disorders is not destined – most children do not develop such disorders, and there are various initiatives to reduce rejection, promote social skills and positive relationships between children, and guard against disorders (Bierman, 2004; Schneider, 2016).

Summary of Part II

1 Peer relations refer to a broad set of direct and indirect experiences with non-familial age mates which constitutes a social setting that exerts immediate and proximal influence on the child. In *vertical* relationships, one part has more knowledge and social power than the other. In a *horizontal* relationship, social power is more equally distributed.

2 Siblings are part of the child's immediate environment. They share many experiences and have positive interactions as well as conflicts, which may have to be resolved by their parents. Although they can support each other in difficult situations, these can also put a strain on the relationship. It is a combination of warmth and conflict that uniquely contributes to the social learning and development among siblings.

3 When one of the siblings is disabled, the relationship is often characterized by more warmth and care than other sibling relationships. As they generally spend less time together, they also experience less conflict and shared prosocial behavior.

4 Children show an early interest in other children and spend increasing amounts of time together throughout childhood, while leisure time with adults decreases. Preschoolers essentially represent a collection of separate individuals; groups begin to form during school age, and children have to reconcile their friendships with the competing demands of the groups they belong to. Adolescence sees a growing number of relationships across the sexes.

5 *Friendship* is a horizontal relationship with a strong emotional bond. By the age of 4 years, children usually have well-established friendship relations, and the number of friends increases slightly with age. For preschoolers, friends are the children they do things

together with. For older children and adolescents, friendship is more about perceived closeness and emotional fellowship. Whereas schoolchildren describe their friends as understanding, loyal and trustworthy, older children place more weight on similar values and attitudes. In adolescence, descriptions of friendship include shared secrets and feelings, and opportunities for emotional support. Friends have as many conflicts as non-friends, but they are better at resolving them. In adolescence, intimacy and personal issues becomes increasingly important for friendships.

6   Toddlerhood friendships typically last for 1–2 years. At preschool age, friendships are somewhat more variable, and, at school age, many children regularly change best friends. In the course of adolescence, friendships become more stable and selective. At preschool age and in childhood, girls have a slightly smaller network of friends than boys, but in adolescence the trend reverses.

7   *Social selection* means children choose friends who are similar to themselves, *social deselection* that they choose not to become friends with children who are different from themselves. Friends affect each other's attitudes and behaviors through *social influence*. Male friends tend to be similar in terms of physical activity, female friends in attractiveness and the size of their social network. Female friends share more similarities in prosocial and antisocial behavior than male friends. The opposite is true of shyness, which is less problematic for girls than for boys.

8   One-third of all children and adolescents say they have *enemies*. Mutual antipathy is an active relationship and integral part of a child's social network, even if its dynamic is negative. Adolescents with many enemies are less accepted and subjected to more bullying. Some enemy relationships are founded on bullying.

9   *Popular children* are often physically strong, with an attractive appearance, but their willingness to share, their ability to cooperate and other social skills are equally important for their popularity. About 50 percent of the *unpopular* group show socially disruptive, aggressive behavior, while socially withdrawn and submissive children make up 10–20 percent. Some rejected children are immature and childish compared with their peers. *Neglected* children are neither accepted nor rejected. *Controversial* children share common traits with both popular and unpopular children and are both accepted and rejected. *Neutral* children are not particularly popular, rejected or controversial, but are not neglected either.

10   Popular and unpopular children have a different understanding of other children's perspectives and intentions and may have completely different motives and expectations. Aggressive unpopular children often mention rivalry, whereas popular children express interest and pleasure in companionship as such. Some unpopular children put the blame on others when conflicts and problems arise. Other unpopular children believe their social success is the result of external circumstances, while blaming social failure on their own personal characteristics. *Cultures* differ with regard to the types of characteristics they consider positive and thus also the characteristics of popular and unpopular children.

11   Most children take part in the process of relational learning and *enculturation* a reciprocal friendship usually involves. Younger children learn to cooperate, resolve conflicts and other social skills. Among older children and adolescents, peer relations contribute to the development of identity and a broader understanding of other people. Unpopular children are at risk of social isolation and missing out on social skills, especially when they do not have friends.

12   Adolescents influence the groups they are part of and are in turn influenced by them. The groups' rules, values and norms are important for their attitudes and behaviors and can both promote and inhibit the development of prosocial and antisocial behavior patterns. A high degree of conformity with friends and groups is typical of adolescence, but, in relation to society, the attitudes and norms of a group can either be conformist, non-conformist or anti-conformist.

13   Studies have found relations between early social acceptance and later disorders. Friendship and group affiliation can contribute to a strengthened self-image and protect against disorders. Children in the aggressive rejected group are vulnerable to developing behavioral disorders and antisocial behavior, submissive rejected children to developing anxiety, depression and low self-esteem. Children who experience chronic rather than intermittent rejection have the greatest risk of later disorders. Nonetheless, most unpopular children without good peer relations do not develop disorders, and there exist interventions that can reduce rejection, promote social skills and positive relationships, and guard against disorders.

Core Issues

- Emotional closeness and conflict among siblings.
- The behavioral bases of peer acceptance and rejection.
- Selection and deselection processes in friendship formation.
- Risk and protection related to friends and peers.

Suggestions for Further Reading

Abecassis, M. (2003). I hate you just the way you are: Exploring the formation, maintenance and need for enemies. *New Directions for Child and Adolescent Development, 102,* 5–22.

Cuskelly, M., & Gunn, P. (2003). Sibling relationships of children with Down syndrome: Perspectives of mothers, fathers, and siblings. *American Journal on Mental Retardation, 108,* 234–244.

Dishion, T. J., et al. (1995). Antisocial boys and their friends in early adolescence: Relationship characteristics, quality, and interactional process. *Child Development, 66,* 139–151.

Dunn, J. (2004). *Children's friendships: The beginnings of intimacy.* Oxford: Blackwell.

Haselager, G. J. T., et al. (1998). Similarities between friends and nonfriends in middle childhood. *Child Development, 69,* 1198–1208.

Howe, N., et al. (2018). "I'm an ogre so I'm very hungry!" "I'm assistant ogre": The social function of sibling imitation in early childhood. *Infant and Child Development, 27,* e2040.

Rubin, K. H., et al. (1994). "Birds of a feather . . .": Behavioral concordances and preferential personal attraction in children. *Child Development, 65,* 1778–1785.

Part III

Self and Identity

Finding a Place in the World

The key issues in this chapter revolve around the forming of the individual self and the emergence of self-understanding and typical and atypical self-esteem and identity. An important aspect of this development is that the self and the identity both change and remain the same (Hammack & Toolis, 2015; Koh & Wang, 2012). The self is an inner experience and awareness of being a unique individual. Identity is a continuation of reflections of the self and an experience of sameness, difference and affiliation with other people, of being part of a larger social context (Hammack & Toolis, 2015). Self and identity have to do with changing variations and answers to the question "Who am I, and what is my place in the world?" (Brummelman & Thomaes, 2017).

DOI: 10.4324/9781003292579-21

The Beginnings of Self-perception

The self comprises two main aspects: the **self as knower**, or *I*, is the experience of being a unique individual. It is a sense of being and acting in the world that comes from within. The **self as known**, or *me*, is the self-perception of an individual, an awareness of being in possession of certain characteristics and qualities and an evaluation of one's own abilities relative to those of others (James, 1890). One method of studying early self-perception is to observe when children recognize themselves in a mirror or a picture. Lewis and Brooks-Gunn (1979) found that children on average have passed the age of 20 months before they touch their nose when they look in a mirror after their mother, unknown to them, has put a red mark on their nose (Box 19.1). Other studies have similar results (Courage et al., 2004) but have also found cultural differences. German and Greek toddlers, for example, showed earlier self-recognition than toddlers from a village in Cameroon, a result that did not seem to be related to differences in the children's access to mirrors but rather to different **parenting styles**. German and Greek children had more face-to-face interaction with adults than the children from Cameroon (Keller et al., 2004, 2005).

The ability to recognize oneself in a mirror is a skill human beings share with few other species. Some elephants seem to understand that they are looking at a mirror image of themselves (Plotnik et al., 2006, 2010), and magpies pass the "mark test" as well (Prior et al., 2008). Self-recognition is rare even among primates: not all chimpanzees show this type of recognition, and only about one-third of all gorillas that have been studied recognize themselves in

DOI: 10.4324/9781003292579-22

Box 19.1   Early Self-recognition in the Mirror (Lewis & Brooks-Gunn, 1979)

The study involved 96 children, aged 9, 12, 15, 18, 21 and 24 months, with eight boys and eight girls in each group.

The children and their mothers were first observed in a room with a mirror for 1.5 minutes. The children looked at the mirror, but almost none of them touched their nose during the observation. Following this, the mother was given a cloth with rouge and, without the child noticing, the mother put a red mark on the child's nose. The mother was instructed not to talk about the nose or direct the child's attention to the nose. She turned the child toward the mirror and he or she was observed for the same length of time, 1.5 minutes. None of the children in the two younger groups touched their nose when they looked into the mirror after the rouge was applied. Nineteen percent of the 15-month-olds and 25 percent of the 18-month-olds touched their nose when they looked into the mirror. It was only after the age of 21 months that a majority of the children touched their nose: 63 percent of the 21-month-olds and 66 percent of the 24-month-olds.

a mirror (Suddendorf & Collier-Baker, 2009). Most animals with a mirror placed in their cage for some time will explore the mirror rather than what the mirror reflects. This demonstrates that it is cognitively more demanding to recognize oneself than to recognize others, something most animals are capable of.

Studies using variations of the mark test have found that children recognize themselves later on video and in photographs than in a mirror. In one study, the experimenter placed a sticker on the head of 2–4-year-olds, without their knowledge, and then took a photograph or video-recording and immediately showed it to the child. None of the 2-year-olds and only one-quarter of the 3-year-olds reacted to the sticker on their head when they saw the photograph or video of themselves they had seen being taken moments earlier, whereas a majority of the 4-year-olds reacted immediately (Povinelli et al., 1996). Experience is of importance for the development of this form of self-recognition, however: toddlers recognize themselves earlier when they have experience using camcorders and digital cameras (see Book 3, *Perceptual and Motor Development*, Chapter 3). The development of self-perception is also reflected in the emergence of **self-referential emotions** such as pride and shame at the same age

"Do it myself"

(see Book 6, *Emotions, Temperament, Personality, Moral, Prosocial and Antisocial Development*, Chapter 7), as well as claims of objects as their own by saying "*It's mine!*" (Levine, 1983; Lewis, 2011). Another milestone in self-development is when children recognize their name. Toddlers begin to refer to themselves by name or *I* and rarely make a mistake between *you* and *I*. Understanding who is referred to by *you* and *I* requires situational awareness, as the personal reference depends on who is talking. Without visual clues, this is more difficult to do, and, although blind children generally develop language at the same time as other children, their use of these particular words is often delayed (Fraiberg, 1977). This does not mean, however, that their self-understanding is any less developed.

20

Theories of Self-development

Self-awareness and knowledge of oneself as a reflective agent in the world are central to human development, and there are many different views on this process. Here is mainly room for the influential theories of Margaret Mahler, Daniel Stern and Michael Lewis.

Separation-Individuation Theory

The distinguishing feature of Mahler's psychoanalytic theory is the inability of the newborn child to differentiate between herself and the mother (Mahler et al., 1975). According to this theory, the human child starts in a symbiotic phase where she experiences oneness with the mother and does not distinguish between self-object and mother-object; the early self thus includes both herself and the mother (see p. 9). After about 5 months, the child begins to differentiate an individual **concept** of self from the early symbiotic concept through what Mahler calls separation-individuation processes. The infant incorporates a representation of herself and the mother and, by the age of 12–18 months, she is able to fully distinguish between them, although the processes continue over the first 3 years of life. During the *separation process*, the child's sense of being a self separated from others gradually increases. She develops feelings of both separateness and connection with the outside world, particularly the connection between her own body and that of the mother. The process of *individuation* allows the child to get a sense of herself as an individual with characteristics independent of the mother. The child's increasing mobility plays an important role in this development. Individuation is dependent on the mother's availability and her ability to match the child's feelings, but the primary goal of this process is independence,

DOI: 10.4324/9781003292579-23

rather than the development of a mother–child relationship such as in Bowlby's attachment theory (see Chapter 2, this volume).

Mahler's theory has been historically important, and its basic views are shared by many within psychodynamic psychology (Blom & Bergman, 2013). For example, Donald Winnicott (1960) describes a development where the child first goes through an *undifferentiated phase* in which she cannot be described independently of the mother. The child's development of self-perception is determined by maternal reactions, and the child's experience of self is an extension of how he experiences the mother's subjectivity. It is the mother's *mirroring* of the child's movements during play and other activities that allow the child to perceive himself as powerful and unique. If the mother is sufficiently empathetic, the child will develop a "true self" that reflects his unique potentials. If the mother lacks the necessary **empathy**, the child will adapt to the mother by developing a "false self" that protects the real self from negative maternal influences. A child's self-perception is therefore directly linked to the mother and makes significant demands on how the mother relates to the child.

Several authors – also within **psychoanalytic** and **psychodynamic psychology** – have pointed out that the assumption that children start with an undifferentiated experience of themselves and their mother is not supported by the early competencies revealed in modern infant research (Blum, 2004; Silverman, 2004; Stern, 1998). Studies have found that newborns show a preference for their mother's voice and learn to distinguish the outline of their mother's head from those of other women early on (see Book 3, *Perceptual and Motor Development*, Part I). The fact that infants react to separation from their mother in unfamiliar surroundings is a further indication that they distinguish between themselves and their mother, and between the mother and other people (see Chapter 4, this volume). Studies of social referencing show that children seek adult help in evaluating the environment as early as the first year of life (see Book 6, *Emotions, Temperament, Personality, Moral, Prosocial and Antisocial Development*, Chapter 6). Although very young children have a limited understanding of the fact that other people can have states of mind, intentions, experiences and skills that differ from their own, they have no problem distinguishing between themselves and others.

The criticism of the early symbiotic phase has led to several revisions of the separation-individuation theory, either by omitting this aspect of the theory and instead maintaining the existence of a core self at birth (Blum, 2004; Silverman, 2004), or by redefining the nature of such a self-experience (Blom & Bergman, 2013; Pine, 2004). However, the theories still maintain that separation-individuation is a self-process, from dependence to independence. Separation-individuation is an intra-person process of becoming a separate person, an independent self (Blom & Bergman, 2013).

Six Senses of Self

Stern (1998) describes the development of a multilayered self (Figure 20.1) whereby each layer develops in parallel and remains an

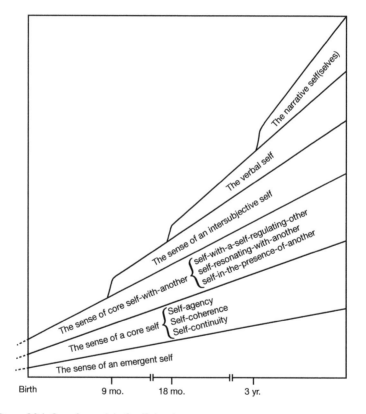

Figure 20.1 Stern's model of self-development.

Three senses of self are present at birth, while the three others emerge at a later age (based on Stern, 1998, p. 47).

independent but integrated part of the mature individual's self. An inadequately developed or severely impaired sense of self will lead to aberrant social functioning or mental health disorders. According to Stern, the self develops through transfer of the caregiver's emotions to the child by means of empathy. He rejects the idea that children go through a phase in which they do not distinguish between their mother and themselves and argues instead that children are born with a sense of independence and agency. Although Stern belongs to the psychodynamic tradition, his description of the development of self-experience differs considerably from those of Mahler and Winnicott.

The Emergent Self

Children's earliest sense of self is the experience of connecting isolated objects and events and discovering their permanent characteristics. They consist of internal signals, including momentary states, arousal, activation, muscle tension, motivation and satisfaction. All these bodily signals come from the self. According to Stern, newborns experience the *process* itself through an increasing degree of organization. It is a form of "primary consciousness" that is not reflective, cannot be formulated verbally, and only lasts for a brief moment, a "now" of what occupies the mind. It is "an awareness of the process of living an experience. The contents of the experience could be anything" (Stern, 1998, p. xviii).

The Core Self

The core self is not a cognitive construct, a "concept of" or a "knowledge of," but an "experiential integration" (Stern, 1998, p. 71). It consists of two parts:

Core self I: self versus other concerns children's experiences of themselves and is divided into three subcategories. *Self-agency* is the sense of being the force behind one's own actions, as distinct from others. *Self-coherence* is the sense of being a non-fragmented, physical whole with external boundaries and a locus of action. *Self-continuity* is the sense of enduring and, in spite of changes, remaining the same over time.

Core self II: self with other concerns children's experiences with others and is divided into three subcategories. *Self with a self-regulating other* refers to the child's sense of security, attachment, arousal, activation, pleasure, unpleasure, physiological gratification, self-esteem and so on. *Self resonating with another* includes the experiences of being in connection with another by way of other-centric participation. *Self in the presence of the other* is the sense of perceiving, thinking or acting, alone but in physical proximity to a caregiver, whereby the physical presence (without any interactive, psychological presence) serves as a framing environment in which the infant can continue to be psychologically alone, on his own. This subcategory is a special variation of the self-regulating other.

According to Stern, children form *representations of interactions that have been generalized* (RIGs), which are activated when children have an experience that reminds them of something they have done before. They are an early form of **script**, mental representations of events children have participated in that are modified and eventually become an organized network of self-experience (see Book 4, *Cognition, Intelligence and Learning*, Chapter 10). One example would be the mental representation of a **generalized** version of peek-a-boo. The game is never exactly the same. This first time, Daddy may be hiding his face behind his hands, something the child remembers as a specific event. The next time, he hides his face behind a teddy bear or a book. With each variation, recollections of the game increasingly change into a generalized event that represents a **prototype** for the child's experiences with the game.

Mental representations of generalized interactions that include other people allow children to form a basic sense of belonging and to acquire new perspectives: their subjective social world is transformed through human interaction. When children activate a mental representation of events that include being together with someone else, they meet what Stern calls an *evoked companion*. The evoked companion is a sense of being with, or in the presence of, a self-regulating other, a sense the child may be, or not be, aware of. The companion is not a separate working model or the concept of a person but part of a generalized event. As the companion can be evoked (mentally activated) in the presence as well as absence of the caregiver, the evoked companion represents a form of **internalization** that provides children with a sense of security and continuity in the absence of the caregiver.

The Intersubjective Self

According to Stern, early on, infants start to sense "that there are other minds out there as well as their own." Although infants' experience

of **(primary) intersubjectivity** nearly goes back to the beginning
of life (see Book 5, *Communication and Language Development*, Chapter 3),
it is the **(secondary) intersubjectivity** that emerges around the age
of 9 months that Stern describes as the sense of an intersubjective
self. Children draw conclusions about mental states that are invisible,
ascribe intentions and feelings to other people and "read" their minds.
This paves the way for the establishment of **joint attention, intersubjectivity**, intimacy and closeness. Initially, it involves an *implicit*
understanding apart from conscious reflection. Nonetheless, this new
relational awareness, based on mind understanding, represents a major
qualitative leap compared with the more physical relational experience of the core self, according to Stern.

Shared awareness of emotional states is one of the key aspects of
the intersubjective self. Stern particularly emphasizes the importance
of **affect attunement** for establishing intersubjectivity. The mother
(or another person) mirrors or matches the affective content of the
child's action, the feeling underlying the action (see Chapter 6, *Emotions, Temperament, Personality, Moral, Prosocial and Antisocial Development*, Chapter 6). Affect attunement results in a sharing of feelings, an
intersubjectivity that provides children with knowledge of their own
emotional state and contributes to the development of a sense of self.

The Verbal Self

With the acquisition of language, children's sense of self becomes
more explicit and conscious. Children can tell themselves what they
are experiencing, such as, *I am thirsty*. The verbal self begins to form
around the age of 15 months and identifies and categorizes properties,
opens up to new relationships and enables children to share private
experiences and coordinate knowledge of themselves and others in
new ways and thereby transcend the immediate experience.

The Narrative Self

The narrative self emerges at the age of about 3. It creates a historical context and represents an individual's autobiography, the official
history of one's life. Initially, the development of the narrative self is
co-constructed with others, usually parents and older siblings who
organize individual event components, order them sequentially and
establish the narrative's emotional highpoints. According to Stern,

these narratives are shared by the family and thus emphasize the **role** of the self in a broader social context.

The Status of the Theory

Stern's theory illustrates the complexity of the **self-concept** and has been of major influence, but has also been criticized for conclusions that are difficult to verify empirically. Although insisting that he takes the child's perspective and interprets what children experience, self-experience is private and relatively inaccessible knowledge. Most of the criticism, however, is directed at his claim that young infants are able to recognize the *process* underlying the development of their sense of self, meaning that very young infants not only experience sensations, feelings and actions but are also capable of experiencing the organizing process underneath, and thus a self as known. Stern believes infants have a level of insight into their own mind and those of others, along with complex beliefs about social issues, for which children at this age lack the developmental prerequisites according to many theorists (Cushman, 1991; Lewis, 1997).

Four Levels of a Representational Self

Lewis (1991, 2011) describes the development of a representational self in four phases, or levels, that emerge in the first 3 years of life. Level 1 is *knowing*, or *I know*. It is an implicit awareness that exists from birth. Children are able to mentally store events and remember, but are not aware of doing so. It is a self that knows, an *I*. Level 2 is *I know I know*. It involves the capacity to reflect on one's own self and knowledge and represents the beginning of self-referential behavior. This level of mental representation is usually described as self-awareness and typically shows up between the ages of 15 and 24 months. Children are not only able to remember events, but are also aware of remembering them. It is a self as known, a *me*. Level 3 is *I know you know*, a form of knowing that begins to develop at the age of 2 and involves children's understanding that they are not the only ones who know that others know something and have a mind. This level forms the basis for sharing opinions. Level 4 is *I know you know I know*, a form of self-awareness that approaches the adult level. Children understand that others can experience events from different perspectives. Additionally, they are aware of the fact that they can be the subject that experiences as well as the "object" being experienced.

Other Views on Early Self-perception

Kagan (1991, 1998b) rejects the notion that children have an early experience of themselves. He maintains that it makes little sense to ascribe self-perception to children before they are able to take an external perspective on themselves, recognize themselves physically and have an awareness of experiencing or doing something, that is, *a self as known*. He points out that it is not enough for children to act and regulate their interactions with the environment as mice do the same thing without anyone claiming they have self-perception. Children must also show that they have the experience of doing so. This, according to Kagan, does not happen until well into their second year, but even this early form of self-awareness is rudimentary in nature.

Thus, the main points of dispute are how to define self-perception and the extent to which very young children can be said to have such a perception of themselves. To a certain extent, the issue revolves around the classic distinction between the self as knower and the self as known. The first represents a sense of being a separate sentient individual who acts and feels; the second involves the capacity for self-reflection, an awareness of one's own abilities. If self-perception is defined as the experience of a meaningful outside world and purposeful action, the only requirement is a "minimal self" (Rochat, 2013), or what Lewis (1991) calls "the machinery of the self," an *I*. There can be little doubt that young infants have such a perception. If one assumes that self-perception implies an understanding of oneself as an individual with certain characteristics subject to opinion and reflection, at least in a simple sense, then an "evaluative" or "personified" self, a *me*, develops in early childhood (Neisser, 1997; Rochat, 2013).

21

Further Development of Self-perception

With age, children become more self-aware and begin to distinguish between a private and a public self: their way of being (private self) and how they appear to others (public self). Older children increasingly consider the private self to be the one that is "real" (Harter, 2006). Adolescents tend to be conscious about themselves and how they appear to others. Rankin and associates (2004) found that younger adolescents were more self-conscious about public appearance than older adolescents who were more self-reflective and privately self-aware than the younger group, and that girls tended to be more self-aware than boys. Adolescents also describe *several selves*, saying they experience themselves to be different in different contexts with parents, friends, romantic partners, classmates and so on. An adolescent may, for example, be talkative among close friends and quiet together with the family (Harter, 2006; Ruble, 1987).

Children's development of self-perception cannot be seen separately from their perception of others. They are unable to notice their own characteristics before these have been contrasted with their presence or absence in others. Toddlers with older siblings show more self-awareness than toddlers without an older sibling (Taumoepeau & Reese, 2014). Children have *first-person knowledge* about themselves (from within) but use *third-person knowledge* to understand themselves (from outside). What comes first is like the question about the chicken and the egg: one is a prerequisite for the other (Bruner & Kalmar, 1998). Although the sense of self is private, children use the same categories to describe themselves and others, with parallel shifts in their descriptions (van Aken et al., 1996).

DOI: 10.4324/9781003292579-24

Self-descriptions

Children's and adolescents' descriptions of themselves change with age and provide insight into their self-perception. Damon and Hart (1988) divide the contents of these descriptions into four domains or aspects: physical, active, social and psychological (Table 21.1). The *physical* aspect includes properties such as height, weight and gender. *Activity* consists of what the child says and does. *Psychological* refers to inner qualities such as smartness or kindness. *Social* includes children's descriptions of relationships and other social factors, especially those involving family and friends.

According to Damon and Hart, examples of all four aspects can be found in children's descriptions at all ages, but their distribution changes with age. Physical self-descriptions dominate among toddlers, for example that they are a boy or a girl, that they have blue eyes and so on. These types of descriptions decrease in middle childhood but increase once again in adolescence. In preschool age, children typically describe what they do, for example that they like to play football, help their mother and go bicycling. Around the age of 7, the number of psychological characteristics increases and reaches a peak in the descriptions of adolescents, which are often characterized by soul-searching and reflection on their own inner qualities, the private self. In answer to the question, *who am I?*, children may also comment that their mother works in an office or that they are popular with other children. In adolescence, descriptions include fewer such social relations.

With age, children's descriptions become more differentiated and consistent, and their self-concepts more complex and relative. Whereas younger children use simple categories to describe the properties of the body, older children tend to compare their physical traits more with those of others. Younger adolescents comment on the importance of physical traits for their relationships with others, whereas older adolescents are concerned with the influence of their physical traits on personal choices. A similar development can be found in children's descriptions of activities. Toddlers talk about what they usually do – play football or fight with their brother. Adolescents talk about actions that reflect personal choices and moral standards, for example that they do not cheat because they think it is wrong, and that they are good losers. When it comes to psychological characteristics, younger

Table 21.1 A model of the development of self-understanding (the model includes four forms of the self as object or known (physical, active, social, psychological) and three aspects of the self as subject or knower (continuity, distinctness and agency) at four different age levels: (a) early childhood, (b) middle and late childhood, (c) early adolescence and (d) late adolescence (Damon & Hart, 1988, p. 56)

Developmental level	General organizing principle	The self as object				The self as subject		
		Physical self	Active self	Social self	Psychological self	Continuity	Distinctness	Agency
Late adolescence	Systematic beliefs and plans	Physical attributes reflecting volitional choices, or personal and moral standards	Active attributes that reflect choices, personal or moral standards	Moral or personal choices concerning social relations or social-personality characteristics	Belief systems, personal philosophy, self's own thought processes	Relations between past, present and future selves	Unique subjective experience and interpretations of events	Personal and moral evaluations influence self
Early adolescence	Interpersonal implications	Physical attributes that influence social appeal and social interactions	Active attributes that influence social appeal and social interactions	Social-personality characteristics	Social sensitivity, communicative competence and other psychologically related social skills	Ongoing recognition of self by others	Unique combination of psychological and physical attributes	Communication and reciprocal interaction influence self
Middle and late childhood	Comparative assessments	Capability-related physical attributes	Abilities related to others, self or normative standards	Abilities or acts considered in light of others' reactions	Knowledge, cognitive abilities and ability-related emotions	Permanent cognitive and active capabilities and immutable self-characteristics	Comparison between self and other along isolated dimensions	Efforts, wishes and talents influence self
Early childhood	Categorical identifications	Bodily properties or material possessions	Typical behavior	Facts of membership in particular social relations or groups	Momentary moods, feelings, preferences, and aversions	Categorical identifications	Categorical identifications	External, uncontrollable factors determine self

children describe immediate feelings and what they like and dislike. Older children also mention cognitive skills. Younger adolescents talk about their social and communicative skills, whereas older adolescents describe their values and fundamental philosophical attitudes. Children with disabilities may mention characteristics related to their disability (Cheong et al., 2016).

Autobiographical Narrative

Memories are core elements of the self. When children have a memorable experience, such as a trip to an amusement park or to visit grandma and grandpa, they can reflect over it for a long time after. When children reflect on past events, they become aware of their former self as both different and similar to their current (reflecting) self. It is an external understanding of themselves that requires language skills, and both the development of memory and the cultural categories embedded in language contribute to the temporal stability of the self (Moore & Lemmon, 2001; Nelson, 2007b).

Children's early life histories are mainly formed in conversation with adults who fill out children's descriptions and give context and meaning to their fragmented narratives (see Book 4, *Cognition, Intelligence and Learning*, Chapter 10). Children do not distinguish between their own early memories and what others have told them – everything is "self-experience" (Nelson, 2007b). However, toddlers' private "crib talk," without anybody present, often has a narrative form. In this monologue, Emily, at 32 months, is placing herself in several everyday events (Nelson, 2015, p. 173):

Tomorrow when we wake up from bed, first me and Daddy and Mommy, you, eat breakfast like we usually do, and then we're going to p-l-a = y, and then soon as Daddy comes, Carl's going to come over, and then we're going to play a little while. And then Carl and Emily are both going down the car with somebody, and we're going to ride to nursery school, and then we when we get there, we're all going to get out of the car, go into nursery school, and Daddy's going to give us kisses, then go, and then say and then we will say goodbye, then he's going to work and we're going to play at nursery school. Won't that be funny? Because sometimes I go to nursery school cause it's a nursery school day. Sometimes I stay with Tanta all week. And sometimes we play mom and dad. But

*usually, sometimes, I um, oh go to nursery school. But today I'm going
to nursery school in the morning.*

Nelson suggests that "for Emily her speech for self seemed to serve as a
space for exploring her place in an expanding universe of knowing in
conjunction with active experience and social speech in conversation
with parents" (2015b, p. 178). Such elaborations of events are part of
an emergent autobiographical narrative and self-development.

Around 3 years of age, children begin to form a clearer understanding of their own life history, and the development continues
through childhood. The autobiographical narrative is not an individual collection of memories but the result of co-construction with others (Thompson, 2006). Through conversations with adults children
become aware that people experience and remember different events,
and that different minds can remember the same event in different
ways. Peers, too, contribute to children's self-history through self-
disclosure (see p. 103) and participation in events parents are not part
of, leading children to focus on new aspects of themselves. In adolescence, new life events and participation in a broader range of activities
influence the autobiographical narrative and self-concept (Negele &
Habermas, 2010). Some life histories make up an integrated whole,
whereas others are more independent parts of the life cycle, but
they are always unified by the sense of having occurred to the same
individual – oneself (Ferrari, 1998).

Cultural Perspectives

It is a general assumption that interactions with others contribute to
the development of children's self-perception. It is a social construct:
children learn to understand themselves through interacting with others (Fivush & Buckner, 1997; Markus & Kitayama, 2010). Cooley
(1902) compares other people to a social mirror in which children
discover themselves.

Considering the social foundation of the self, it follows that children's self-concepts reflect the culture they grow up in. Adults guide
children onto culture-specific "selfways" that reflect the society's self-
ideas and self-values. Children's self-perception is thus the result of
both cultural selfways and individual experience. It lies at the core of
the unique individual, albeit constructed through the cultural filter
represented by the surrounding social world (Markus et al., 1997).

The *cultured self* is primarily individualistic and autonomous, or *independent*, in some cultures, and more social and relational, or *interdependent*, in others (Markus & Kitayama, 2010; Wang, 2014). In the United States, the most prominent notion about the self is independence; in Japan, it is relations. The Japanese word for "self" is *jibun* and refers to "one's part of the shared living space." In one study, half of Japanese adolescents' self-descriptions were about relationships with others, compared with only one-quarter of American adolescents' descriptions. The difference is explained by the fact that American adults encourage children to compare themselves with others, and that children develop an early habit of identifying their own positive qualities and the belief that they are better than their peers. In Japan, adults spend far more time talking about children's relations with other people and how children's actions depend on their relationship with others (Dennis et al., 2002; Markus et al., 1997). Another view is that there are two main selves, an individual-oriented self and a social-oriented self, and that it is the strength of these that varies across cultures (Sun, 2017). This means that the two selves change with cultural changes. In China, for example, cultural influences from Western countries seem to increase the role of the individual self (Lu, 2008).

Self-disclosure

Self-disclosure – giving personal information about oneself to others – is an important element in the development of self-perception in older children and adolescents. This can include factual information or opinions, such as how they feel about an event or person (Rotenberg, 1995), and may take place face-to-face or via social media (Valkenburg et al., 2011). Children and adolescents typically communicate this type of information to parents and siblings, and a central characteristic of close friendships among older children and adolescents is the ability to talk about one's innermost thoughts without being ridiculed (see Part II, this volume). However, children and adolescents do not usually disclose everything. Experiences that they disclose are part of the narrated and shared self, but experiences that they remember but do not want to tell others about also have an impact on their construction of the self (Pasupathi et al., 2009).

For younger children, parents' acceptance is most important; recognition by peers becomes more important toward the end of adolescence. In the course of development, disclosure to friends increases, while disclosure to parents remains stable or decreases slightly. This means that self-disclosure on the whole increases throughout childhood and adolescence, only to slow down again around the age of 18–20 years (Buhrmester & Prager, 1995). The pattern is similar across cultures, even though the content of disclosure varies (Hunter et al., 2011).

Parents are not always the most fitting partners for these conversations involving self-disclosure. They typically lack the necessary insight into youth culture, and self-disclosure often involves issues young people do not want to share with their parents. Besides, holding back information about oneself is a way of marking one's independence and autonomy (Howe et al., 1995; Hunter et al., 2011). Some adolescents continue to confide mainly in their parents, especially when their mothers are warm and do not control their personal lives too much. Adolescents who fear **punishment** if they tell a secret to their parents, or who are involved in delinquent activities, have low levels of self-disclosure to their parents (Keijsers et al., 2010; Smetana et al., 2009). Both boys and girls disclose a great deal to their mother, and boys disclose to their father relatively more often than girls do. Disclosure to the father declines among adolescent girls but not among boys. Fathers often are more restrictive toward their daughters than their sons, and girls may confide less in their father to avoid being restricted in their freedom of action (Buhrmester & Prager, 1995).

Until the age of about 9, the amount of self-disclosure to peers is the same for boys and girls. After this age, female friends exchange more self-disclosing information than male friends. The increase in self-disclosure usually begins around 10–11 years for girls and 13–14 years for boys, and the transition from mainly confiding in parents to mainly confiding in friends also occurs earlier among girls than boys. These differences are probably related to puberty and physiological **maturation** in males and females, but the characteristics of social interaction among male and female groups also seem to contribute to differences between genders. The emphasis on status and dominance among boys can inhibit self-disclosure, whereas emphasis on relationships can create a need for intimacy and promote self-disclosure among girls. These differences, however, only apply to *groups*: many male friendships are characterized by closeness, intimacy and a high degree of disclosure, while many female friendships are not. In middle adolescence, a rapid change takes place in self-disclosure between males and females. Before this age, few relationships between genders are close enough to open up for self-disclosure. In romantic relationships, self-disclosure is expected (Berndt & Hanna, 1995; Buhrmester & Prager, 1995).

Self-disclosure allows children and adolescents to achieve *self-clarification* by formulating their thoughts and ideas. They are either *validated* in their beliefs and attitudes through agreement with and recognition from parents or friends, or they realize that their thoughts and viewpoints are unacceptable (Derlega & Grzelak, 1979). As the amount of self-disclosure increases, conversations between peers progressively include more negative gossip about others. Both help to establish group standards based on shared beliefs and attitudes. Thus, conversations between adolescents about themselves and others are closely linked, just like their perception of themselves and others. Reciprocal disclosure helps adolescents construct each other's life stories (Berndt & Hanna, 1995). For today's adolescents, the use of social media may have a significant role in this process through online communication about personal topics that are typically not easily disclosed, such as one's feelings, worries and vulnerabilities. The self-disclosure hypothesis states that online self-disclosure may have beneficial effects on social connectedness and well-being (Huang, 2016; Valkenburg & Peter, 2009).

Self-evaluation

As children grow older, their self-concept also includes evaluations of the characteristics they ascribe to themselves and others. Self-esteem is children's subjective evaluation of their own worth as a person (Donnellan et al., 2011). Children develop an internal standard against which they evaluate their characteristics, a standard that also includes an ideal self, how they would like to be. Some develop a positive evaluation of themselves, others a more negative perception of their own worth. Self-perception is dynamic and may change over time, but also shows some degree of continuity (Chung et al., 2017).

Views differ on how and when children develop the ability for **self-evaluation**. From the perspective of attachment theory, children's self-concept develops in parallel with the establishment of *working models* for the child–parent relationship. Relationships are based on reciprocity: when parents are caring, the child is worthy of being cared for (Bowlby, 1969). Working models thus incorporate the beginnings of self-evaluation (see p. 5). According to Neisser

(1997), children's *evaluating self* begins to develop around the age of 2–3 years and entails a conscious self-understanding and reflection on their own characteristics. One sign of an evaluative self-perception is children's ability not only to express their feelings, but to talk *about* them. Kagan (1998b), however, maintains that children under the age of 5 years are not capable of self-evaluation as they lack the necessary cognitive development to reflect on whether their characteristics meet their own standards and those of society.

At preschool age, children's self-evaluations generally show little reflection. They confuse effort with achievement and often have a far too high opinion of their own abilities when they start school. Even when children are told how they are doing compared with others, they do not seem to use this information in evaluating their own performance (Ruble, 1987). Children are well into school age before they start comparing themselves with others in a way that affects their self-evaluations, and their main motive for comparing themselves with peers seems to be to determine their own competence. Adolescence is characterized by self-consciousness, and adolescents make increasing use of comparisons to ascertain reactions to themselves and others and as a basis for changing their own behavior.

Harter (1987) investigated how children rate their own competence in various areas – academic skills, sports, popularity, acceptance, physical appearance and behavioral conduct – and found that children's self-evaluations gradually became more differentiated. The children below 8 years of age tended to have the same perception of themselves in all areas; they described themselves as capable, bad, kind or mean. Older children evaluated themselves differently in each area. They said they could be good at one thing and bad at another, or kind in some situations and mean in others. Physical appearance has a major impact on self-evaluation in both children and adolescents. Girls focus more on appearance than boys, and many girls perceive themselves as being unattractive. One consequence of this seems to be that girls as a group have lower self-esteem than boys (Baumeister, 1993). It is often maintained that low self-esteem may lead to poor academic achievement, and there are many school programs directed at increasing children's self-esteem (Baumeister, 2005). However, the modest correlations found between self-esteem and academic achievement in typically developing children indicate that low school grades lead to low self-esteem rather than the other way around (Baumeister et al., 2003; Trautwein et al., 2006).

The reactions of people in the surroundings is an important basis for self-evaluation. These reactions reflect both the children's behaviors and their compatibility with the characteristics of important people around them. For example, active children whose parents react negatively because they have trouble dealing with the child's activity level can develop an image of themselves as being disruptive. Other children may be just as active, but their parents react in a way that leads to a positive self-perception, for example as someone with "lots going on" (Eder & Mangelsdorf, 1997). Many adults believe that praise is the best medicine for raising a child's self-esteem, and parents may lavish their children with praise. Brummelman and associates (2017) found that parents of children with low self-esteem gave more "inflated" praise – "Your drawing is amazing" – than parents of children with average or high self-esteem, probably with the intention of raising their child's self-esteem. However, inflated praise seemed to work in the opposite direction and to lower, rather than raise, the child's self-esteem, while inflated praise to children with high self-esteem seemed to increase narcissistic features (see p. 112). Instead of praise, it may be better to influence a child's self-esteem indirectly, by showing affection and positive interest in their activities (Brummelman et al., 2016; Brummelman & Thomaes, 2017). Studies have found that children with warm, sensitive and responsive parents have better self-esteem and evaluate themselves more positively than children with cold and unresponsive parents (Clark & Symons, 2000). Parents with realistic expectations of the child's abilities and needs tend to promote positive self-evaluation. Children with parents whose expectations do not match the child's interests and abilities might believe their parents are dissatisfied with their achievement and develop low self-esteem. A low self-esteem is also a key characteristic of children who have been subjected to mistreatment and abuse. These children may feel that they have little worth and are unworthy of love and can experience themselves as being a bad person, "rotten to the core" (Harter, 2006).

Self-efficacy

Self-efficacy is an important aspect of self-evaluation: the experience of personal agency and control over one's own life (Bandura, 1997, 2008). Children with low self-efficacy feel that they lack such control and that their lives are controlled by external forces. For example, they may believe that they will continue to do poorly in school even if they work harder. Comparisons with others are important for children's development of self-efficacy, for example whether the children they use for comparison succeed in tasks they themselves master or do not master. School is another factor with a major impact on children's self-efficacy (Bouffard & Vezeau, 1998). Adolescents with low self-efficacy may experience **learned helplessness**; they have learned that what they do will not matter and do not attempt to succeed because they believe they will be unsuccessful no matter what (Seligman, 1975). It may become a self-fulfilling belief and lead to underachievement and a failure to learn and experience mastery.

22

Self-perception in Atypical Development

It is generally acknowledged that children's self-perception is influenced by how other people react to them. These reactions are influenced by the children's characteristics, including the presence of disabling conditions. In **typical development**, physical attractiveness is associated with self-esteem (see above), but there is not a direct relation between degree of disability and self-esteem. In children with physical disabilities such as cerebral palsy and spina bifida, minor disabilities were found to have a moderate impact and severe disabilities only a mild impact on their general self-esteem (Miyahara & Piek, 2006). One reason may be differential reactions to disabilities: severe disabilities are visible, and any achievement by children with such disabilities may be met with positive reactions, whereas minor disabilities may not be noticed, and the children's difficulties may be seen as a result of a lack of effort, and the children are therefore met with less favorable reactions. Another explanation may be that the results reflect the comparison group the children used when they evaluated themselves. According to social comparison theory, children's self-esteem depends on who they compare themselves with (O'Byrne & Muldoon, 2017). The children with minor disabilities may score lower on self-esteem because they compare themselves with peers with typical development, whereas children with more severe disabilities feel they do better and have higher self-esteem because they compare themselves with children with similar disabilities.

It has been hypothesized that the social difficulties of children with autism spectrum disorder will have an impact on their self-perception. However, studies have found that the self-images of adolescents with autism spectrum disorder are similar to those of adolescents with typical development, but, in line with their problems with mind understanding

DOI: 10.4324/9781003292579-25

(see Book 4, *Cognition, Intelligence and Learning*, Chapter 23), they had problems telling how others might perceive them (Farley et al., 2010). There is a somewhat higher prevalence of low self-esteem among children with autism spectrum disorder than among children with typical development (16 vs 6 percent). This may reflect the social difficulties of children with autism spectrum experience and their problems understanding what they perceive as the "mindreading abilities" of other people. However, the results also show that most of these children had comparable levels of self-esteem to those of children with typical development (McChesney & Toseeb, 2018).

One study found that the self-perception of adolescents with intellectual disability was similar to typically developing children matched for **mental age** (Nader-Grosbois, 2014). However, in another study, children with intellectual disabilities in the seventh grade had lower self-efficacy than non-disabled children, even when they obtained comparable grades. This probably reflected their struggle with schoolwork, continuous frustration and the large efforts they invested to achieve grades comparable to their peers'. Some of the children in this group said that they felt that they worked all the time and had little life outside school (Lackaye et al., 2006).

23

Self-perception and Emotional and Behavioral Disorders

It is a common finding that low self-esteem is associated with emotional and behavioral disorders, and that high self-esteem may protect against **psychopathology** (Zeigler-Hill, 2011). One study found lower self-esteem in 8–14-year-old children with psychiatric disorders than in peers without such disorders (Stadelmann et al., 2017). Other studies have found high correlations between self-report measures of self-esteem and depressive symptoms among children and adolescents with typical development (Moksnes et al., 2016; Pauletti et al., 2012), as well as among children with intellectual disabilities and **learning disorders** (Alesi et al., 2014). However, correlational studies do not say anything about causal direction. Low mood may influence self-esteem, and low self-esteem can lead to lower mood levels (Harter, 1987). Moreover, it is not easy to distinguish the effect of self-esteem from other factors. Studies suggest that positive or negative self-esteem is a marker and not a causal factor in social and personal development (Baumeister et al., 2003; Boden et al., 2008). Marsh and O'Mara (2008) argue for reciprocal influences, that self-perception influences the way children and adolescents act, and that the reactions to their actions from other people in turn influence their self-perception.

Eating Disorders

Self-perception is a main element in eating disorders. These disorders usually start in adolescence, but body dissatisfaction and worries about weight are common already at early school age and may become an adolescent's constant focus of attention (Evans et al., 2017; Saunders & Frazier, 2017). The age at onset seems to be decreasing, which may reflect an increasing body focus in today's children (Favaro et al.,

DOI: 10.4324/9781003292579-26

2009). Misperception of the physical self, of the weight and size of one's own body compared with peers, intense fear of gaining weight, and low self-esteem or self-worth are core features of eating disorders, which may also include overeating and self-induced vomiting. They may start with dieting, sometimes after comments from peers or others about weight, but most adolescents who diet do not develop eating disorders (Carr, 2016; Evans et al., 2013). Eating disorders are often associated with girls but also occur in boys, especially binge eating, although with a lower prevalence. A higher age at onset among boys may be related to the later puberty in boys compared with girls (Mitchison & Mond, 2015).

Amianto and associates (2016) consider **anorexia nervosa** a deficit in the integrative function of the self, that is, its ability to integrate cognitive, affective and conative – intrinsically motivating – functions. Reported risk factors in preadolescence are perceived pressure to be thin and thin-ideal internalization. Body dissatisfaction has also been seen as a risk factor but may develop in parallel with symptoms of eating disorders and may thus be a sign of the disorder rather than a precursor (Amaral & Ferreira, 2017; Evans et al., 2017; Rohde et al., 2015). Disordered self-perception is a core feature, but eating disorders are complex and have been linked to a range of biological and social factors, including puberty and dieting, as well as attachment, sexual abuse and trauma (Bryant-Waugh & Watkins, 2015; Klump, 2014). Eating disorders occur in most countries, but the prevalence differs considerably and may be influenced by the focus on beauty and the ideal self in mass media and society (Becker et al., 2011; Smink et al., 2012).

Self-esteem and Narcissism

Some years ago, it was a common belief that aggressive behavior and bullying were signs of low self-esteem and insecurity (Baumeister et al., 1996). However, assertiveness and aggression are not typical behaviors of children and adolescents with low self-esteem, who rather tend to be careful and avoid conflict (Baumeister et al., 2003; Zeigler-Hill, 2011). Aggressive and bullying children tend rather to have high but unstable self-esteem and to put the blame on others when their interactions run into problems (Baumeister et al., 1996; Crick & Dodge, 1996). Moreover, bullying and aggression have been connected to narcissism. Narcissistic personality disorder is only diagnosed in adults, but narcissistic traits, such as grandiosity in fantasy or behavior, self-enhancement, an unrealistic sense of importance and entitlement, sensitivity to criticism, need for admiration and lack of empathy can be apparent in middle childhood and may be particularly common in adolescence (American Psychiatric Association, 2013; Thomaes et al., 2008). In a longitudinal study, Carlson and Gjerde (2009) found that narcissism scores increased from middle to late adolescence, followed by a decrease into emerging adulthood.

> High self-esteem means thinking well of oneself, whereas narcissism involves passionately wanting to think well of oneself.
>
> (Bushman & Baumeister, 1998, p. 228)

A high positive self-evaluation is a core feature of narcissism, but not all individuals with a high self-evaluation are narcissistic (Baumeister et al., 2003). An important difference is that self-esteem is an evaluation of the actual self, whereas narcissism is characterized by a constant need for social approval and admiration in order to nourish the grandiose self (Pauletti et al., 2012). In young people, genuine high self-esteem is related to positive social relationships and mental health, whereas narcissistic grand self-evaluation is related to aggression and antisocial behaviors (Bushman & Baumeister, 1998; Tracy et al., 2009). Aggression thus appears to be a feature of narcissism rather than of high self-esteem, elicited by a perceived threat to the individual's **ego**. Consistent with this view, studies have found small negative correlations between narcissistic traits and self-esteem in 11-year-olds (Pauletti et al., 2012). Different developmental origins are also indicated by the finding that high self-esteem and narcissistic features in 7–12-year-olds were associated with parental overevaluation of their child, overestimation of her intelligence and overpraising of her performance, whereas high self-esteem without narcissistic features was related to parental warmth, parents treating their child with affection and appreciation, sharing of positive affect, and fostering in their child the feeling that he or she matters (Brummelman et al., 2015, 2016). Research thus supports a developmental distinction between typical and atypical forms of self-esteem.

24

Identity Formation

Identity formation starts in adolescence and entails both the continuing development of the self and **integration** in a "society of minds" (Nelson, 2007a). Personal identity comprises the self-defining characteristic of the individual person, who he thinks he is. Social or collective identity refers to **identification** with groups and social categories to which the individual belongs, who he thinks he belongs with, the meanings that he gives to these social groups and categories, and the feelings, beliefs and attitudes that result from identifying with them. Being a member of several groups and categories may imply having multiple identities, sometimes contradictory (Vignoles et al., 2011), such as when an adolescent with severe hearing impairment identifies with both the culture of his hearing family and the deaf community (Bat-Chava, 2000).

In adolescence, individuals become more aware of who they are, while at the same time developing new roles, independent positions and a clearer sense of belonging to certain groups in society. Adolescents search for coherence and question the nature and meaning of life in a way not found in children. They explore values and attitudes and search for possible roles, affiliations and their future place as an adult and independent individual in society, in relation to gender, sexual orientation, social class, education, occupation, religion and neighborhood affiliation (McLean & Syed, 2015). In modern, multicultural societies, language and ethnicity are important aspects of an individual's identity. Discussions about identity formation are about the *content*, the issues, concerns and topics that adolescents (and adults) are attentive to when they think about who they are and will become, and the *process*, the activities they engage in when they think about this content (McLean et al., 2016). For today's adolescents, the social

DOI: 10.4324/9781003292579-27

media represent opportunities for trying out roles and attitudes (Shapiro & Margolin, 2014; Wängqvist & Frisén, 2016).

The central theorist in identity development is Erik Homburger Erikson (1968). In his theory, adolescence is the fifth of eight phases of social crises, each of which leaves a permanent mark on the individual's personal and social development (see Book 6, *Emotions, Temperament, Personality, Moral, Prosocial and Antisocial Development*, Chapter 14). In phase 5, the individual defines himself actively, becomes aware of the future, unites the inner and outer world and, if successful, achieves an identity. The crisis arises because identification with parents that was so important in childhood is not enough for adolescents to develop their own roles and relationships and find their independent place in a wider social context. Therefore, young people have to seek out other sources of knowledge, inspiration and models to live up to in creating their own adult lives.

According to Erikson, adolescents are in a state of **psychosocial moratorium** during the transition to adult life. Figuratively speaking, the moratorium represents a chasm between the safety of childhood and the autonomy of adulthood, a period in which the individual tries out different roles and can go through frequent changes in attitude and behavior. The outcome of a positive transition through this phase is fidelity and commitment to others. Identity achievement is the experience of being at home in one's own body and knowing what to move toward, as well as an inner certainty of being accepted by the people who are important in one's life. It is not a static experience, but rather a sense of being on the inside of a dynamic process that provides the right direction for a future life. A suboptimal transition through the social crisis in this phase will lead to role confusion and uncertainty about one's own identity. This can take two forms: young people can either become withdrawn and isolate themselves from family and peers or plunge into a world of peers and lose their identity among the crowd.

Erikson builds on Freud, and his theory is met with some of the same criticism as Freud's theory (Arnett, 2015). As his basis lies in clinical experience, the theory is not easily tested by empirical means. In addition, Erikson's theory is deeply rooted in the social and historical context of his time. According to Erikson, career choice is central to the social crisis of adolescence, but today, this aspect of identity formation is part of emerging adulthood, and far more young people go through a long period of student identity before assuming a more permanent professional identity well into adulthood (see Chapter 40, this volume). Another example is Erikson's portrayal of men as oriented toward career and ideology and women toward creating an adult existence centered on taking care of husband and children. Such **gender differences** are disappearing in modern cultures (see Part IV, this volume). These examples demonstrate the importance of viewing identity formation in light of the social changes that take place in society (Hammack, 2015; Kroger, 2004). In addition, longitudinal observations suggest that adolescence does not involve a massive identity crisis, and, even if identity gradually becomes more stable, the process continues throughout adulthood (Meeus, 2011).

Most other theories of identity development build on, or argue against, Erikson's psychodynamic theory. In recent years, *neo-Eriksonians* have revised and clarified numerous aspects of Erikson's theory (Hammack, 2015; Schwartz, 2001). Adams and Marshall (1996) point to the integrative element in Erikson's theory: the integration of the personal identity that distinguishes the individual from other individuals, such as personal tastes and preferences, and the collective identity that involves affiliation with groups and society by means of language, ethnicity, social class, education, political alignment and so on. They emphasize the balance between *differentiation processes* that contribute to the establishment of an independent individual and *integration processes* that involve the individual's affiliation with social and cultural groups – an excessive level of differentiation can lead to rejection *of* others, whereas a low level of integration can lead to rejection *by* others.

Erikson's theory is also a basis for *theories of narrative identity*, together with theories of **autobiographical memory** and narrative development (Fivush et al., 2011; Nelson & Fivush, 2004). Autobiographical memory (see Book 4, *Cognition, Intelligence and Learning*, Chapter 10) integrates individual experiences of self and cultural frames, and narratives are important for the individual's sense of personal continuity. Narrative identity formation builds on autobiographical reasoning around relationships, roles and positions with a basis in the individual's life history. It is a process that serves to create meaning and coherence in the individual's life (Habermas & Köber, 2015; McAdams, 2013; McAdams & Cox, 2010). One example would be all the factors that may lead an adolescent to become a carpenter, such as his or her particular skills, prior experience with woodwork, the wish to take up a profession that does not require an academic education, the career choices of friends and a shortage of carpenters in the local community. This type of integrated identity process requires cognitive and social skills that are not developed until adolescence (Habermas & Reese, 2015). The development of an autobiographical narrative and a sense of continuity, context and social identity are important prerequisites for mental well-being (Habermas & Köber, 2015).

Ethnic Identity

An *ethnic group* refers to individuals who identify themselves with a particular culture *and* have an affiliation that provides the basis for interaction. This may be the majority or a minority group such as the indigenous Sami people in Scandinavia or Mexicans living in the United States. The language is often an important identity element of an ethnic group, and many adolescents with severe hearing impairment see themselves as members of a Deaf ethnic group that shares the use of a **sign language** (Bat-Chava, 2000). When written with a capital D, *Deaf* refers to membership of a social and cultural group, rather than being a bearer of a medical category. An *ethnic category* is defined by an outside source, be it a bureaucrat or a scientist (Gjerde, 2014). Adolescents who are placed in a given ethnic category can be attributed specific ethnic characteristics (which often reflect stereo-typical views), without these characteristics being important for their identity.

Young people in modern multicultural societies have to deal with a greater number of value systems than in previous societies. This offers new opportunities, but also leads to a more complex – and perhaps lengthier – process of identity formation. Adolescents from ethnic minorities go through the same process of identity formation as the majority **population**, but, in addition to the usual characteristics and roles, parts of their identity may be linked to an ethnic group and race (Umaña-Taylor et al., 2014). Phinney (1990, 1993) describes three **stages** in the development of identity as a member of an ethnic minority (Table 24.1).

Ethnic minority adolescents are often in a complex identity situation because they may have to deal with the expectations of society at large, their peers within the majority population, and their own ethnic group (Hedegaard, 2005). Children notice differences in skin color and cultural background, and adolescents become more aware of their cultural background, although the impact of ethnic background on

Table 24.1 The development of identity as an ethnic minority (based on Phinney, 1993)

Stage	Age	Characteristics
1 Unexamined ethnic identity	Childhood	No exploration of ethnic issues Passive acceptance of the majority culture's values
2 Ethnic identity search/moratorium	Early adolescence	Seeking to determine the meaning of ethnicity to oneself Questioning former attitudes May include increased political awareness and anger
3 Ethnic identity achievement	Late adolescence	A clear and secure sense of one's own ethnicity Uncertainty is resolved, and commitments are made Ethnicity becomes internalized

their identity formation varies considerably (Way & Rogers, 2015; Worrell, 2015). The family is important for the development of identity and acquisition of group values and customs in adolescence. Some immigrant parents who have grown up in poverty may warn their children "Don't be like me" and encourage their child to seek education (Maciel & Knudson-Martin, 2014). On the other hand, the obligation to follow tradition and parental expectations are often stronger among minority than majority populations, and this may reduce minority adolescents' available options. Generational conflicts can arise when young people from minority groups wish to create an adult existence that differs radically from what their parents have intended for them (Seiffge-Krenke & Haid, 2012), such as when a Norwegian adolescent with Pakistani parents wants to study art rather than work in the family grocery store. Conflicts between generations can also be more extensive and profound. A break with ethnic heritage can have lasting consequences for adolescents' relationship with parents and their ethnic group. At the same time, adolescents can have a strong desire to pattern their adult existence along the same lines as that of their peers in the majority population. For many young people from ethnic minorities, such dilemmas get in the way of identity formation and can lead to crises in the more literal sense of the word, not least for asylum seekers who come to a new country as children and have strong feelings for both their old and new country (Umaña-Taylor et al., 2014).

Another problem is that young people from ethnic minorities do not always have positive role models to identify with and may therefore struggle to transcend the majority population's expectations of them as members of a minority, even when this has the support of their parents and others. One example is the relationship between the values of the White majority and the Black minority in the United States, which represents an obstacle for many Afro-American adolescents. While some of them identify with the White majority and take on their values, their skin color and cultural background prevent many White people from fully accepting them. Others distance themselves completely from White majority values and ways of life and thereby limit their own options. Still others try to balance the two value systems in their search for a future role. The same applies to adolescents from Asian and other ethnic backgrounds (Way & Rogers, 2015; Worrell, 2015). Studies show that positive feelings about one's ethnic identity and race contribute to social adjustment and mental health (Rivas-Drake et al., 2014).

Summary of Part III

1   The *self as knower*, or *I*, is the experience of being a unique individual acting in the world. The *self as known*, or *me*, is the individual's perception of self, an awareness of being in possession of certain characteristics and qualities.

2   In the middle of their second year of life, children begin to realize that a mirror shows a reflection of themselves and, sometime later, also recognize themselves in a photograph or a video. Toddlers start referring to themselves by name or *I* and rarely make a mistake between *you* and *I*.

3   According to Mahler, the newborn child is unable to differentiate between herself and the mother. Through a *separation process*, children gradually develop a sense of being a self separate from others. During the *individuation process*, they develop a sense of themselves as autonomous individuals with characteristics independent of the mother. Winnicott suggests children first go through an *undifferentiated phase* and gradually develop a sense of self through the mother's *mirroring* and other maternal reactions. Later theorists are critical of the assumption that infants starts with a differentiated experience of themselves and their mother and have revised this part of the theory.

4   Stern describes a multilayered self that experiences being both independent and part of a social world. Some layers are present at birth; others emerge later in development: *emergent self, core self I* and *II, intersubjective self, verbal self* and *narrative self*. Stern emphasizes interaction, social relations and *affect attunement* in the development of the self. His theory has been of major influence, but has been criticized for the assumption that very young infants

can recognize the *process* underlying their development of self-perception and conclusions that are difficult to verify.

5 Lewis describes four levels in the development of a *representational self* that emerges in the first 3 years of life: level 1 is *I know*, level 2 is *I know I know*, level 3 is *I know you know* and level 4 is *I know you know I know*. Children become aware that they may be both the subject that experiences and the "object" being experienced.

6 Questions about the self revolve around the distinction between the self as knower and the self as known. Kagan believes children must have a primitive sense of self-as-known before they can acquire a sense of self-perception.

7 Children's self-descriptions include four aspects: *physical, activity, psychological* and *social*. The distribution of these changes with age, and children's descriptions become more differentiated and integrated. Adolescents experience themselves to be different in different contexts and describe *several selves*. Self-descriptions also reflect the culture.

8 Memories are a core element of the self, and the *autobiographical narrative* is an essential part of self-perception and the result of co-construction with others, initially in conversation with adults, later also with peers.

9 The culture constitutes a foundation for self-development. Some cultures are individualistic and autonomous; others are more socially and relationally oriented. *Selfways* reflect the culture's ideas and values about the nature of the self, and children's self-perception is the result of cultural selfways and individual experience.

10 *Self-disclosure* is the sharing of personal information with others, face-to-face or on social media. Self-disclosure to friends increases with age, whereas self-disclosure to parents remains stable or decreases slightly. Children and adolescents achieve *self-clarification*; they are either *validated* in their beliefs and attitudes through agreement with and recognition from parents or friends, or they realize that their thoughts and viewpoints are unacceptable. Gender differences in self-disclosure seem to be partly due to the different characteristics of male and female group interaction.

11 Younger children rarely compare themselves with others and use the reactions in their surroundings as a basis for *self-evaluation*. At school age, they start comparing themselves with peers, seeming

to determine their own competence. Adolescents use comparisons to ascertain reactions to themselves and others and as a basis for changing their own behavior. Parents with realistic goals for their child promote positive self-evaluation, whereas parents with expectations that do not match the child's prerequisites can contribute to low self-evaluation. Inflated praise from parents may lead to lower self-esteem or to an increase in narcissistic features.

12 *Self-efficacy* is the experience of personal agency and control over one's own life. Children with low self-efficacy feel their lives are controlled by external forces. Comparisons with others are important for children's development of self-efficacy, for example whether the children they use for comparison succeed in tasks they themselves master or do not master. Adolescents with low self-efficacy may have learned that what they do will not matter – learned helplessness.

13 Self-perception varies somewhat in children with *atypical development*, but most show comparable development to typically developing children. Children with minor disabilities may have lower self-esteem than children with more severe disabilities. The self-images of adolescents with autism spectrum disorder are similar to those of adolescents with typical development, but they have problems telling how others might perceive them.

14 Studies have found associations between emotional and behavioral disorders and self-esteem, and the influences may be reciprocal. Disordered self-perception is a core feature of eating disorders, but these disorders are complex and have been linked to a range of biological and social factors.

15 Research indicates a developmental distinction between typical and atypical self-esteem. Narcissism may be rooted in parental overevaluation, and high self-esteem in parental warmth. Aggression and bullying may imply unstable self-esteem and have been connected to *narcissism.*

16 *Identity formation* involves the exploration and selection of different values and attitudes and finding one's place in society. In Erikson's theory, a positive transition through the social crisis of the fifth phase leads to a mature identity, whereas a suboptimal transition leads to role confusion and uncertainty about one's identity. The theory is deeply rooted in the social and historical context of Erikson's time, and neo-Eriksonians have revised the theory in various ways and adapted it to today's social reality,

including an increased emphasis on integration of personal and social identity, and the development of narrative identity theory.

17 *Ethnicity* and *race* are essential elements in identity formation. Adolescents gradually develop an awareness of their cultural background, with varying impact on their identity. Phinney describes three phases in the development of *ethnic identity*. Multicultural societies lead to new processes in identity formation. Young people from ethnic minorities have to deal with the expectations of society at large, their peers within the majority population and their own ethnic group.

Core Issues

- The newborn infant's ability to distinguish psychologically between herself and the mother.
- The process of self-perception development.
- Self-esteem and narcissism.
- Identity formation and culture.

Suggestions for Further Reading

Brummelman, E., et al. (2015). Origins of narcissism in children. *Proceedings of the National Academy of Sciences, 112*, 3659–3662.

Erikson, E. H. (1968). *Identity: Youth and crisis*. New York, NY: Norton.

Fivush, R., et al. (2011). The making of autobiographical memory: Intersections of culture, narratives and identity. *International Journal of Psychology, 46*, 321–345.

Habermas, T., & Reese, E. (2015). Getting a life takes time: The development of the life story in adolescence, its precursors and consequences. *Human Development, 58*, 172–201.

Markus, H. R., & Kitayama, S. (2010). Cultures and selves: A cycle of mutual constitution. *Perspectives on Psychological Science, 5*, 420–430.

Pine, F. (2004). Mahler's concepts of "symbiosis" and separation–individuation: Revisited, reevaluated, refined. *Journal of the American Psychoanalytic Association, 52*, 511–533.

Swanson, S. A., et al. (2011). Prevalence and correlates of eating disorders in adolescents. Results from the national comorbidity survey replication adolescent supplement. *Archives of General Psychiatry, 68*, 714–723.

Umaña-Taylor, A. J., et al. (2014). Ethnic and racial identity during adolescence and into young adulthood: An integrated conceptualization. *Child Development, 85*, 21–39.

Part IV

Gender Development

Gender in Society

Gender or sex is a salient biological characteristic, as well as a social and cultural construct, in the sense that societies attribute different abilities and behaviors to being male or female. Gender is a characteristic of both individual and collective identity (I'm a girl/boy; we are girls/boys) and impacts the life patterns of boys and girls, men and women, and society's activities in general. This chapter is about the development of gender knowledge, of the understanding of being a boy or a girl, and biological and environmental factors that may influence the development of **gender identity** and gender-related behavior.

DOI: 10.4324/9781003292579-29

The Development of Gender Understanding

Most children develop an early awareness of differences between boys and girls and actively begin to look for traits that distinguish the two groups. At the end of their second year, children show a growing understanding of the words *boy* and *girl*. They acquire concrete knowledge such as the fact that men have beards and women have breasts, as well as cultural knowledge and attitudes related to typical male and female tasks in the society in which they grow up. Although the content of children's gender concepts changes with age, it continuously affects their interpretations and recollections of events involving boys and girls, men and women. Furthermore, children internalize the **gender roles** and **gender stereotypes** of their culture (Martin & Ruble, 2009).

Gender Identity, Stability and Constancy

Kohlberg (1966) describes three stages in children's development of gender awareness. During the first stage, beginning around 2 years of age, children develop gender identity and are able to distinguish boys and girls. Initially, they have slight difficulties answering whether they themselves are a girl or a boy, but manage to choose correctly when they are shown pictures of a boy and a girl and asked which of them is like themselves. Once children begin to identify with their own gender, they also start to perceive gender as a central and positive aspect of themselves (Ruble et al., 2007). However, toddlers are unaware that gender remains stable over time and that boys turn into men and fathers, and girls into women and mothers. During Kohlberg's second stage, beginning at 3–4 years of age, children develop gender stability: the understanding that people maintain the same gender throughout

DOI: 10.4324/9781003292579-30

life. The percentage of children who show gender stability increases from age 4 to 5 (Halim et al., 2017). The third stage, **gender constancy**, begins around 6 years of age. Now children begin to understand that gender is related to biological characteristics rather than the types of clothes people wear and similar external features. Once children have developed gender constancy, they also become increasingly aware of other aspects of male and female characteristics and categorize people spontaneously by gender. At this age, children often have rigid views on traits that characterize boys and girls (Halim & Ruble, 2010).

It is generally agreed that children's gender awareness develops in the order described by Kohlberg, but with considerable variation in age for each of the stages and the length of time children remain in a given stage (Ruble et al., 2007). In one study, 40 percent of 3–5-year-olds answered that children maintain the same sex even if they put on clothes belonging to the other sex (Bem, 1989), earlier than the average indicated by Kohlberg.

Gender Roles

Gender roles consist of all the expectations society has of children and adults by virtue of their gender, that is, how males and females in a given culture are expected to behave in different contexts. These expectations vary within different areas of life, from culture to culture and from era to era (Hewlett, 2000). For example, among the Aka tribe in Central Africa, young children spend much of their time with both parents, and gender roles are relatively egalitarian (Box 26.1).

It seems that fathers' greater participation in childcare and housekeeping is both a result of and contributes to greater gender equality. This is one reason why some countries have introduced child-birth leave that can only be used by the father (Eydal et al., 2015; Karu & Tremblay, 2017; O'Brien & Wall, 2017). This policy has contributed to a change in the father role as well as an increase in work equality in the home, but in most societies mothers still do most of the childcare and housework (Almqvist & Duvander, 2014; O'Brien & Wall, 2017). The general change in gender roles taking place is well illustrated by the fact that, in around 1900, women were not expected to study. One hundred years later, female students outnumbered male students at universities in many countries

Box 26.1   Gender Roles among the Aka Tribe (Hewlett, 1991, 1992, 2000)

The Aka tribe lives off hunting and gathering in the tropical forest regions of the southern Central Africa Republic and northern People's Republic of the Congo. The husband–wife relationship is close and cooperative, and the gender roles are relatively egalitarian. Aka husbands and wives engage in a variety of tasks together, including hunting with nets and childcare. Women are held in high esteem, and food preparation and childcare are not considered feminine activities. In fact, fathers provide more direct infant care than in other societies. Young children spend much of their time with both parents. The Aka fathers do not play with their children, but they hold them a lot and talk with them and they spend a lot of time together. Through this, father and child develop strong attachment and relationships. It is believed that both the shared hunting and housework and the large amount of time both parents spend in caregiving contribute to the egalitarian gender roles in this society. Although hunting methods have changed somewhat, and mobility has reduced since the 1980s, the caregiving pattern of mothers and fathers of the Aka tribe has remained stable together with cultural features such as egalitarianism, sharing and autonomy (Meehan et al., 2017).

Thanks to Barry S. Hewlett for the photograph.

(Eggins, 2017). For example, in 2014, 56 percent of US students were female (Snyder et al., 2016).

Boys and girls show different preferences for toys early on (see Chapter 27). However, preschool children rarely justify their choice of toy based on whether it is fitting for boys or for girls, but instead base it on personal preference (Eisenberg-Berg et al., 1982). Thus, young children's behavior is not shaped by gender roles and general expectations of how boys and girls should play. Instead, children's experiences with their own and other children's preferences and behaviors contribute to sex-typing and eventually lead to a conscious understanding of what being male or female means for oneself and others.

Once children start in school, they already have a good understanding of what is expected of boys and girls and of characteristics and activities considered male and female. As children gain increasing insight into these expectations (gender roles), they also become less conforming and more flexible in their attitudes toward them (Ruble et al., 2006). It is a developmental trend that the female role is less rigid than the male role, and younger boys are under greater pressure to comply with their gender role than younger girls. It is more acceptable for girls to be boyish than for boys to be girlish (see p. 141).

In adolescence, gender roles once again become less flexible, probably because gender-related expectations are strengthened by the focus on sexual relationships typical for this age (Clemans et al., 2010).

Gender Stereotypes

In most societies, social gender categories have evolved general views about what it means to be a boy, girl, man or woman, and what characterizes typical male and female activities and traits. Within a culture, there is usually widespread agreement on what defines these characteristics, and **stereotypes** are often activated without any awareness on the individual's part (Banse et al., 2010; Brandt, 2011).

Once gender identity has been established, children begin to form gender stereotypes. *Boys hit people, Girls talk a lot, Girls often need help, Boys play with cars* and *Girls give kisses* are examples of statements made by 2½–3½-year-olds (Schaffer, 1996, p. 192). In one study, 3–5-year-olds were asked what they thought of two infants. Half of the children were told that child A was a boy and child B a girl, while the others were told the opposite. Regardless of whether A or B was a "boy," the "boy" was labeled big, fast, strong, loud, smart and hard, and the "girl" was labeled little, scared, slow, weak, quiet, dumb and soft (Haugh et al., 1980). The children attributed these qualities solely based on their knowledge of who was a boy and who was a girl. Similar studies have been made with adults (see p. 140), and the gender label appears to have a stronger effect on children and adolescents than on adults (Stern & Karraker, 1989; Vogel et al., 1991). When toddlers are asked what kinds of jobs men and women have, they largely respond in line with attitudes typical for their society (Gettys & Cann, 1981). From 5 years of age, children increasingly say that men and women have different personality traits. Five-year-olds expect women to be calmer than men, and men to be more aggressive and competitive than women (Best et al., 1977).

Gender stereotypes also affect the way in which children remember events. Children aged 5–6 years were shown pictures depicting a male doctor and a female nurse. A week later, they were asked what the pictures had shown and had no problems describing it. Other children were shown pictures of a female doctor and a male nurse. When asked 1 week later what the pictures had shown, they had a tendency to associate the man with the doctor and the woman with the nurse (Cordua et al., 1979). Children aged 5–9 years were shown a film of a boy playing with a doll and another film of a girl playing with a truck. When the children were asked to describe the films, 58 percent of them changed the gender of one of the children, and 22 percent changed both, with the youngest children relabeling gender more often than the older children.

A common stereotype is that girls are concerned about their appearance. In another study, 4–10-year-olds were told: "I think you know a lot of girls (boys). Tell me what you know about girls (boys). Describe them." The most frequent answers dealt with appearance ("girls wear dresses") for girls (31 percent) and personality traits ("boys are mean" or "girls are sensitive") for boys (27 percent). Personality traits came in second place for girls (19 percent), and appearance came in third place for boys (13 percent). The same pattern was found from preschool to fifth grade, but descriptions of personality traits and other internal characteristics increased with age (Miller et al., 2009; see also Book 6, *Emotions, Temperament, Personality, Moral, Prosocial and Antisocial Development*, Chapter 15).

Gender stereotyping increases until the age of 11–12 years. From 8 years of age, children's perceptions largely coincide with those of adults

In many countries, fathers participate more in the care of the children.

within the same culture. At the same time, children become more flexible in their own attitudes, beginning around 6–8 years of age, with girls somewhat more flexible than boys (Banse et al., 2010; Halim & Ruble, 2010). When school-age children were asked to draw their preferred future occupation, many boys and few girls wanted to be football players and policemen, while the gender pattern was opposite for hairdresser, veterinarian and kindergarten teacher (Tzampazi et al., 2013). To some degree, stereotyping has a normative function, with significant social consequences for the relationships between the sexes and choices related to education and work (Brown & Stone, 2016).

Sex-typing

Gender roles are about attitudes and expectations, while sex-typing reflects what children actually do. Children gradually learn to act in accordance with what their culture considers appropriate behaviors and attitudes for boys and girls. However, they may have a clear understanding of what is appropriate for boys and for girls without necessarily conforming to gender roles in every detail themselves. Boys with clear gender stereotypes generally are also more sex-typed in their preferences, but such a connection is not as pronounced among girls (Halim & Ruble, 2010).

Activity Preferences

From early on, boys and girls show different play preferences and behaviors, reflecting both their culture's stereotypes and children's own preferences (McHale et al., 2004). Boys engage in more rough-and-tumble play than girls, a fact that may be related to boys' generally higher activity level (Goldstein, 1994). One-year-old boys prefer cars, tools and other forms of active play. Girls prefer dolls, soft toy animals and building blocks. By 20 months of age, these preferences have stabilized. Although girls are somewhat less biased in their choices than boys, they too make clear gender-typical choices at 3 years of age (O'Brien & Huston, 1985; Todd et al., 2017). Gender differences in toy preferences are maintained throughout childhood (Cherney & London, 2006). However, children's actual use of toys depends on availability. During a visit to an orphanage in Uganda where there were almost no toys, I observed what happened when the children were given dolls and doll equipment – toys that are mainly favored by girls. Both boys and girls of all ages played happily with the dolls: caring, dressing, bathing and feeding them.

DOI: 10.4324/9781003292579-31

Gender-specific preferences for color emerge around 2 years and are well established by 3 years (Wong & Hines, 2015). One study found that over half the girls showed "clothing rigidity," with a preference for pink frilly dresses around the age of 3–4 years in particular, but also that about 25 percent never had such a preference. For boys, the opposite was true: approximately one-quarter were preoccupied with clothing, especially with *not* wearing pink, while more than half never went through a period of clothing rigidity (Halim & Ruble, 2010). The preferences of boys and girls thus show clear differences as well as significant overlap.

Boys are often more interested in construction play than girls, but the relatively organized play activities in kindergarten show no differences. In home observations, which may more clearly reveal children's own preferences, 5–6-year-old boys spent about 16 percent of the time with construction games, and girls spent less than 7 percent (Christie & Johnson, 1987). Although boys and girls spend about equal time on **pretend play**, the content varies: while girls prefer activities such as shopping and washing the baby, boys pretend to be policemen, firemen, Superman and the like. Generally, girls prefer small groups with one or two best friends, while boys prefer to play in larger groups. These differences in emotional and behavioral style are probably important for sex-typing. Even when boys and girls share the same object preferences, such as a cart and similar items that can be pushed along, they use them in different ways. Boys tend to bash them around, whereas girls use toys more gently. Girls who often join in with groups of boys tend to be particularly good at sports. Boys are rougher, engage in more teasing and fighting, have more conflicts and are more competitive and status-oriented than girls. They interrupt each other, talking, directing and threatening, and often refuse to follow the directions of others (Liben & Bigler, 2008). Traditionally, boys have spent more time than girls on team activities such as football or other types of ball games, but this is changing. In many countries, handball and soccer have become common sports among girls as well (Figure 27.1).

There are general patterns in sex-typing but also individual differences. By the age of 5, some children have established distinct gender-typical preferences for activities and games. Other children show a slower and more gradual development with stabilization of clear gender-typical preferences around the age of 10 (Trautner, 1992). Studies have found a connection between gender-typical preferences in early childhood and sex-typed behavior in later childhood. Children

Figure 27.1 In many other countries, soccer has become a common activity among girls.

who show the most sex-typed behavior at the age of 2½ years tended to show the same type of behavior at the ages of 5 and 8 years. One reason for this stability may be that the children with the most sex-typed behavior played more with same-sex children, thereby strengthening their sex-typed behavior (Golombok et al., 2008, 2012).

Boys and girls continue to show sex-typed behavior in adolescence, but also more interest in gender-neutral activities. Their activity choices become more varied, and girls continue to be more flexible than boys (Su et al., 2009). It is important to remember, however, that sex-typing refers to *group differences* with a considerable overlap between male and female groups. Within each group, there is significant individual variation in degree of sex-typed behavior.

Gender-Segregated Interaction

A preference for same-sex playmates can be observed as early as toddler age, and somewhat earlier among girls than boys. At 3 years of age, girls mainly play with girls and boys with boys. In addition, preschoolers are more positive about their own than the opposite sex and are more open to praise and recognition from same-sex than

Girls tend to prefer small group activities, and boys play in larger groups.

other-sex peers (Fagot, 1985; Halim et al., 2016). There is little reason to believe that children have an innate tendency to seek out same-sex peers. Nor does research indicate that parents make a particular point of encouraging play with children of the same sex or are averse to play with children of the opposite sex (Golombok & Fivush, 1994). When children "naturally" seek out same-sex peers, their shared play preferences are probably an important contributing factor, but also the wish to identify with children of the same sex as their own (Martin et al., 2014). Boys play somewhat differently with boys than with girls (and vice versa) and are less aggressive in playing with girls than with boys. Preschoolers, however, prefer children of their own sex in gender-neutral activities as well, such as playing with a swing or laying a puzzle. They also feel more competent and comfortable when playing with children of the same sex as their own. These factors strengthen each other (see Figure 27.2). In my observation of doll play in an orphanage in Uganda mentioned previously, there was a clear gender segregation even though all the children played with dolls.

The tendency to play with children of the same sex becomes more pronounced with age, although joint play and activities are found

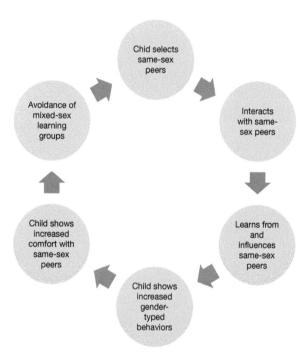

Figure 27.2 The gender-segregation cycle (based on Martin et al., 2014, p. 162).

at all ages (Maccoby, 2002). Participation in physical activity may influence gender segregation. In a study of 3–5-year-olds, the girls with a high activity level spent more time with boys – and thus less time in segregated play – than the less active girls. The boys with a high activity level spent most time in segregated play. This indicates that girls with a high activity level prefer boys with a moderate activity level over girls with a moderate activity level, but not boys who have a high activity level (Bohn-Gettler et al., 2010). In another study, around 6 years of age, US children played 11 times more often with same-sex peers than with peers of the opposite sex (Maccoby & Jacklin, 1987).

School has a major influence on gender-segregated interaction, both in and outside the classroom (see the following) – learning and development seem to be best promoted by mixed-sex classes (Martin et al., 2014). When British children were asked about friends of the opposite sex, 8-year-olds responded that they had several such friends, although these consisted mainly of family and children they had known since preschool age. Eleven-year-olds answered that they would probably have more friends of the opposite sex once they were older (Abrams, 1989). Toward mid-adolescence, gender-segregated groups are gradually replaced by mixed groups as romantic relationships become more common. Also friendships with the opposite sex are increasingly being established (see Part II, this volume).

Gender-segregated play can be found in most cultures, albeit to varying degrees (Best, 2010; Boyette, 2016; Munroe & Romney, 2006). This means that most children's upbringing environment provides a basis for sex-typing. Mixed-gender groups are generally the result of limited access to same-sex peers. In such cases, the preferences of boys and girls usually differ, even though the playgroups in practice are mixed. Nor does early play interaction between boys and girls prevent sex-typing and the development of distinct sex-typed behavior patterns in adulthood (Harkness & Super, 1985; Maccoby & Jacklin, 1987). Mixed-gender groups can be encouraged with the support and organization of adults, but children tend to return to gender-segregated interaction patterns as soon as adults stop encouraging mixed groups (Serbin et al., 1994; Thorne, 1986).

Some societies place higher demands on girls' than on boys' participation in housework, leaving girls with less time for games and play. In non-industrialized societies, boys can have up to one-third more leisure time than girls, but around 10 percent is more typical. In industrialized societies, there are no significant gender differences in regard to playtime (Larson & Verma, 1999).

Differential Treatment

It is a general observation that boys and girls in many ways are met and treated somewhat differently by their environment from an early age. Newborn boys are dressed in blue and girls in pink, and their rooms are decorated in keeping with their gender (LoBue & DeLoache, 2011). Advertisements and shops use pink and blue to mark things for girls and boys (Fine & Rush, 2018). One experimental study found that adults reacted differently to the same 1-year-old, depending on whether they had been told it was a boy or a girl. As a "boy," the child was treated far more roughly than as a "girl" (Bem et al., 1976). In a similar study, adults were shown a video of a 9-month-old who was called either "David" or "Lisa." When the adults were asked to describe the child, David was perceived as angry and Lisa as scared when a jack-in-the-box jumped up, even though the video was identical (Condry & Condry, 1976). These studies demonstrate that external characteristics alone do not lead to different perceptions and treatment of boys and girls. Stereotyped views of children and adults and the different expectations associated with boys and girls are significant as well (see p. 131). Children's behavior, however, is more closely linked to the parents' gendered behaviors than to the parents' gender attitudes and ideologies (Halpern & Perry-Jenkins, 2016). However, same-sex parents do not seem to have much influence on sex-typing. Children aged 2–4 years who had been adopted by same-sex couples showed typical sex-typed behavior, but with slightly smaller differences between boys and girls than in heterosexual families (Goldberg et al., 2012).

Parents accentuate gender by talking about *boys* and *girls* when referring to other children's actions, instead of using the gender-neutral label *child*, for example, "See that boy running fast" or "The girl is laughing" (Zosuls et al., 2009). They talk more with their daughters than with their sons, make more of an effort to involve them in conversation and talk more with them about emotions, especially positive ones. They also tend to talk about an experience itself with their daughters, whereas they discuss causes and consequences with their sons, often involving negative emotions such as anger. Girls are encouraged to show their distress, whereas boys are told to control their anger, influencing boys and girls differently to regulate their own and others' emotional expressions. School-age girls, for example, expect more positive parental responses when they feel sad than boys do (Brody & Hall, 1993; Kuebli & Fivush, 1992).

Studies show that parents respond positively to girls using "girl toys" and boys using "boy toys," but this is more the case for boys than for girls. Parents largely encourage their child's own interests, and children rarely get negative reactions, but, as early as 1 year of age, gender-atypical play among boys – but not girls – is actually met with negative reactions. Boys are generally under greater pressure to live up to their gender roles than girls, especially in relation to their fathers. "Tomboy" is not perceived to be as derogatory as "sissy." Whereas it is relatively acceptable for girls to show boyish behavior, boys face considerable social sanctions if they show effeminate behavior (Hines, 2015).

At least as important as the influence of parents and other adults on the development of gendered behavior is the influence of peers (Martin & Fabes, 2001). Children expect gender-typical behavior when playing with same-sex peers and are extremely critical when other children violate their expectations of gender roles. At school age, they tend to tease or otherwise penalize children with friends of the opposite sex. Both children and adolescents respond with severe sanctions to boys who deviate from male gender roles, whereas they find it more acceptable for girls to participate in boy activities. Atypical gender behavior in preschool age may be associated with **open** and **relational aggression**, exclusion and bullying. A similar pattern of negative reactions may be found at school age and in adolescence, but friendship with and acceptance by same- and other-sex peers can protect against such sanctions (Toomey et al., 2014; Zosuls et al., 2016). Nonetheless, more in-depth studies have shown that the influence of friends is a complex process. One study found that negative peer sanctions led 10-year-old boys with many male friends to become more gender-typical, whereas boys with few male friends had a more atypical development. Girls developed more gender-typical traits, but only those with many male friends. Girls with many female friends and few male friends did not change, possibly because they did not perceive their problems to be related to gender-typical behavior (Ewing Lee & Troop-Gordon, 2011).

School can have a major impact on gender-typical behavior. The way in which teachers relate to students contributes to promoting or reducing students' sex-typed behavior (Bhana, 2016; Stromquist, 2007). Yet some authorities argue that the differences in boys' and girls' brains and their competitive mentalities, cognitive processing, activity levels and so on make it impossible to teach them effectively in the same classroom (Gurian, 2011). In 2012, the United States had 699 schools with gender-segregated classes and 106 single-sex schools (67 for girls, 39 for boys; Klein et al., 2014). Research, however, shows that both girls and boys learn as well or better in mixed- than in single-sex classes. Classes with both boys and girls also seem to have a regulating effect on sex-typed play and other behavior among both sexes; boys, for example, do not engage in physical fights when playing with girls. **Segregation** of girls and boys or teachers who in other ways stress gender as a category in the classroom seem to contribute to underlining and reinforcing gender stereotypes. Mixed-sex classrooms thus lead to more positive gender attitudes than segregation (Hilliard & Liben, 2010; Martin et al., 2014).

The gender roles of society have a general impact, and it is a common finding that boys and girls are treated differently in children's literature and mass media. As nearly all children watch television, it is likely that television programs affect gender attitudes, and that existing gender stereotypes are reflected in how males and females are portrayed. The traditional literature for children and adolescents has represented men and women based on stereotypes. Since the 1980s, authors have placed greater emphasis on equality between the sexes, but women continue to be portrayed as more in need of help than men (Ruble et al., 2006). Moreover, a gender bias may still be found in schoolbooks (Moser & Hannover, 2014).

28

Atypical Development

Children vary in their development of gendered preferences, behaviors and interests. Despite many emotional experiences, development proceeds without problems in most cases. A minority of around 3 percent have difficulty finding their role as a male or female in society and show a "non-conforming" development of gender identity (Becker et al., 2017). They may experience a discrepancy between their anatomical and their perceived gender and feel they belong to a different sex than the one they were "assigned." This is a small group, estimated at 2–14 in 100,000, but the numbers are quite uncertain. Boys dominate among those who are referred for sex identity problems, and, although slightly more girls than boys report they would rather belong to the other sex, this need not be related to gender identity (Gender Identity Research and Education Society, 2006; Zucker & Seto, 2015).

There seem to be two atypical develop mental pathways. The first consists of an "early" group, with atypical development from early childhood. The second group begins to show signs closer to puberty when gender identity is affected by the body's first sexual responses and feelings of love. Whereas the majority of children in the early group become homosexual, this is not the case for the latter group, which instead is characterized by cross-dressing and the like. The reasons for atypical development are uncertain, but twin studies suggest both genetic and non-genetic contributions. Individuals with atypical prenatal sex hormones have a far higher **incidence** than the general population, but the majority of this group do not show atypical gender development (Hines, 2015; Ristori & Steensma, 2016; Zucker & Seto, 2015).

The experience of atypical gender identity development can be an extremely difficult one for children and adolescents. Younger

DOI: 10.4324/9781003292579-32

children can react by crying when their parents tell them that they belong to their anatomical sex. The children might dislike their own genitalia and other bodily sexual characteristics, have a strong desire to belong to the other sex, dress up like the opposite sex and play with other-sex children and their gender-typical toys. They often take on the role of the opposite sex in pretend and fantasy play (Zucker et al., 2014).

When this type of development creates severe distress and problems in daily life, children or adolescents may meet the criteria for a diagnosis of "gender dysphoria" (American Psychiatric Association, 2013) or "gender incongruence of childhood" (Reed et al., 2016; World Health Organization, 2018). The duration of dysphoria varies and, for most children, it does not last into adolescence (Box 28.1). However, for some, the problem will not desist until they have decided

Box 28.1   Desistence and Persistence of Childhood Gender Dysphoria (Steensma et al., 2013)

How long gender dysphoria lasts varies considerably. Seventy-nine children with a natal gender of boy and 48 children with a natal gender of girl who were referred to a gender specialist clinic and diagnosed with gender dysphoria before the age of 12 years were followed up in adolescence and were 15 years and older at the follow-up, from 2008 to 2012. Twenty-three of the 79 natal boys and 24 of the 48 natal girls reapplied for treatment and were considered "persisters." Two-thirds of the natal boys and half of the natal girls thus did not return to the clinic. It was assumed that they no longer had a desire for gender reassignment and thus that the gender dysphoria had desisted. Those who had more intense gender dysphoria were more likely to persist. When asked "Are you a boy or a girl?" those who expressed cross-gender identification had a greater probability of persisting. Nearly half of the boys who persisted had started the social transition in childhood, whereas only a small minority of the desisters had started early. Among the girls, the difference was small, around half of both the persisters and the desisters had started early. Thus, among the natal males, early transition predicted the developmental course but it did not among the natal female group.

to change gender, and a small percentage choose sex change surgery (Ristori & Steensma, 2016). One interview study found a difference between those who said they *were* the other gender and those who said they *wished* they were the other gender. Gender dysphoria was persistent in the first group, whereas it showed more desistence in the second group (Steensma et al., 2011).

Atypical gender behavior and the experience of being different from others typically lead to severe problems with personal relationships in childhood and adolescence. Many among this group develop behavioral disorders and emotional responses involving depression, anxiety and social withdrawal. This may be related to a lack of tolerance and acceptance from peers in childhood and adolescence (Bos & Sandfort, 2015; Eden et al., 2012). Self-harm and suicidal ideation are much more common than in the general population and increase throughout childhood (Aitken et al., 2016).

In line with the broad range of variation among this group, the aim of intervention can differ considerably: reduction of gender-atypical and promotion of gender-typical behavior, conversations with children and parents about social consequences, or determining whether the child actually identifies as transgender. Whatever the goal may be, any intervention entails major professional and ethical issues (Ehrensaft, 2017; Ristori & Steensma, 2016).

29

Theoretical Perspectives on Gender-Typical Behavior

Theorists largely agree on the development of sex-typed behavior and the role of cultural factors in this development, but differences between the genders have various explanations, particularly with regard to the emphasis on nature versus nurture. Theories must be able to explain the trajectories and variations of both typical and atypical development.

Although men and women show clear biological differences related to reproduction, it is not as clear how biological differences affect the development of male and female behavior. According to **evolutionary psychology**, many forms of behavior that typically distinguish the sexes have their origin in hormonal processes related to maturation, such as choice of partner, caring for children and emotional relationships (Buss, 2009; Kennair et al., 2011; Wilson, 1998). A major argument in favor of this theory is that variation in prenatal sex hormones seems to contribute to individual differences in sex-typed behavior (Cohen-Bendahan et al., 2005; Hines et al., 2016). One study found that mothers of young girls with more male-typed behavior had higher testosterone levels than mothers of girls with more female-typical behavior (Hines et al., 2002). Hormones organize the brain, and activity interests are linked to prenatal androgen exposure (Berenbaum & Beltz, 2016). Girls who have been exposed to abnormally large amounts of male hormones during fetal development will exhibit more boy-like characteristics, even if their hormonal balance is restored after birth, their parents encourage them to engage in more girl-typical activities than other parents, and the children clearly develop as females (Hines, 2015). The girls in this group do better than average on tasks requiring spatial perception (an area in which boys generally outperform girls)

DOI: 10.4324/9781003292579-33

and tend to be boy-like in their selection of toys, such as choosing cars over dolls (Nordenström et al., 2002; Servin et al., 2003). For the majority of girls, the hormonal disturbance does not lead to changes in gender identity and self-perception as females, but only in the development of gender-typical behavior. Children who are genetically male, but were insufficiently exposed to male hormones during the **fetal period**, do not have a corresponding tendency to develop female-typed behavior. This may be because the environment places more pressure on boys than on girls to conform to sex-typed behavior. It is easier for girls to follow their actual preferences without incurring social sanctions (Meyer-Bahlburg et al., 2006; Ruble et al., 2006).

Some boys (with **sex chromosomes** XY) do not have male genitalia owing to congenital anomalies, and, on rare occasions, the penis has been accidentally cut off during circumcision. In some of these cases, attempts have been made to transform a male into a female by surgically forming a vagina, initiating hormone treatment and raising the child as a girl (Money 1975; Money & Ehrhardt, 1972). Such attempts have shown widely differing results. Although most of the children developed a female identity, nearly all were characterized by male interests. Some experienced themselves as a male in a female body, with a far higher incidence of sex reassignment surgery than among the general population. The results suggest that prenatal hormones impact individual interests, but that hormones alone do not determine gender. Parenting, too, can have a significant effect on gender identity formation (Meyer-Bahlburg, 2005).

Behaviorist theories represent the counterpart to evolutionary psychology, in that the rearing environment is believed to have the greatest impact. Sex-typing is the result of differential treatment, as people in the environment encourage and penalize various types of behavior among boys and girls (Lamb et al., 1980). Furthermore, children observe the behavior of boys, girls, men and women and other people's responses and thereby get to know their own and the opposite sex. They learn to behave in different ways with different people, and gender is one of the main categories of division. Studies show that children imitate older children and adults of the same sex more than children and adults of the opposite sex (Novak & Peláez, 2004). Just like other acquired behavior, traditional behaviorism views sex-typing as primarily driven by external influences. **Cognitive behavioral theory** unifies learning-based theories with the formation of gender concepts (see below). Bussey and Bandura (1992, 1999) describe a development from external control to internal regulation of gender-typical behavior. By observing many people, children form an abstract and generalized understanding of how boys, girls, men and women behave. It is this understanding, together with the knowledge of their own gender, which forms the basis for children's actions in situations in which gender has a bearing on their choice of action.

Other theories focus on the development of *cognitive gender* **schemas** or *gender concepts*, the beliefs children form about boys' and girls' behavior. According to Kohlberg (1966), part of children's cognitive development entails that, as soon as they have established gender identity and gender constancy (see p. 128), they begin to interpret the outside world based on gender as a main category and to infer what it means to belong to a certain gender. Boys discover that they are boys and instruct themselves to do "boy things." Similarly, girls instruct themselves to do "girl things." What is typical for "boy things" or "girl things" depends on the differences between boys' and girls' activities in the society they grow up in and that "labels" them as belonging to one or the other gender. Kohlberg's theory thus views children's gender-typical behavior as the result of a conscious effort to be like children of the same sex as their own. Therefore, gender constancy is a prerequisite for gender-typical behavior, but studies show that children have gender-typical toy preferences before they know whether they are a boy or a girl. Although 3-year-olds have only developed gender stability, they have a good understanding of typical boy and girl things and the play preferences of boys and girls (Martin et al., 2002). This suggests that the development of understanding gender as a permanent individual trait occurs in parallel with the acquisition of knowledge about gender roles in society.

Also, Bem (1981) suggests that sex-typing has its origins in the development of gender concepts or schemas. Children establish a gender concept through learning to evaluate what is right and wrong from a gender perspective and thus how they should act based on their own gender. The organization of behavior based on one's own gender identity is not driven by cognitive development but is the result of adults directing children's attention to the gender-typical traits of other children and adults from an early age. Although Bem's *gender schema theory* places greater emphasis on gender as a social construct than Kohlberg's theory, both agree that children seek to be similar to others who share the same biological attributes.

According to *developmental intergroup theory*, children identify with other children based on certain characteristics. Gender is an important group characteristic in society, and affiliation with either the "boy" or the "girl" group represents a key element in children's social identity (Bigler & Liben, 2007). Sex-typing is assumed to have its origins in the biological characteristics of males and females as well as in children's perceptions and concepts of what boys and girls do. Their social identity as a boy or a girl makes children see the world through "male lenses" or "female lenses" and represents a strong incentive to act in accordance with what is considered appropriate for one's own sex and avoid acting like the other sex (Liben, 2014; Maccoby, 1998).

This short overview shows that the theoretical perspectives on gender development vary considerably. For example, evolutionary psychology and behaviorism make very dissimilar assumptions about the foundation of gender-typical behavior. Other theories are complementary rather than contradictory, making it possible to unify several theoretical perspectives. Biological factors undoubtedly play an important role in the development of gender-typical behavior, but biological differences alone are unable to explain the variation in interests and behavior among boys and girls. Nor do parents relate so differently to boys and girls that this alone would be able to explain the differences between genders (Hines, 2015; Maccoby, 2000). Besides, these differences only represent an average – men and women show a wide range of characteristics and behaviors, and there are significant cultural differences (Buller, 2005, 2008; Lickliter & Honeycutt, 2003). Overall, research suggests that biology imposes certain **constraints** that contribute to the different development in males and females. Boys and girls are biologically "primed" to develop gender-typical behavior, but the content of their gender schemas and identities can be affected by upbringing. Although biological factors are of importance to children's early preferences, the social environment can have a decisive impact on whether the differences between boys' and girls' preferences and behaviors are maintained or modified (Archer, 1992). The same developmental processes can result in cultural differences in relation to gender roles and behavior. Cultural differences and the changes that have occurred in many countries with regard to gender roles and women's participation in the workplace, in team sports and in men's and women's choice of profession are examples of how culture contributes to maintain or change areas of activity that may be perceived to be biologically determined and gender-specific in a given culture. However, identifying as a boy or a girl need not be the only reason for gender-specific behavior. Other differences can lead boys and girls to form different concepts and beliefs about the world. Maccoby (2002) points to peer groups as an important influence on sex-typing. It is the multiple interactions between biological differences impacting temperament, **cognition** and action, the typical activities and experiences of boys and girls, and the responses and influences from their surroundings that form the development of children's perception of the social world.

Summary of Part IV

1   Gender is a salient biological characteristic as well as a social and cultural construct. Children are, at an early age, aware of differences between boys and girls and begin to acquire society's expectations of males and females.

2   Kohlberg describes three stages in the development of *gender awareness*: *gender identity*, *gender stability* and, finally, *gender constancy*.

3   *Gender roles* consist of the expectations society has of children and adults by virtue of their gender. Boys seem to be under greater pressure than girls to live up to their gender role and incur more social sanctions for behavior typical of the other sex.

4   *Gender stereotypes* are beliefs about the characteristics of adults and children solely based on their gender. From 3–4 years of age, children gradually adopt culturally transmitted attitudes about the typical vocations and personalities of men and women.

5   *Sex-typing* refers to the acquisition of what culture regards as appropriate play, behavior and attitudes for boys and girls. Children vary in their developmental trajectories of gender-typical activity preferences. Adolescents continue to show sex-typed behavior, but also more interest in gender-neutral activities.

6   Children prefer to play with same-sex peers, but joint play and activities take place at all ages. In mid-adolescence, mixed groups replace gender-segregated groups, and friendships with the other sex become increasingly common.

7   Boys and girls are, in different ways, met and treated somewhat differently by their environment, in the home, in kindergarten and school, among peers and in children's literature and mass media.

8   A small percentage of children experience a discrepancy between their anatomical and their perceived gender. Some children and

adolescents meet the criteria for a diagnosis of "gender dysphoria" or "gender incongruence." In the majority, the problems are temporary, but for some they do not desist until the person has decided to change gender. Atypical gender behavior typically leads to relationship problems and emotional disorders, and any intervention entails major professional and ethical issues.

9   *Evolutionary psychology* stresses the biological basis of gender-typical behavior patterns. One argument in favor of the theory is that variation in the prenatal sex hormones seems to contribute to individual differences in sex-typed behavior, although the influence on gender identity is small. Studies suggest that biology imposes certain constraints, but that gender identity is also affected by upbringing.

10   *Behaviorist theories* largely view gender differences as the result of the environment encouraging and penalizing various types of behavior among boys and girls. According to *cognitive behavioral theory*, children gradually form a generalized understanding of what boys and girls are and how they behave, leading to a development from external control to internal regulation of gender-typical behavior.

11   Kohlberg's theory views children's development of gender concepts as part of their general cognitive development. *Gender identity* forms the basis for developing gender-typical behavior: boys do "boy things" while girls do "girl things." According to Bem, sex-typing is the result of adults helping children to develop gender concepts by directing children's attention to the characteristics of the child's own and others' gender-typical behavior from an early age. *Developmental intergroup theory* views gender as an important group characteristic in society and therefore as a key element in children's social identity. Children's social identity as a boy or a girl leads them to view the world through "male lenses" or "female lenses" and act in accordance with what is considered appropriate for their own sex and avoid acting like the other sex.

12   Overall, research suggests that boys and girls are biologically "primed" to develop gender-typical behavior, but that the content of their gender schemas and identities is affected by upbringing. Cultural differences and changes in women's participation in the workplace and sports are examples of how culture affects gender roles. The multiple interactions between biological differences

impacting temperament, cognition and action, the typical activities and experiences of boys and girls, and the responses and influences from their surroundings form the development of children's perception of the social world.

Core Issues

* The biological and social bases of gender-typical behavior.
* The evolutionary basis of gender roles.
* The cultural and historical variation in gender roles and behavior.

Suggestions for Further Reading

Banse, R., et al. (2010). The development of spontaneous gender stereotyping in childhood: Relations to stereotype knowledge and stereotype flexibility. *Developmental Science*, *13*, 298–306.

Halim, M. L. D. (2016). Princesses and superheroes: Social-cognitive influences on early gender rigidity. *Child Development Perspectives*, *10*, 155–160.

Halpern, H. P., & Perry-Jenkins, M. (2016). Parents' gender ideology and gendered behavior as predictors of children's gender-role attitudes: A longitudinal exploration. *Sex Roles*, *74*, 527–542.

Karu, M., & Tremblay, D. G. (2017). Fathers on parental leave: An analysis of rights and take-up in 29 countries. *Community, Work and Family*, *21*, 344–362.

Maccoby, E. E. (2002). Gender and group process: A developmental perspective. *Current Directions in Psychological Science*, *11*, 54–58.

Munroe, R. L., & Romney, A. K. (2006). Gender and age differences in same-sex aggregation and social behavior: A four-culture study. *Journal of Cross-Cultural Psychology*, *37*, 3–19.

Ristori, J., & Steensma, T. D. (2016). Gender dysphoria in childhood. *International Review of Psychiatry*, *28*, 13–20.

Part V

Play

Participation in Play

The activities children participate in are a basis for their enculturation. In the first years of life and throughout childhood, play is an important activity for children in many societies. A clear-cut definition of play is difficult to find. In fact, most authors point to the difficulty defining play and avoid defining it (Glenn et al., 2013; Sheridan et al., 2011). They point out that play is not a group of activities but defined by the underlying motives – play actions are voluntary, do not distinguish between reality and fantasy, are enjoyable and have no goal beyond themselves; they may or may not involve others (Lifter et al., 2011; Pellegrini, 2013). Thus, running up a hill to get to school on time is not play. When children run up and down a hill without any other purpose than perhaps to see who can run the fastest, they are playing. Except on occasions when children don't know what to do with themselves, they need neither encouragement nor reward for playing. Play actions are motivating in and of themselves and are typically accompanied by joy and other positive emotions.

This chapter describes different forms of play and their developmental trajectories and discusses the functions of play in children with typical and atypical development.

DOI: 10.4324/9781003292579-35

Forms of Play

Play takes many forms and can be categorized in different ways (Lillard, 2015; Mertala et al., 2016). Some of the more common categories are listed in the following, but the boundaries between them are often blurred.

Sensorimotor play and **exercise play** are forms of *physical play* (Pellegrini & Smith, 1998). Infants and toddlers can keep up rhythmic movements with their arms and legs for long stretches at a time and engage in *locomotor play* involving gross motor activities such as running, jumping, climbing and sliding, or activities such as pulling, grasping and throwing objects, all without a clear outside purpose other than the activity itself. Many animals, too, spend a lot of time on gross motor play (Burghardt, 2005). Objects can be used in fitting ways for play, such as when children have a long "conversation" on a telephone that is not connected, or in unfitting ways, such as when a child persistently hits a toy car on a table top. Whereas very young infants and children engage in pure motor activities, in later activities the physical actions have a broader basis of meaning, often **imitations** of adult activities. However, the aim of such actions does not lie in their practical consequences, but solely in the pleasure of mastering them. When children do the dishes or sweep the floor in the kitchen or the dollhouse, they do so not in order to clean, but to master an adult activity. When children perform actions to help adults with their work and perceive their own actions as goal-oriented and helpful, they are no longer playing. This type of cooperation also introduces children to culturally valued activities, but here they are "trainees" rather than play partners.

Rough-and-tumble play is physical but also a form of *social play* in which children chase each other – pushing, tickling and the like – or

DOI: 10.4324/9781003292579-36

engage in play fighting. The fact that the fighting is not for real is signaled by children's facial expressions and verbal communication and by the way in which they fight. These episodes usually last for a short time, and children do not hit as hard as when they fight for real. Such play can nonetheless lead to arousal, and, for children with self-regulation problems, play fighting tends to develop into real fighting (see Book 6, *Emotions, Temperament, Personality, Moral, Prosocial and Antisocial Development*, Chapter 27). This type of play is also common among many animal species and provides insight into their communication (Palagi et al., 2016; Pellegrini & Smith, 1998).

Constructive play involves creating something, such as building a house with blocks or Lego, forming a clay figure or assembling a Meccano vehicle. Children putting bricks on top of each other and knocking them down again is not considered constructive play. Constructive play can occur alone or together with others and often has symbolic elements. Children can use their constructions in role-play and pretend play, often accompanied by a story, such as dolls living in a house built of blocks or puppets "eating" a clay cake the child has made (Christie & Johnson, 1987). Piaget (1951) and Pellegrini (2013), however, argue against the role of construction as play, contending that construction has an extrinsic goal – the completed structure – and therefore cannot be considered play. There are no clearly defined boundaries, however. Playing out a story in a dollhouse or racing toy cars can be as goal-oriented as building a house with Lego, and neither the act of constructing nor making up a story has a goal other than the joy of carrying out the activity itself.

In **symbolic play** or *pretend play*, children take on the role of a person or an animal and assign a function to objects other than their usual one. It involves both symbolic objects and objects used for their actual function, but without fulfilling that function in reality. When children pretend to be drinking from an empty cup, the cup is used for its intended purpose, but the action is make-believe. One of the characteristics of play is that it can transcend the constraints of reality and incorporate *counterfactual* reasoning (Amsel & Smalley, 2000). The child can be a nurse, a firefighter or a pirate, and a building block can become a house or a car. It is the object's role in the context of play that defines its use and function. When a building block acts as a toy car, it is the properties of cars, rather than blocks, that determine what the block can do and how it can be used in play (even though "cars" sometimes begin to fly in the air). The same applies to children's make-believe roles. When children become nurses or pirates, it is their make-believe role that determines the possibilities and limitations of their actions. Play reflects children's imagination, but also the basic human tendency to think in **metaphors** (see Fauconnier & Turner, 2002; Lakoff & Johnson, 1980). Pretend play is often social and particularly common when children play together with their parents or other children.

Symbolic play is often considered the "true" form of play, but many types of play can include symbolic elements and take place both in a social context and alone. For example, children can run on their own for the sake of running, or play cops and robbers and run after each other.

32

Solitary, Parallel and Group Play

The earliest form of play takes place in interaction with adults, such as playing peek-a-boo or retrieving an object that falls outside the infant's reach. Over time, children become more self-reliant and able to play on their own (Christie & Johnson, 1987; Pellegrini, 2013).

The first form of play involving several children is **parallel play**. Children play *next to* rather than *with* each other. The reason for this may be that coordinating several actions and people at the same time exceeds younger children's cognitive capacity. In the early years, children also spend a good deal of time watching other children's activities without participating themselves (Veiga et al., 2017).

With increasing age, **group play** becomes more common. In **associated group play**, children play with the same toys and interact to a certain extent. They might play side by side with dolls, for example, and occasionally put their own doll in the bed of another child's doll. **Collaborative play** involves complementary roles and tasks. One child bathes the doll while another makes up the doll's bed. One child assembles the train tracks into a circle while the other finds the locomotive and wagons and puts them on the tracks (Parten, 1932).

Among slightly older children, play has traditionally been social and collective, but, in the course of the twentieth century, solitary play has become significantly more common in Western industrialized countries among children not attending kindergarten (Sutton-Smith, 1994). This may be owing to the smaller size of families, less access to play areas and more time spent playing at home, as parents today often feel it is unsafe for their child to play outside, especially in cities (Frost, 2012; Wridt, 2004). This development is also reflected in the manufacture of many toys children can play with on their own (including tablets and online games).

DOI: 10.4324/9781003292579-37

Most children spend a lot of time playing, but play patterns vary from one child to another. Solitary play is more common among shy children not because they are not motivated to play with others, but because they feel anxious about engaging in new activities and being judged and evaluated socially (Coplan et al., 2015). Much time spent on solitary play can also be the result of rejection by other children (Coplan et al., 2014). At preschool age, this can be a warning sign of social isolation or atypical social development, particularly when caused by rejection, but solitary play can also be constructive and creative (Coplan et al., 2015; Luckey & Fabes, 2005). *Nonsocial play* means that children play alone even when possible play partners are present. This can reflect a preference for solitary play that need not be related to developmental problems, whereas children who actively show *social avoidance* are at risk of being rejected by their peers and developing social anxiety and other internalizing disorders (Coplan et al., 2015).

33

The Development of Play

Different forms of play do not represent separate stages or periods of development. Some appear earlier than others but continue to be part of children's repertoire as long as they play. Thus, there is no clear timeline between the different play forms.

Exercise play is the most common form of play in the first 3 years of life. Reaching a peak at the age of 4–5 years, it continues throughout childhood, while physically active play becomes common in the first few years of school. Initially, this type of play consists of motor repetitions for the sheer pleasure of executing them and manipulating objects in the environment, but it gradually becomes more symbolic and involves more participants (Pellegrini, 2011). Rough-and-tumble play begins around the age of 3. Play fighting increases throughout childhood, making up 3–5 percent of play at preschool age, peaking at around 8–10 percent in middle childhood and decreasing to 5 percent in early adolescence (Pellegrini & Smith, 1998).

Simple constructive play starts in the beginning of the second year. Around 2 years of age, constructive play increases significantly and represents 40 percent of all play at the age of 3–4, especially in kindergarten, which often is well equipped for this type of play. Although constructive play stands for about half of all play in kindergarten from the age of 4 to 6, it makes up only 12–13 percent of the time spent playing at home and features twice as much among boys as girls (Christie & Johnson, 1987). The simple constructions of young children and toddlers are gradually replaced by train sets, complicated Lego structures and model airplanes.

According to Piaget (1951), the earliest symbolic play can be observed in the second year of life, when children begin to perform familiar activities with novel objects. When Piaget's own daughter,

DOI: 10.4324/9781003292579-38

Jacqueline, was 18 months old, she said *cry, cry* to her toy animals and made crying sounds for them. Two months later she was scrubbing the floor with a sea shell, similar to the action she had seen the cleaner perform with a scrubbing brush. Pretend play is central to the third of Vygotsky's and Elkonin's six stages of leading activities in the period from 3 to 7 years (see Book 4, *Emotions, Temperament, Personality, Moral, Prosocial and Antisocial Development*, Chapter 6).

Fenson and Schell (1985) describe three parallel developmental trends in pretend play. The first is related to **decentration**, meaning that play gradually involves other people as well. One example of a developmental sequence is that the child first pretends to be drinking from an empty cup, then feeds a doll from an empty cup and finally lets the doll drink from the empty cup. Usually, this last type of play action emerges during the second year of life (Largo & Howard, 1979a, b). The second parallel developmental trend is *decontextualization*. This means that the child gradually moves away from concrete actions, for example by first drinking from an empty cup, then drinking from a shell or similar item and finally pretending to drink without a cup or other substitute object. Around the age of 3–4 years, children usually use their finger as a toothbrush when asked to pretend to brush their teeth, whereas children above the age of 6 perform this make-believe action with their hand without replacing the missing toothbrush with a finger or an object. Using invisible objects to make-believe is considered a more advanced form of pretend play, as the absence of a concrete object shows that it exists only in the child's mind (Weisberg, 2015). The third trend is the gradual *integration* of multiple actions in the same play activity. A possible developmental sequence can start with the child pretending to feed a doll, followed by feeding several dolls in turn and finally feeding, washing and putting the doll to bed. Performing several actions within the same play activity usually also occurs before the age of 2.

The onset of pretend play seems to vary among cultures, depending on the extent to which adults encourage such play, but in all cultures it starts before the age of 3 years. By this age, most children have also developed a good understanding of the difference between reality and fantasy (Ma & Lillard, 2006). Symbolic play has a central place in children's activities between the age of 3 and 5 years (Lillard et al., 2013). In a **retrospective survey** of university students, 92 percent responded that pretend play had been a daily activity at 4–5 years of age. The percentage decreased at early school age, and, after the age of 10–11 years, pretend play gradually became less common, although a small group of students said they continued to play beyond the age of 18 years (Table 33.1).

Many children have an *imaginary companion*, a fantasy person who accompanies them everywhere. This is also considered a form of pretend play (Weisberg, 2015). Some children create extensive worlds that include farms, railways, countries and islands filled with people, animals and things. These companions and worlds can be private and secret, or children can tell their parents and siblings about them (Cohen & MacKeith, 1990). This form of pretend play is most common during preschool age. In one study, 31 of 100 children aged 3;4–4;8 years responded that they had such a companion. Three years later, only three of the children still had one (Taylor et al., 2004). There is a possible relation between imaginary companions and verbal imagination. On average, children with imaginary friends tend to be better at telling stories than children without such friends (Trionfi & Reese, 2009).

Helping Children Play

Younger children need help to develop play skills. Adults often help children get started with pretend play and thereafter withdraw so children can develop these skills on their own (Shmukler, 1981). How children play also depends on whether they are playing alone

Table 33.1 The development of pretend play (113 students were asked how often they engaged in pretend play throughout childhood and adolescence (based on Smith & Lillard, 2012). Asterisks (*) indicate cells where the observed count was significantly higher than the expected count (p < 0.01).)

Age (years)	Never	Rarely	Monthly	Weekly	Daily
4–5	0	0	0	21	92*
6–7	0	1	2	34	76*
8–9	1	5	16	56*	35*
10–11	7	11	34	46*	15
12–13	11	33	43*	21	5
14–15	29	44*	23	13	4
16–17	35*	52*	13	9	4
18+	48*	43*	8	9	5

or together with someone else. Slade (1987) found that toddlers' play was more advanced and lasted longer when the mother took an active part than when they were playing on their own. Verbal encouragement alone, without the mother's participation, had little impact on the children's play. Another study found a difference between children's pretend play with their mothers and with their peers: playing with the mother, children largely followed her suggestions and directions, whereas peer play was more active, equal and flexible (Howes & Matheson, 1992).

Play is also central to fathers' parenting style. In fact, fathers spend more time playing with the child than in other care-taking activities (Fletcher et al., 2011). There are, however, differences between father–child play and mother–child play. In a study of children aged 2–4½ years, the mothers structured the play, supported learning through teaching, guided the child's behavior and engaged in empathic conversation. The fathers engaged in physical play, behaved more like an age mate, let the child lead the activity and supported learning by motivating and challenging the child (John et al., 2013). It is suggested that fathers' involvement in rough-and-tumble play may support the child's development of self-regulation (Fletcher et al., 2013).

The influence of parents' participation depends on the play skills of the child and what is being played. O'Connell and Bretherton (1984) observed that explorative and exercise play increased among 20–28-month-olds when their mother was present. Among 28-month-olds, the mother's presence only affected symbolic play. All the mothers supported both forms of play to an equal degree, but maternal interaction only helped children develop their most advanced form of play. The mothers' attempts to help their child with previously mastered play skills were overlooked by the children. This is in line with Vygotsky's theory that learning support must occur in the child's **zone of proximal development** and within the relevant area (see Book 4, *Cognition, Intelligence and Learning*, Chapter 36). Help from more competent adults and peers is important for children's learning and development, but only as long as the child needs help and is able to understand the task itself and what the help involves. This emphasizes the importance of offering individualized help and support to children with both typical and atypical development.

34

The Functions of Play

Depending on the theoretical point of view and the type of play involved, psychology offers various explanations and attributes different functions to play in children's development (Burriss & Tsao, 2002). Some give particular weight to the biological basis of play and its importance for children's enculturation. According to evolutionary psychology, exercise play is biologically determined as a way of discovering and practicing new skills in a safe environment before they are applied. It is an **adaptive function** that has given human beings and other species an evolutionary advantage (Pellegrini et al., 2007; Pellegrini & Smith, 1998). From a different theoretical perspective, Piaget (1951) ascribes a similar function to exercise play.

Other theorists have focused on pretend play. From a psychodynamic perspective, Winnicott (1971) sees play as a "third zone" between inner mental life and external reality. Play promotes the development of emotional relations, allows children to use their creativity fully and contributes to establishing the self (à Beckett et al., 2017). In line with this, psychodynamic psychology uses play as a tool in psychotherapy for children with psychiatric disorders (Axline, 1964; Mumford, 2012; O'Connor & Braverman, 1997).

Building on **logical constructivism**, Furth and Kane (1992) view pretend play above all as a way of constructing an understanding of society. Children "play society" and co-construct societal knowledge together, such as when two girls play they are going to bed and create going-to-bed rules based on their age in the pretend play role. The lack of access to free play with peers that characterizes many of today's Western urban communities can therefore have an impact on children's enculturation (Jarvis et al., 2014). Others see pretend play in the context of developing mind understanding (Lillard, 2001).

DOI: 10.4324/9781003292579-39

Montessori (1910) believes that constructive play develops sensory and motor skills, but maintains that pretend play is a primitive escape from reality without functional value: children should set real tables and sweep real floors instead of performing such activities in a dollhouse. Piaget (1951) disagrees with Montessori and views imagination and symbolic play as important aspects of cognitive functioning. Pretend play does not primarily fulfill an exercise function: the purpose of washing and putting a doll to bed is not for children to learn to wash themselves and go to bed, but for the sheer joy and sense of mastery.

Vygotsky (1967) mainly discusses pretend play, to which he ascribes major developmental importance, but holds a somewhat different view than Piaget. According to Piaget's theory, pretend play contributes to development through the activities children participate in, but as the *result* of cognitive development, not as a means of promoting such development. Vygotsky's theory views pretend play as a way of overcoming the limitations of the immediate situation and fulfilling unattainable desires, thereby contributing to the development of higher mental functions. Pretend play is learned through social activities, often in interaction with the parents, but in such a way that children eventually can play on their own, incorporate more people into their pretend play and create more roles by themselves (Bodrova & Leong, 2015; Karpov, 2005; Nicolopoulou, 1993).

Despite the importance often attributed to play in connection with children's learning and development (Ginsberg et al., 2007; Singer et al., 2006), it has been difficult to demonstrate the developmental effects of children's participation in play (Lillard et al., 2013). This may be owing to the fact that play is not a uniform set of activities but includes many different elements and forms of interaction. Johnson and colleagues (1982), for example, found a positive relation between children's constructive play and their scores on intelligence **tests**, but not between **role-play** and intelligence. Connolly and Doyle (1984) found a similar relationship between children's role-play and social skills. The results probably reflect the fact that intelligence tests include construction tasks such as puzzles and copying of dice patterns, whereas social skills require knowledge of social relationships. Thus, it is possible that constructive play promotes skills relevant to many of the typical tasks on intelligence tests, whereas role-play promotes social skills. Another possibility is that an aptitude for construction skills leads to advanced constructive play, and an aptitude for social skills leads to better role-play. Whatever the case may be, studies suggest that children's play reflects not their general cognitive ability, but rather different abilities related to specific activities.

It is commonly asserted that play-based teaching leads to better learning results than other forms of teaching (Weisberg et al., 2015). However, comparisons of play-based and other forms of teaching have not been able to uncover systematic differences, except that play-based teaching seems to promote children's social participation (Smith & Simon, 1984; Trawick-Smith, 1989). Such participation may in itself be positive but does not necessarily lead to more learning. Moreover, some researchers believe that focusing on educational benefits in play may lead to a loss of the very nature of play, that play has no purpose outside the enjoyment of playing (Singer, 2013). Fun and interesting instruction is not the same as play. If a teacher presents schoolwork as play – that is, without an overriding objective – students may find it disparaging to their effort to learn.

35

Play in Different Contexts

Play does not depend on the presence of playgrounds or the availability of ready-made toys. When children are asked, they say they can play anywhere, but the type of play depends on the context: being indoor or outdoor affords different types of play (Glenn et al., 2013). In some countries, manufactured toys are a rarity (Gosso et al., 2007; Göncü et al., 2000).

Culture defines the settings for play, and the environment in which children are raised influences how they play. The same forms of play can be found in many countries, but their specific content varies with the economic and cultural characteristics of each society. For example, in small societies such as the Aka and Ngandu people in Central Africa, children tend to spend much more of their playtime in pretend work than in other forms of pretend play. The Ngandu people are rather competitive, whereas the Aka people are more group-oriented, and a study found that the Ngandu children spent much more time playing games than the Aka children, who participated more in various forms of object play (Boyette, 2016).

Also, the amount of time children spend playing varies from one country to another. First-graders in Japan and the United States play about 3 hours per day. American fifth-graders play approximately the same amount of time, whereas Japanese fifth-graders play 1 hour less because they spend more time on schoolwork (Stevenson & Lee, 1990). In a number of non-industrialized societies, children are expected to contribute to adult work from a relatively early age. They spend less time together with other children than children in industrialized societies and therefore play less and become "apprentices" under adult supervision (Morelli et al., 2003; Rogoff, 2003). This may also be reflected in parental attitudes to play: US mothers believe play promotes children's cognitive development, and Chinese mothers

DOI: 10.4324/9781003292579-40

that it benefits social and physical development, whereas Mexican mothers believe participation in work and work-related activities is more important for the children's development. Japanese mothers see play as a means to promote social interaction and communication, whereas US mothers see play as a means to get world knowledge. In some cultures, it is siblings rather than parents who **scaffold** children's play (Kazemeini & Pajoheshgar, 2013).

Children's household chores will affect how much they play. In the United States, 5-year-olds spend an average of 15 minutes a day on chores, whereas 15–17-year-olds spend 41 minutes. Western European adolescents spend 10–20 minutes on housework, whereas the average in Korea is 6 minutes. In Bangladesh, the amount of time girls spend on chores increases from 1.9 hours at 4–5 years to 6.7 hours at 10–12 years. Time for play and other leisure activities is correspondingly reduced (Alsaker & Flammer, 1999; Larson & Verma, 1999). Children's contribution to housework is related to economic factors but also to cultural attitudes. In Bangladesh, children's work contribution is a necessity, whereas, in the United States, sharing in housework is motivated by the wish to help children become independent and self-reliant individuals. Parents in China and Japan place few demands on children's participation in housework because they are afraid it will affect their children's school performance.

Although children in some cultures have a limited amount of time for play with each other, it has been difficult to ascertain any developmental consequences of participating in housework and other activities rather than play. The extent to which children are given the opportunity to play in the traditional sense has not been shown to affect their development (Sutton-Smith, 1986), and children who spend a lot of time playing do not seem to have an advantage in terms of social or cognitive development. This may be because most children get to play enough, or because their other activities promote development in similar ways as play. It is also possible that most children in Western cultures play so much that it does not make a difference whether they play slightly more or less. Children grow up in different environments and acquire skills and knowledge through play or by performing tasks of various kinds, but this does not seem to lead to general developmental differences between them. Meaningful activities must be part of children's everyday life, but several **developmental pathways** lead to good cognitive and social functioning (Karpov, 2005; Larson & Verma, 1999; Maccoby, 1990).

36

Play among Children with Atypical Development

Play reflects children's cognitive, social and language skills and abilities, and atypical development in these areas will affect both the form and function of children's play. Compared with children without disabilities, children with many types of disabilities more often become spectators and spend more time playing alone and less with peers (Barton, 2015; Hestenes & Carroll, 2000).

Children with intellectual disability typically show a similar delay in play as in other areas and need more help than other children to initiate and carry out play activities (Layton et al., 2014; Venuti et al., 2009).

Children with severe congenital visual impairment are delayed in the development of all forms of play and generally play less than other children and more often alone (Lewis et al., 2000; Preisler, 1993). Delayed motor development is common in this group, and problems with spatial orientation puts restraints on many forms of exercise play, including social play such as rough-and-tumble. Celeste (2006) describes a 4½-year-old blind girl who showed typical development in most areas but played little and mostly on her own. In addition to the girl's lack of relevant experiences, this may reflect the fact that it was difficult for the other children to adapt their pretend play so that she, too, could take part in it. Another study with older children (6–9 years) found near normal pretend play in blind children without other social or cognitive disorders (Bishop et al., 2005). The fact that children with visual impairments begin with pretend play, albeit slightly later than others, shows that it is possible to develop such play without the use of visual make-believe cues. Voice and touch, for example, can provide cues that something is make-believe rather than real. With age, blind children usually become more integrated into

DOI: 10.4324/9781003292579-41

play as their dependence on specific objects in symbolic play decreases and language gains a more prominent place (see Book 3, *Perceptual and Motor Development*, Chapter 3).

As much of children's early play involves motor functions, movement disorders affect the development of play (Pfeifer et al., 2011). Even moderate movement disorders can inhibit children's participation in locomotor play and changes of activity in the group. Symbolic play with objects and pretend play can be problematic when children cannot make full use of their hands. Children with more severe motor disorders typically play on their own and together with adults (Skär & Tamm, 2002). This group depends on much help and support from adults and peers in order not to be left out and become spectators rather than active partners in play (Graham et al., 2014). The physical environment can, however, be adapted to facilitate more participation, both indoors and outdoors (Woolley, 2013). When children's motor disorders prevent them from constructing or performing other play actions with their hands, they can use speech, graphic symbols or written text to instruct peers and adults to perform the actions they themselves are physically unable to perform (Batorowicz et al., 2016). In this way, by using *language for action*, they develop personal autonomy in spite of their physical limitations and dependence on others to perform the actions.

Children with autism spectrum disorder generally have difficulty understanding other people, imagining and planning the future and realizing that another person can perceive the world as different from how it actually is (see Book 4, *Cognition, Intelligence and Learning*, Chapter 23). Pretend play appears difficult for this group, and a number of studies have shown that children with autism spectrum disorder rarely initiate pretend play, even if they are able to perform pretend actions when explicitly asked to do so (Jarrold et al., 1996; Kasari et al., 2013; Lam & Yeung, 2012). For example, one boy could sit for long periods and explore an action figure, balancing it, bending its legs and arms, taking it apart, putting it back together again and the like, seemingly without a play story. He joined peers and adults when they initiated role-play but did not engage in role-play on his own (Papacek et al., 2016). In a comparison of 15-minute school recess activities among 51 5–12-year-old high-functioning children with autism spectrum disorder and 51 children with typical development, the children with autism spectrum disorder spent three times as much time alone (30 versus 9 percent) and just over half as much time interacting (42 versus 72 percent). The children with autism spectrum disorder initiated fewer interactions than the children with typical development and, in addition, were less likely to get a response when they initiated (Locke et al., 2016). At the same time, gender differences in play preferences among boys and girls with autism spectrum disorder are similar to those of other boys and girls (Harrop et al., 2017). Studies have found that support of play activities increases social participation and interaction with peers and helps children with autism spectrum disorder develop communication and the ability for pretense (Chang et al., 2016; Goods et al., 2013; Papacek et al., 2016).

Strategies to promote play and making physical and social adaptations to enable all the different forms of play are central elements in early intervention for all children with disabilities.

Summary of Part V

1   Play is difficult to define. Important characteristics are that play has no extrinsic goal and is motivating in itself. *Exercise play* is the most common form of play in the first 3 years of life. *Rough-and-tumble* play is a form of social play. Exercise play aims not at the practical consequences of an action but at the joy of mastery. Simple *constructive play* shows up in the beginning of the second year and stands for a major part of toddlers' play, especially in kindergarten. *Symbolic play* or *pretend play* involves imagination, taking on the role of a person or an animal and using objects for other functions than their usual ones. Pretend play often involves several children but can also be solitary.

2   The earliest form of play takes place in interaction with adults, whereas *solitary play* becomes more dominant in the second year. In *parallel play*, children play side by side with each other. In *associated group play*, children play with the same toys and interact to a certain degree, while *collaborative play* involves complementary roles and tasks. *Nonsocial play* can reflect a preference for solitary play, while children who show active *social avoidance* are at risk of being rejected by their peers and developing internalizing disorders.

3   Different forms of play first appear at different ages and continue as part of children's repertoire as long as they play. Play gradually becomes more symbolic and involves more participants. *Decentration* means that play includes others than the child himself, *decontextualization* that children move away from concrete actions and use substitute or imaginary objects in play, and *integration* that children include several actions in the same play activity. Younger children need help to initiate and sustain play.

4   There are several views on the *function of play*. According to
Piaget, play reflects cognitive development but also contributes
to development through the activities children participate in.
The increase in interactive play is the result of cognitive development. In Vygotsky's theory, pretend play is learned through
social activities that eventually enable children to play on their
own. Although play is fundamentally social and cultural, the individual child gradually develops the ability to create the various
roles independently.

5   The same forms of play are found across *cultures*, but their content varies with the economic and cultural characteristics of each
society. In some societies, children spend a lot of time playing,
whereas, in others, they have many tasks in and outside the home.
The extent to which the amount of play affects development has
been difficult to ascertain.

6   Play reflects children's motor, cognitive, social and language skills
and abilities, and any *atypical development* in these areas will affect
how they play. Children with disabilities may need help to initiate and carry out play activities. However, play is equally important for children in this group as for other children.

Core Issues

- The evolutionary bases of play.
- The functions of play.
- The role of play in education.

Suggestions for Further Reading

Boyette, A. H. (2016). Children's play and culture learning in an egalitarian forag-
ing society. *Child Development, 87,* 759–769.
Christie, J. F., & Johnson, E. P. (1987). Reconceptualizing constructive play:
A review of the empirical literature. *Merrill-Palmer Quarterly, 33,* 439–452.
Lewis, P. J. (2017). The erosion of play. *International Journal of Play, 6,* 10–23.
Lifter, K., et al. (2005). Developmental specificity in targeting and teaching play
activities to children with pervasive developmental disorders. *Journal of Early
Intervention, 27,* 247–267.
Lillard, A. S. (2017). Why do the children (pretend) play? *Trends in Cognitive Sci-
ences, 11,* 826–834.
Papacek, A. M., et al. (2016). Play and social interaction strategies for young
children with autism spectrum disorder in inclusive preschool settings. *Young
Exceptional Children, 19,* 3–17.

Part VI

Media and Understanding of Society

37

Becoming Part of a Larger Society

This chapter discusses children in a media world and how children come to learn about the functions of society – two quite different aspects of the expansion of the social environment. Through exposure to and exploration of the digital world children get experience with real and fictional realities that are not part of their immediate surroundings. With the use of social media they communicate with friends and a wider circle of people.

The development of societal understanding begins in childhood and gains momentum in adolescence. Children and young people learn about the functions and roles of society, societal groups, local and national political leaders, the importance of money, power and status, and prevailing conflicts of interest. These insights represent important aspects of their societal understanding and becoming citizens.

DOI: 10.4324/9781003292579-43

38

Children and Adolescents in a Media Society

Digital media are an important part of modern life and take up a major amount of children's time from early childhood on (Haughton et al., 2015; Rideout, 2013). Most digital media provide passive or interactive access to information and entertainment. *Social media* involve online communication between two or more people via cell phone, tablet or computer (Calvert, 2015; O'Keeffe, 2016). Key issues are how the new media affect children's knowledge and cognitive development, prosocial and antisocial behavior and their general well-being. Much knowledge has been gained about the influence of television and video, but knowledge about other media remains limited, especially their long-term effects (Anderson & Kirkorian, 2015; Calvert, 2015). Since the internet began to take shape in 1993, development has been rapid, but children who have had today's massive exposure to digital media are barely into adolescence.

> Children are in the midst of a vast, unplanned experiment, surrounded by digital technologies that were not available but five years ago.
>
> (Hirsh-Pasek et al., 2015, p. 3)

Extent of Media Use

Most people living in modern societies own a cell phone, and almost every home has a television set as well as a computer, tablet or similar device, but, in many economically developing countries, electronic media are less common. Television and video (via different sources)

DOI: 10.4324/9781003292579-44

continue to be the most prevalent forms of media in environments with children. In the United States, about 40 percent of all children are regularly exposed to television and video from the age of 3 months, and, by the age of 2, 90 percent of all US children regularly watch television and video (American Academy of Pediatrics, 2011). One-year-olds watch on average 1 hour a day, increasing to about 1.5 hours by the age of 2, more time than the average child is being read to (Barr et al., 2010; Zimmerman et al., 2007). As a result, many of today's children are experienced media users by the time they start school. In 2015, average daily media use in the United States was nearly 6 hours among 8–12-year-olds. This included about 2½ hours of television, video and DVD, 1½ hours of electronic games, nearly an hour of music, a quarter of an hour of social media and half an hour of reading. Between the ages of 13 and 18 years, the corresponding figures were about 2½ hours of television, video and DVD, 1½ hours of electronic games, 2 hours of music, just over 1 hour of social media and half an hour of reading. The adolescents spent a total of 9 hours in media activity, of which 6½ hours were screen activities (Rideout, 2016). This shows that the use of social media and music particularly was increasing among this age group. Similar time use has been reported in other countries (Kanz, 2016; Padilla-Walker et al., 2016; Yu & Baxter, 2016).

Children and adolescents thus spend a lot of their time on screen-based media. An Australian survey found that this accounted for one-quarter of girls' and one-third of boys' waking time (Olds et al., 2006). By the time they finish high school, with current media use, today's adolescents in the United States will have spent more time in front of a screen than in school (American Academy of Child and Adolescent Psychiatry, 2015). These average figures conceal large individual differences, however. Some children watch very little television and video and almost never use a tablet or computer, whereas others spend most of their leisure time on these activities. One study found that some 4-year-olds spent 4 hours a day watching TV at home (Fletcher et al., 2014). The central place of media in modern daily life is evidenced by the fact that around 16 percent of 0–1-year-olds in the United States have a television set in their bedroom. This percentage gradually increases to nearly 60 percent among 13–18-year-olds. The majority of children and adolescents also own a cell phone, and many have gaming consoles, tablets and similar devices (Rideout, 2013, 2016). According to one study, more than 40 percent of 8–10-year-olds and 90 percent of 15–17-year-olds owned a cell phone. Forty percent of the 8–10-year-olds sent daily text messages, and nearly half of the 15–17-year-olds sent more than 30 messages a day (Lauricella et al., 2014).

A small group of adolescents spend a great deal of time online. A study of 11–16-year-olds from 25 European countries found that 4.4 percent made moderately excessive use of the internet (over 4 hours a day), while 1.4 percent made very excessive use of it (over 5 hours a day). The average for all the adolescents was 1¾ hours (Blinka et al., 2015). Some adolescents show signs of withdrawal when the internet is unavailable (see p. 192).

Parental Attitudes and Children's Media Environment

In addition to their own active use, many children are passively exposed to media. In some homes, the TV is on all the time, even when no one is watching. One study found that about one-third of parents of children aged 3–27 months left the TV turned on all or most of the time (Wartella et al., 2013). According to another study, the TV was on during half or more of the playtime of a large majority of children aged 4–19 months, when they played both alone and with their mother. This reduced some of their attention as well as the quantity and quality of play (Masur et al., 2015). In a study of 0–6-year-olds, the children from homes with the TV on in the background much of the time participated less in reading and other activities (Vandewater et al., 2005). Both children and parents talk less when the TV is on, as the sound makes it more difficult to understand what others say (Christakis et al., 2009). Taken as a whole, conditions such as these may affect children's language development.

By comparison, American parents daily spend nearly 3 hours watching television, 2 hours using their computer (outside of work) and under 1 hour playing video games (Vittrup et al., 2016). To some degree, parents control how much and what their children get to watch, and naturally there is a relationship between the media use and attitudes of parents and the extent of their children's use. For some people, media take up a major part of life, with an average of over 11 hours of screen exposure per day. Less than 20 percent of US parents of children aged 0–8 years expressed concern about their children's media use (Wartella et al., 2013). In one study, nearly 70 percent of parents of 2–7-year-olds agreed with the statement that early use of technology better prepares children for working life, and two-thirds disagreed that children under the age of 2 years should not watch television, as suggested by the American Academy of Pediatrics (Shifrin et al., 2015). Nearly the same number of parents believed that today's children have an early and natural understanding of how to use computers and similar technologies and generally seemed to overestimate children's competence (Vittrup et al., 2016). But there are cultural differences. Many British parents, for example, are concerned about the use of e-books among their 0–8-year-old children (Kucirkova & Littleton, 2016).

To some extent, parents use electronic media – mainly television and video – together with their children, especially at younger ages, and fathers take more part in electronic games than mothers (Connell et al., 2015). Children quickly become independent, however, and the time children and parents spend on media together diminishes significantly between early childhood and the beginning of school (Rideout, 2014; Wartella et al., 2013). The fact that a majority of children have media access in their room also reflects the differences in media use between parents and children. When adults and children watch television together, it is usually to watch the adults' programs. Many preschoolers and younger schoolchildren watch adult-directed programs such as news, entertainment and movies. Younger schoolchildren can become anxious watching news about fires, floods and other disasters, whereas older children think that reports about murder and other types of crimes are most frightening (Smith & Wilson, 2002; Valerio et al., 1997). Several studies have additionally shown that younger children and adults communicate less while watching television than when reading a book or playing together (Nathanson & Rasmussen, 2011; Pempek et al., 2014).

Many parents establish rules for using games and video, for example that homework and other tasks must be finished first, but what children are allowed to do also depends on the parents' activities. If they themselves are often busy, they allow children more leeway and also use media access as reward or punishment to mediate other behaviors. Many parents, however, try to teach their children to regulate their own time in front of the screen (Jago et al., 2016; Schaan & Melzer, 2015). On the other hand, parents' emotional involvement in children's online use seems to contribute to fewer restrictions (Schaan & Melzer, 2015).

The use of media is an integral part of modern society. The large differences in media use and access among children and families are related to factors such as children's temperament, gender, geographic location (urban or rural), siblings, parenting style, attitudes to and use of media, socioeconomic background and schools' policies on electronic media use. This makes it difficult to separate the effects of media from general changes in technology and society. It becomes a question of whether media contribute to **shaping** children's worlds, or whether their content merely reflects the world as it is.

Media and Learning

As electronic media occupy such a major part of children's lives, it is important to understand their possible impact on learning and the acquisition of knowledge. A myriad of educational computer programs and apps exists today, but, with the exception of television and video, many applications of electronic media are fairly new, and knowledge about their impact on development and learning remains limited. Although the use of electronic media has become part of children's curriculum in many schools, no one knows how the content of these vast electronic offerings affects thinking and learning (Guernsey, 2017; Lauricella et al., 2017).

Research shows a complex picture. It is a question not simply of time use, but of content and how impressionable children are (Guernsey, 2017; Wartella et al., 2016). Any positive or negative impact will depend on (a) the content of the media, (b) how it is adapted to the child's age, cognition and language, and (c) the context in which the media are used, for example whether the child is alone or together with other children or adults (Barr & Linebarger, 2017). Videos with engaging stories and educational content adapted to the child's age can promote imaginative thinking. Ready-made stories and little quiet, empty time for reflection, on the other hand, can reduce children's creativity and imagination (Calvert, 2015). Although educational videos can benefit children's understanding and knowledge, experiencing two-dimensional images on a screen cannot replace the experience of a three-dimensional physical world. Infants and toddlers in particular have a poorer understanding of something presented on a screen as against in the real world – Anderson and Pempek (2005) refer to this as "video deficit." Any possible benefits for very young children are uncertain, especially considering that the time spent in front of the screen inevitably displaces other toys and activities (Haughton et al., 2015). Nonetheless, many parents still consider early media use to be educational and believe that younger children in particular learn a lot by watching television and video (Rideout, 2014). Video series such as *Baby Einstein* claim to promote infants' and toddlers' exploration and learning, but studies show that young children learn little from these videos. When parents were asked to assess how much their child learned from a video, their assessment had more to do with how much the parents themselves liked the video than with how much their child actually learned (DeLoache et al., 2010).

Although slightly older children can benefit from educational media (Gentile, 2011; Gentile et al., 2009), their usage decreases with age (Rideout, 2014), and studies generally find little effect on learning (Anderson & Kirkorian, 2015). A number of US studies found a greater vocabulary increase in preschool children who watched programs that included explanations of vocabulary than in children who did not watch these types of programs (Rice et al., 1990; Wright et al., 2001). Not all television programs designed to promote reading skills had a measurable effect on children's reading skills, however, even if the programs were popular and the children enjoyed watching them. It is possible that the development of good reading skills requires a more active effort, and that the television medium is not suited to this type of learning (Huston & Wright, 1998; Linebarger & Walker, 2005). Furthermore, television programs generally make small demands on vocabulary: 3,000 words stand for 95 percent of the words used in American children's and entertainment programs (Webb & Rodgers, 2009). In addition, television and video can promote passive viewing behavior. The content, often well designed and ready-made, can reduce children's reflective thinking and problem solving (Anderson & Kirkorian, 2015). Children become consumers and experience the world in a different way than the active and exploratory child Piaget places such emphasis on.

Educational games encouraging active participation can lead to better learning. Some video games, for example, have been found to promote spatial skills (Powers et al., 2013; Redick & Webster, 2014) or enhance performance on tasks requiring visual attention and quick reactions (Spence & Feng, 2010). Educational programs designed to improve children's math skills have also shown positive results (Drijvers et al., 2016). Nonetheless, there remains considerable disagreement about the effect of interactive computer games on everyday cognitive functioning (Bavelier et al., 2010; Owen et al., 2010).

Extent of Media Exposure and Learning

Media use can have both positive and negative effects, but always involves less time for other activities, including sleep. Adolescents in the United States sleep less than just a few years ago: more screen time leads to later bedtimes and less sleep (Hale & Guan, 2015). There is no link between regular television viewing (2 hours per day) and learning, schoolwork and attention problems. A moderate amount of television and video, with a certain proportion of informational programs, seems to increase children's level of know ledge, whereas a lot of time spent watching ordinary entertainment content has a negative effect on academic performance (Anderson & Kirkorian, 2015). There is a positive relation between the time spent on educational games and school performance (Hastings et al., 2009), but a negative one between total screen time and school grades (Kirkorian et al., 2008). One study found that 10–19-year-old boys who played online games spent 30 percent less time on reading, and the girls spent 34 percent less time on homework, than those who did not play (Cummings & Vandewater, 2007). Studies show that the acquisition of reading skills can be inhibited by little time spent reading during the first few years of school (Koolstra & Van Der Voort, 1996).

Rideout and associates (2010) found that nearly half of a group of 8–18-year-old heavy media users had fair or poor grades, compared with light media users where under a quarter had such grades at school. However, what is cause and effect remains uncertain. It is possible that children watch a lot of television and video because they have little or poor contact with their peers and participate in few other activities. When adolescents spend a lot of time playing video games, it may be that they experience social and personal problems but feel they master the game (Gentile, 2009; Kowert et al., 2015; Rasmussen et al., 2015). Adolescents in this group have higher rates of depression than those with light or moderate media use, and suicide attempts are more frequent among this group (Johansson & Götestam, 2004; Messias et al., 2011). One study found that children and adolescents with excessive use of online gaming showed anxiety and depression, and that these symptoms were reduced when they stopped playing online games (Gentile et al., 2011a). Such findings underline the importance of parents and teachers following up children and adolescents with an atypical amount or pattern of media use.

Prosocial and Antisocial Effects of Media

Research has particularly focused on how television and other media content affects the attitudes and behavior of children and adolescents (Anderson et al., 2010; Prot et al., 2014). Television and streaming media offer a wide range of content: family idylls among ethnic groups, everyday environments of adolescents and young adults or "reality" shows showing young people in a variety of life situations. Observing how relational problems are resolved, for example, can promote development of both prosocial and antisocial attitudes. A study of 13-year-olds in Singapore found that those who preferred TV programs with prosocial content were more positive about helping and sharing and less accepting of aggressive attitudes than children who preferred programs with other content (Gentile et al., 2009). Studies have found that exposure to a number of such programs – rather than total viewing time – had an impact on young people's self-esteem and attitudes toward parenting (Ex et al., 2002; Martins & Jensen, 2014). The way in which problems and **moral dilemmas** are solved in programs watched by children and adolescents can thus affect their self-perception, values and attitudes.

Television and Aggression

Violence is common in media: Studies show that 70 percent of all TV programs for children include physical violence in one form or another, more than programs aimed at adults, with a violent episode about every 4 minutes (Potter, 1999; Wilson et al., 2002). Children and adolescents express a greater preference for violent games than for television and video with violent content (Funk et al., 2004).

There have been two key assumptions about the impact of observing violence and aggressive behavior on television and other media: that it leads to either an increase or a decrease in children's aggression. From the perspective of *psychodynamic* theory, observing violence should lead to a reduction in arousal (catharsis) and therefore a reduction in actual violent behavior (Feshbach, 1961). This point of view has little support in research. There are no studies that show a relation between exposure to violent media and a decrease in aggression, whereas nearly all studies have found positive correlations between exposure and aggression, although the effects are moderate (Greitemeyer & Mügge, 2014; Huesmann et al., 2003).

Studies thus suggest that violent media content can affect children's and adolescents' attitudes to violence and increase their likelihood of getting involved in violent situations themselves (Kanz, 2016). This is in line with most theories of aggression, including Crick and Dodge's social cognitive model (see Book 6, *Emotions, Temperament, Personality, Moral, Prosocial and Antisocial Development*, Chapter 27). According to *cognitive behavioral theory*, children imitate the people they see on television, and their aggressive behavior increases when they observe others performing violent actions. In addition, their **inhibition** to aggression can be weakened by exposure to violence (Bandura, 1994). One US longitudinal study found that boys who watched a lot of videos with violent content at 2–5 years of age showed more antisocial behavior at the age of 7–10 years than boys who did not watch as many violent videos. There was no corresponding connection for girls, and the children's total TV viewing time had no impact on the development of antisocial behavior (Christakis & Zimmerman, 2007). Another explanation is that media content contributes to forming children's and adolescents' expectations of other people's behavior and their perception of how conflicts are resolved. This can result in both prosocial and antisocial behavior, depending on the content and the way it is interpreted. For children who observe a lot of violence in the media, violence will appear to be a normal solution to conflicts. They form scripts (see Book 4, *Cognition, Intelligence and Learning*, Chapter 10) containing aggressive elements, whereas children who watch prosocial programs more often form scripts with prosocial content (Huesmann, 2007; Huesmann et al., 2003).

Thus, children are affected by their media experiences, but the effects are complex (Anderson et al., 2010; Prot et al., 2014). How children react to screen media depends on characteristics such as age, gender and cognitive skills (Wiedeman et al., 2015) and whether they can identify with the situation. In cases in which it is difficult for children to distinguish between fantasy and reality, media have a greater impact on their perception of the world. Studies show that toddlers more often imitate the actions of real-life people than those they have seen on video (Nielsen et al., 2008). As cartoons seem less real than movies with people, they more clearly represent fantasy. In one study, many children stated that they enjoyed watching programs designed for adults, but also that they had felt scared and gotten nightmares. This, too, supports the assumption that films in which real people show violent behavior have a greater impact than violence in cartoons (Gunter & McAleer, 1997). Also, the presence of adults viewing may influence how children perceive the violence they see. A comment made by an adult can sometimes change a child's view of what is happening, and children can interpret the silence of an adult co-viewer as supporting the behavior observed on the screen (Cantor & Wilson, 2003). Additionally, children are more likely to imitate the violent behavior of a "hero" who is rewarded for his aggressive actions than that of a ruthless killer who is caught and put in jail (Huesmann, 2007). Children do not merely imitate, but make sense of the actions they observe based on their general social understanding.

Computer Games

Over 90 percent of computer games considered suitable for 10-year-olds include hitting, shooting and other violent elements (Gentile & Gentile, 2008). Compared with video and television, computer games require more active participation. While children and adolescents who watch television are in a certain sense passive onlookers, computer games often involve performing make-believe destructive actions and being rewarded with a higher point score (Hastings et al., 2009). Much time spent on gaming seems to lead to higher levels of arousal, more aggressive thoughts and behavior, and less empathy and helping behavior. This is mainly related to physical aggression in boys and relational aggression in girls (Anderson et al., 2010; Gentile et al., 2011b; Huesmann, 2010). Playing games alone in particular leads to increased aggression, whereas gaming together with others can reduce aggression (Velez et al., 2016). Gaming is not a minority phenomenon: many adolescents spend many hours a week on video games containing a lot of violence (Rideout, 2015), and gaming may therefore bring with it major social consequences (Anderson, 2004). Studies in other countries report similar findings, but the effect on behavior shows some variation depending on cultural attitudes (Krahé, 2016). However, studies have also found that prosocial computer games lead to more prosocial behavior and less aggression (Greitemeyer & Mügge, 2014).

A possible reason for the connection between aggression and violent computer games may be that aggressive children are drawn to such games. A greater likelihood of aggressive behavior may also be due to the fact that games with violent content prime children and adolescents to form scripts containing violent elements (see above) and thus more easily activate aggressive thoughts (Greitemeyer & Mügge, 2014). When violence becomes an appropriate and expected response to certain situations, it will affect the attitudes of children and adolescents. Moreover, exposure to violent games can lead to a *desensitization* to violence and fewer negative emotional reactions to observing violence (Hastings et al., 2009; Krahé et al., 2011; Orue et al., 2011). The effect of violence in videos and games is furthermore compounded: children who are exposed to violent content are affected by the content while at the same time losing out on the positive effects of being exposed to more prosocial content.

Many factors thus contribute to the impact of more or less exposure to electronic media. Studies have generally shown small or moderate correlations between media exposure in childhood and later violent and criminal behavior. This is not to say that their effect is insignificant, but underlines the fact that media are among several sources that influence children's development of interaction strategies and behaviors (Anderson et al., 2015; Bushman & Anderson, 2015). At the same time, it is important to emphasize that only a small percentage of children and adolescents show high levels of aggression. Nor do most adults become involved in criminal behavior, aside from traffic offenses and similar, regardless of whether they do or do not like movies with a lot of violent content.

Social Media

Social media such as *Facebook*, *Twitter* and *YouTube* are systems that enable two or more people to communicate and share content. They are used to communicate with individuals and groups, friends, classmates and other people who share a particular interest, such as geology, Harry Potter, bird watching or sports. Some people use social media to spread their views or to sell their music, their fashion designs or other products and services. The most active and frequent users of social media are adolescents and young adults, and their numbers have increased dramatically in recent years. In the Netherlands, about 60 percent of 10–11-year-olds and almost 90 percent of 12–16-year-olds used the internet to communicate via chat groups or messaging, with an average of 11 hours per week (van den Eijnden et al., 2010, 2011).

Similar figures apply to the United States, where 20 percent of adolescents said they checked social media more than five times a day (Lauricella et al., 2014; Rideout, 2012). When children and adolescents spend a lot of time on social media, it leaves less time for face-to-face communication with one or more other persons.

In today's society, cell phones and social media contribute to shaping the social patterns of children and adolescents in significant ways. Gatherings and activities are largely coordinated via e-mail and cell phone calls or text messages; established meeting places play less of a role than before (Kaare et al., 2007; Lenhart et al., 2010). This means that children and adolescents depend on being contacted by others – or initiate contact themselves – in order to take part in social events. Some of them will miss out on many social events, not because they are unpopular or actively being avoided, but because they are overlooked.

Negative social patterns are changing as well, and children and adolescents in many countries are bullied on social media, via e-mail and cell phone messages (Navarro et al., 2016). *Cyberbullying* has the same consequences as other types of bullying: depression, low self-esteem, learned helplessness, social anxiety and alienation (Giumetti & Kowalski, 2016; see Book 6, *Emotions, Temperament, Personality, Moral,*

The cell phone plays a key role in the social life of children and adolescents.

Prosocial and Antisocial Development, Chapter 27). Moreover, this form of bullying can be more pervasive than direct bullying because it is impossible to protect oneself without severing all electronic connections with the outside world and thereby isolating oneself from the social community at large (Patchin & Hinduja, 2010; Wong-Lo & Bullock, 2011).

Studies show that most children and adolescents follow up existing friends on social media, while some also look for new relationships. Some socially anxious adolescents report that they find it easier to open up for *self-disclosure* (see p. 103) and communicate about intimate topics online than face-to-face. This applies especially to people they know in real life, whereas pure online contacts are perceived to be less close (Liu & Brown, 2014; Valkenburg & Peter, 2007). Some children are drawn to social media because they feel socially isolated and have difficulty establishing social relationships in the real world. Some adolescents show atypical development, with signs of internet addiction (see Book 1, *Theory and Methodology*, Chapter 35). Their thoughts are dominated by the internet, which they use to escape negative thoughts and feelings, experiencing discomfort when they do not have online access and continuing their online activities although they have decided to stop. In many cases, social media are the main factor contributing to dependency (Johansson & Götestam, 2004; van den Eijnden et al., 2011).

The use of social media is considerable and may rise even higher, and the long-term positive and negative consequences of this will only show themselves in the future. From the perspective of developmental psychology, it is important to monitor how they impact the cognitive, emotional and social development of children and adolescents, their communication and interaction patterns and their perceptions of themselves and others.

39

Societal Knowledge

All children grow up in a society. As they grow older, children gain an understanding of how the society functions, of societal structures and social similarities and differences (Buchanan-Barrow, 2005). Societal cognition is an extension and further development of understanding individual thought and action and entails the construction of a set of concepts and a "theory" of society (Hatano & Takahashi, 2005). Children's experience of themselves and their own position in society and that of others provide an important basis for the development of societal knowledge (de França, 2016; Killen et al., 2016).

Economics and Social Structure

As early as toddlerhood, children begin to understand that money is used to buy things, but they have little understanding of where money comes from (Berti, 2005; Webley, 2005). In the following example, Berti talks to 3;6-year-old Esther about work and salary (Berti & Bombi, 1988, p. 61):

B: *How do daddies come to have the money they need?*
E: *They take it.*
B: *How do they take it?*
E: *They take in their pocket.*
B: *The money they have in their pocket, was it also there yesterday?*
E: *Yes.*
B: *And before then?*
E: *It was in their pockets.*

DOI: 10.4324/9781003292579-45

B: *When it's finished what does Daddy do?*
E: *He takes it from his other pocket.*
B: *And when that one's also empty what does he do?*
E: *He takes more.*
B: *Where from?*
E: *From wallets.*

Six-year-olds only have a nascent understanding of economic reality, such as the fact that shop owners have to pay for the goods they sell (Jahoda, 1984, p. 72):

I: *What do you do when you buy something?*
S: *Give the shop lady the money.*
I: *What does she do with it?*
S: *Gives the money back.*
I: *Is it the same money?*
S: *Yes.*
I: *Can you tell more about this?*
S: *The people pays her, she pays the people.*
I: *Where does the milk in the shop come from?*
S: *Cows – the man brings it.*
I: *Does the lady have to pay for the milk?*
S: *The lady pays the man and the man pays the lady because he gives her milk.*

Around the age of 7–8 years, children begin to form a basic under-standing of the parts of society they themselves belong to, but have no knowledge of public institutions and governance and usually are unaware that a shopkeeper makes money by selling things. They believe that any profits are given to poor or disabled people, but their explanations also reflect their personal experiences. Children who have sold things at garage sales or in the street have a more developed understanding of profit than children without this type of experience (Berti, 2005; Webley, 2005).

Around 9–10 years of age, children realize that someone must be supplying the supermarket with groceries, and that these are bought from farmers, fishermen and others, but they fail to understand the larger picture and the various functions of the people in the system. Children do not understand the relationship between bank deposits and loans, that a principal has to get money from someone in order to run the school, or that a shopkeeper must generate earnings. This is from an interview with a 10-year-old (Jahoda, 1984, p. 74):

I: *Who pays the shop lady?*
S: *The manager.*
I: *Where does he get the money from?*
S: *Off some of the money out of the till.*
I: *Is the manager doing a job?*
S: *No.*
I: *Where does he get the money for his food?*
S: *He might have another job.*

Not until the age of about 13 do children begin to understand how the person who pays wages earns his or her money.

School is the first social institution children encounter, and by the age of 11 they have gained an understanding of how school works as a system, like Jaqui (Emler, 1992, pp. 71–72):

J: *They [teachers] could make classroom rules but they would not be able to make whole school rules.*
I: *Who can make school rules?*
J: *Headmaster.*
I: *Could he make a rule to say children should come to school?*
J: *No, that would be the government.*

At this age, children accept the teacher's authority in the classroom, but are also aware of its limits. They consider it ridiculous, for example, that the teacher should decide when they have to go to bed. Younger children are more willing to accept this type of authority from teachers (Emler, 1992).

According to Furth (1980), children's general cognitive development furnishes the basis for their understanding of society as a **hierarchical structure**. Jahoda (1984) emphasizes the fact that children and adolescents construct knowledge based on the information they have about different areas, rather than merely reproducing what they have learned at school or heard from adults. Children's incomplete understanding of societal functions is due to the relative complexity of these issues as well as children's lack of **domain-specific** knowledge. The answers in the previous dialogues above reflect the children's efforts to use their own experience to create meaning and context in areas they have little knowledge about.

Social Inequality

Children notice differences between people early on. At preschool age, many children become aware that some people earn more than others, especially those they perceive to be in a position of power, such as policemen. When asked to describe a person in a picture, they often name the person's profession, such as plumber, doctor or businessman (Emler & Dickinson, 2005). At this age, children also begin to pay attention to clues about wealth and status, such as how people dress and live and, in some areas, the color of their skin. Children use these clues to evaluate the abilities and popularity of other people and whether they themselves would want to be friends with them (Shutts et al., 2013).

Sigelman (2012) found that 6-year-olds had difficulties explaining why some people are rich, even though some of them said they had a good job. Marco, aged 6;8 years, believed that everyone who worked was rich (Berti & Bombi, 1988, p. 70):

B: *How come there are rich people and poor people?*
M: *Because the poor don't have any money.*
B: *And why don't they have any money?*
M: *Because they don't work.*
B: *And the rich, on the other hand?*
M: *They go to work.*

Many of the 10-year-olds in Sigelman's study mentioned a good job in addition to effort and inheritance, while the 14-year-olds additionally included abilities and education. Another study found that children aged 10–12 years had a relatively good understanding of the social class they belonged to, but also associated poor people with fewer positive traits than rich people (Mistry et al., 2015).

At the same time, younger children are concerned with equality and justice and often argue that differences are unjust (Almås et al., 2010), such as 6-year-old Mary (Leahy, 1983, p. 99):

M: *Some people don't got no refrigerators, nothing to eat . . . if they don't eat they gonna die.*

At 7–8 years of age, children begin using more judgmental terms to describe different professions. Some are great, others are bad jobs or regular jobs. Common explanations for why some people earn more than others is that some jobs are important or strenuous, or require knowledge or education: doctors earn more than bus drivers because "drivers just drive a bus, while doctors cure people."

In late childhood and adolescence, explanations of social inequality involve more psychological factors and differences in traits, thoughts and motives. Social class differences collide with principles of equality or are justified by ideas about equality, as in the case of 12-year-old Dean (Leahy, 1983, p. 99):

D: *I think that they should all be the same, each have the same amount of money because then the rich people won't think they are so big.*

Adolescents use words such as responsibility, qualifications and abilities when they argue why some jobs are better paid than others. The rich and the poor are perceived to be different types of people with different thoughts, feelings and characteristics. Until the age of about 14 years, arguments in favor of equality dominate, whereas such arguments make up less than half of all explanations after the age of 17 years. Seventeen-year-old Rose is aware of the contradictions on the issue of inequality (Leahy, 1983, p. 99):

R: *If you look at it one way you say, "Why?" It's so unfair. . . . Like why can't it be equally balanced? But I guess people who are rich, they work for what they have.*

Some older adolescents perceive personal economy as a reward merited by individual effort. Seventeen-year-old John argues more clearly in favor of social inequality (Leahy, 1983, p. 99):

J: *They don't want to go for a job. it's their own fault. They deserve to be poor . . . they're just hanging out, doing nothing. A person like that deserves to be poor.*

In later adolescence, factors such as market forces, class and political power become increasingly important (Emler & Dickinson, 2005). People who belong to the same social class are perceived as similar because they share psychological characteristics (Leahy, 1983). Adolescents rank different professional groups approximately the same as adults do, but their own social background impacts their evaluation. Middle-class adolescents are generally more aware of occupational status, whereas adolescents from working-class backgrounds overestimate the status of skilled workers in society. Middle-class adolescents also estimate the wage differences between people with and without an education to be greater than adolescents with a working-class background do (Emler & Dickinson, 2005).

Becoming Citizens

Societal reasoning develops from a primary focus on the individual's own situation to including the needs of others and factors of general importance to a society (Helwig & Turiel, 2002). It is the mental schemas children and adolescents have formed about political processes and the workings of society that are activated when they meet with political dilemmas and begin to fulfill their role as citizens (Torney-Purta, 1992). In adolescence and emergent adulthood, young people come to integrate the understanding of social structure, organization, rules and roles that is necessary to fully become a member of society (de França, 2016).

Summary of Part VI

1 Children are exposed to electronic media early on, with a continual increase in use throughout childhood and adolescence, but with large individual differences. Parents try to regulate their children's media use and to some extent spend time on media together with their younger children. Media take away time from other activities.

2 The learning effect of electronic media is small for toddlers, and two-dimensional images cannot replace the experience of a three-dimensional physical world. Slightly older children and adolescents may profit from media with educational content and purpose, but many educational programs only show a minimal learning effect. There is disagreement about potential positive influences of computer games on cognitive functioning. There is a negative relation between a lot of time spent gaming and academic performance.

3 The *psychodynamic* assumption that watching violence leads to a reduction in violent behavior has little support in research. According to *cognitive behavioral theory*, children imitate aggressive behavior when they see others perform violent actions on video and have less inhibition of aggressive behavior. Another explanation is that the content contributes to shaping children's and adolescents' expectations of other people's behavior and their perceptions of how conflicts can be resolved. Children who witness large amounts of violence in the media form *scripts* containing aggressive elements, whereas children who watch prosocial programs more often form scripts with prosocial content. Exposure to violent games can lead to a *desensitization* to violence.

4   Prosocial games can lead to an increase in prosocial behavior.
    Many electronic games include make-believe destructive actions
    that give a higher score and lead to higher levels of arousal, more
    aggressive thoughts and behavior, and less empathy and helping
    behavior. There is a moderate relation between children's prefer-
    ence for violent games and later violent and criminal behavior.
    Excessive amounts of time spent on electronic games can be an
    expression of social and personal problems.

5   Social media use increases with age, and most adolescents use
    social media daily. Children and adolescents follow up their exist-
    ing friends and look for new relationships online. *Cyberbullying*
    has the same consequences as other types of bullying but can be
    more pervasive because it is impossible to protect against. Some
    children are drawn to social media because they are socially iso-
    lated and have difficulty establishing social relationships in real
    life. Some adolescents show atypical use and signs of internet
    addiction.

6   *Societal cognition* involves the construction of a set of concepts
    or a "theory" about society. At preschool age, children have no
    coherent understanding of society's functions. At early school age,
    children begin to understand the parts of society they themselves
    belong to, and, on their way to adolescence, children acquire a
    basic understanding of societal functions and how different sys-
    tems work.

7   Children notice differences between people early on. At pre-
    school age, they become aware that some people earn more than
    others. At early school age, children begin to use more judg-
    mental terms to describe different professions, but also give more
    rational explanations for differences in wages and status. Children
    typically argue that differences are unjust, whereas positive justi-
    fications become more prominent in adolescence. Social back-
    ground impacts these evaluations.

Core Issues

- The impact of media use on development and learning.
- The impact of media use on social interaction patterns.
- The impact of media on prosocial and antisocial behavior.
- The bases of political attitudes.

Suggestions for Further Reading

Anderson, C. A., et al. (2010). Violent video game effects on aggression, empathy, and prosocial behavior in Eastern and Western countries. *Psychological Bulletin, 136*, 151–173.

Barrett, M., & Buchanan-Barrow, E. (Eds) (2005). *Children's understanding of society*. New York, NY: Psychology Press.

Berti, A. E., & Bombi, A. S. (1988). *The child's construction of economics*. Cambridge: Cambridge University Press.

Blinka, L., et al. (2015). Excessive internet use in European adolescents: What determines differences in severity? *International Journal of Public Health, 60*, 249–256.

Christakis, D. A., et al. (2009). Audible television and decreased adult words, infant vocalizations, and conversational turns: A population-based study. *Archives of Pediatric and Adolescence Medicine, 163*, 554–558.

DeLoache, J. S., et al. (2010). Do babies learn from baby media? *Psychological Science, 21*, 1570–1574.

Huesmann, L. R. (2007). The impact of electronic media violence: Scientific theory and research. *Journal of Adolescent Health, 41*, S6–S13.

Kucirkova, N., & Littleton, K. (2016). *The digital reading habits of children: A national survey of parents' perceptions of and practices in relation to children's reading for pleasure with print and digital books*. Book Trust. Available from: www.book trust.org.uk/news-andblogs/news/1371

Lauricella, A. R., et al. (2015). Young children's screen time: The complex role of parent and child factors. *Journal of Applied Developmental Psychology, 36*, 11–17.

40

Toward Adulthood

Childhood and adolescence are valuable periods in their own right and, at the same time, form the basis for life as an adult. Adolescence completes the developmental pathways of childhood and marks out the course for a more autonomous and independent existence (Smetana et al., 2006). It is a period characterized by puberty and sexual maturation and brings with it new types of relationships and social activities. Adolescence is replaced by *emerging adulthood*, which extends into the 20s and is described in slightly different ways: as an extension of adolescence (Wyn, 2004), a separate stage of development (Arnett, 2006; Arnett et al., 2014) or a transition period to adulthood (Côté, 2014). Emerging adulthood varies in length and shows major variations along the way, but typical of this period is the transition from one's former family to a new one, from dependence to independence and from mandatory school attendance to personal choices regarding education, occupation and lifestyle, with all the changes in social roles, goals and responsibilities this entails. At the same time, young adults spend more time alone than in the periods before and after, in which they generally live together with family (Larson, 1990). It is an age at which many feel uncertain about their future and the world, but it is also a window of opportunity for individuals to make changes to their existence and the course of their lives, for example when those who have grown up under difficult family circumstances show resilience and exploit their independence to create a good life for themselves as adults (Masten, 2016). Additionally, early adulthood is an important element in the development of societies, and community engagement contributes to a positive development (O'Connor et al., 2011).

As many of the choices an individual makes in emerging adulthood affect the remainder of adult life, it is an important phase from a

DOI: 10.4324/9781003292579-46

life-span perspective (Schulenberg et al., 2004). In the past 100 years, higher education has evolved from an elite privilege for the few to become a natural part of the lives of most adolescents and young adults (Snyder et al., 2016). In industrialized societies, education is an important pursuit for many at this age (Arnett, 2006). The current pattern of education also affects cultural continuity and the relationship between generations in fundamental ways. Previously, occupations were largely "inherited," whether this meant following in the footsteps of a physician or a blacksmith, but many millennials choose an education different from the one their parents chose. This applies equally to working-class children who become academics as to children of university professors who choose a non-academic career or no higher education at all. Early adulthood and the transition to adult life are usually shorter for those who do not continue to study but move straight on to working life.

The experience of being an adult comes gradually, and many young adults report a sense of standing between adolescence and adulthood (Arnett, 2001). Nelson and Barry (2005) found that 25 percent of 19–25-year-olds considered themselves adults, while 69 percent felt they were adults in some, but not in all, areas. They have an adult existence in the sense that many of them have left their homes and live on their own, with a spouse or a partner, but are adolescents in the sense that today's financial situation allows parents to influence their child's transition to adulthood but also to maintain a certain degree of dependence in the relationship (Fingerman & Yahirun, 2015). The key role parents or others of the parental generation have played in enculturating their children is completed, however. They have become independent members of society and are in the process of establishing more stable romantic relationships; for them, the role as parent is not merely a biological option, but a cultural probability. Establishing one's own (first) home is a developmental task that belongs to emerging adulthood, and studies show that it often leads to positive changes in the parent–child relationship. But above all, it is a steady job and the independence that comes with it that distinguish the established adult life (Seiffge-Krenke, 2015).

The metaphor "the child is father of the man" denotes that the adult individual is shaped by his upbringing. Nonetheless, development is not finished at the threshold to adulthood – the transition itself is considered a particularly important part of the life span and can entail both continuity and **discontinuity** in social development and mental health (Schulenberg et al., 2004). Prosocial and **moral reasoning** continue to develop (Eisenberg et al., 2005). The formation of identity – which is usually considered part of adolescent development – can in some cases last well into an individual's 30s (Cramer, 2017), and the development of personality undergoes its largest average changes between the ages of 20 and 40 years (Roberts et al., 2006). Nor is it a linear transition – emergent adulthood is characterized by many changes in residence (including moving back home during periods) and partners (Arnett, 2006), as well as in degree of dependence (Cohen et al., 2003). Both the establishment of relationships and experienced loneliness show major individual differences at this age (Bowker et al., 2014).

From a life-span perspective, the functional changes that take place in adulthood can be studied as developmental phenomena in line with the changes taking place in childhood and adolescence (Baltes et al., 2006). This calls for a broader concept of development than, for example, that of Werner (1948), who proposes that traits and abilities become qualitatively and quantitatively more complex, extensive and the like. In the course of the life span, development also includes periods of declining characteristics and skills and the need to adapt to weaker functioning. In this perspective, too, developmental changes are time-bound, but with variations in the direction of change.

Glossary

See subject index to find the terms in the text

Activity   A stable and complex system of goal-oriented activities or interactions that are related to each other by theme or situation and have taken place over a long period of time.

Adaptation   Changes that increase the ability of a species or an individual to survive and cope with the environment.

Adaptive function   Behavioral consequences that contribute to an individual's survival.

Adolescence   The period between *childhood* and adulthood, age 12–18.

Affect attunement   See *emotional attunement*.

Age score   The average age at which children achieve a certain *raw score* on a *test*; sometimes called mental age in connection with *intelligence tests*.

Aggression   Behavior intended to harm living beings, objects or materials; see *open aggression* and *relational aggression*.

Anorexia nervosa   Eating disorder involving excessive dieting, under-eating and weight loss.

Antisocial behavior   Behavior that shows little concern for other people's feelings and needs, and violates the common social and ethical norms of a culture; see *prosocial behavior*.

Assessment (in clinical work)   The mapping of an individual's strengths and weaknesses, competencies and problem areas.

Associated group play   Form of *group play* in which children engage in the same activities and interact to a certain degree.

Association   A link, such as between a stimulus and a reaction or action, or between ideas or thoughts.

Attachment   A *behavioral system* that includes various forms of *attachment behavior*; the system is activated when a child finds herself at a shorter or a longer distance from the person she is attached to, and experiences emotions such as pain, fear, stress, uncertainty or anxiety; the term is also used to describe emotional attachment to a caregiver; Attachment can be secure, insecure and disorganized; see *exploration*.

Attachment behavior   According to Bowlby, any behavior that enables a person to achieve or maintain closeness with another, clearly identified person who is perceived to be better able to cope with the environment; includes signal behavior and approach behavior.

Attention deficit hyperactivity disorder; ADHD   Attention deficit disorder with restlessness and a high level of activity.

Atypical development   Course of development that differs significantly from the development of the majority of a *population*; see *individual differences* and *typical development*.

Autism spectrum disorder   Neurodevelopmental disorder that appears in the first years of life; characterized by persistent deficits in social skills, communication and language, and by repetitive behavior and restricted interests.

Autobiographical memory   Memory of chronologically organized sequences of personally experienced events.

Autonomy   Independence, self-determination. Ability to make independent decisions related to life's everyday tasks; an important element in the formation of *identity* in *adolescence*.

Behavioral disorder   All forms of behavior that are socially unacceptable in one way or another, such as running away from home, screaming, cursing, messy eating manners, bed-wetting, ritual behavior, excessive dependency, poor *emotion regulation*, *aggression*, fighting and *bullying*.

Behavioral system   Innate system shaped by evolutionary factors; activated under certain conditions and terminated under conditions other than those that activated it; the function of a behavioral system is the likely outcome of the behavior.

Behaviorism; Behavior analysis   Group of psychological theories that emphasize the influence of the environment to explain developmental changes.

Bullying   Negative actions, such as teasing and physical or verbal *aggression*, that are repeated over time and directed toward one or several individuals; direct bullying consists of open attacks on the person being bullied, while indirect bullying entails social exclusion.

Caregiving system   According to Bowlby, an innate behavioral system that triggers caregiving behavior in adults.

Cerebral palsy   Impaired muscle function due to prenatal or early brain damage. Characterized by paralysis, poor motor or postural coordination, and increased or varying muscle tension.

Childhood   Age 1–12 years.

Chromosome   Thread-shaped formation in the cellular nucleus that carries genes; always occurs in pairs, with 23 pairs in human beings.

Cognition   Thinking or understanding; includes some type of perception of the world, storage in the form of mental *representation*, different ways of managing or processing new and stored experiences, and action strategies.

Cognitive behavior theory   School within the behavioral tradition built on the basic premise that development is a cumulative learning process, and that learning forms the basis for most individual differences between children; also emphasizes the importance of models and *observational learning*, and cognitive processing and regulation of own behavior; also known as social learning theory.

Collaborative play   Form of *group play* in which children take on complementary roles and tasks.

Communication   Intentional conveyance of thoughts, stories, desires, ideas, emotions, etc., to one or more persons.

Concept   Mental *representation* of a category of objects, events, persons, ideas, etc.; see *extension (of a concept)*.

Conditioning   The learning of a specific reaction in response to specific stimuli; includes classical and operant conditioning. In *classical conditioning*, a neutral stimulus is associated with an unlearned or *unconditioned stimulus* that elicits an unlearned or *unconditioned response*, eventually transforming the neutral stimulus into a conditioned stimulus that elicits a conditioned response similar to the unconditioned response. In *operant conditioning*, an action is followed by an event that increases or reduces the probability that the action will be repeated under similar circumstances.

Conformity   The adoption of other people's attitudes and behavior due to actual or perceived pressure from them.

Constancy (in cognition)   The ability to understand that the attributes of objects and people remain the same, even if they seem to have changed, for example due to a different viewing angle and lighting conditions; see *object permanence*.

Constraint (in development)   The organism's resistance to change and adaptation to new experiences; often used in connection with the nervous system.

Constructive play   Form of play that entails that children construct something, such as a Lego house or a clay figure; may be performed alone or together with others; see *exercise play*, *group play*, *pretend play* and *symbolic play*.

Continuity (in development)   Development in which later ways of functioning build directly on previous functions and can be predicted based on them; see *discontinuity*.

Controversial children (sociometry)   Children who are both accepted and rejected by their peers, and may appear active, aggressive, destructive and angry, or as socially withdrawn; they can also be helpful, cooperative and assume leadership, and at times display socially sensitive behavior; see *neglected children*, *neutral children*, *popular children* and *unpopular children*.

Correlation   Measure of the degree of covariation between two variables, ranging from −1.00 to +1.00; values close to 0.00 show a low degree of correlation; a positive correlation (+) means that a high score on one variable is associated with high score on the other; a negative cor relation (−) indicates that a high score on one variable is associated with a low score on the other.

Correspondence (cognitive)   In Piaget's New Theory, the perception of structural similarity that provides a basis for comparing people, objects, events, actions, etc.

Critical period   Limited time period in which an individual is especially susceptible to specific forms of positive or negative stimulation and experience; if the stimulation or experience fails to take place during this period, a similar stimulation or experience later in life will neither benefit nor harm the individual to any appreciable extent; see *sensitive period*.

Culture   The particular activities, tools, attitudes, beliefs, values, norms, etc., that characterize a group or a community.

Detachment   Discontinuation of an attachment relationship due to prolonged or permanent separation; see *attachment*.

Development   Changes over time in the structure and functioning of human beings and animals as a result of interaction between biological and environmental factors.

Developmental pathway   One of several possible courses of development within the same area or domain.

Difficult temperament   According to Thomas and Chess, temperament characterized by a tendency to withdraw in new situations, general negativity, strong emotional reactions and highly irregular sleeping and eating patterns.

Disability   The difference between an individual's abilities and the demands of the environment.

Discontinuity (in development)   Development in which new functions are associated with qualitative differences rather than merely a quantitative growth in previously established functions, and where the effect of past development can be altered by subsequent experiences; see *continuity*.

Domain   A delimited sphere of knowledge; an area in which something is active or manifests itself.

Domain-specific   Abilities and skills within a specific domain of knowledge.

Down syndrome; Trisomy 21   Syndrome that causes varying degrees of *intellectual disability*; caused by an error in cell division that results in a partial or complete extra copy of chromosome 21.

Ego   In *psychoanalytic theory*, one of the three parts of the human psyche; its purpose is to regulate the drives and impulses of the *id* in relation to the realities of the world and the limitations of the *superego*.

Emotion   A state caused by an event important to the person and characterized by the presence of feelings; involves physiological reactions, conscious inner experience, directed action and outward expression.

Emotion regulation   Implicit and explicit strategies to adapt one's own emotional reactions and those of others in line with social and cultural conventions, especially in regard to the expression, intensity, duration and contexts in which they arise.

Emotional attunement; Affect attunement   A state in which a person is *sensitive* and *responsive* to the emotional state of another. Accord ing to Stern, a process by which the caregiver "mirrors" the experiences of the child without using language and allows the child to understand how he or she is perceived.

Emotionality   The mood of an individual; the amount and intensity of positive and negative emotions.

Empathy   Feel with someone; emotional reaction similar to the emotion another person is perceived to experience.

Enculturation   Acquisition of a culture's practices, customs, norms, values, and the like; the first foundation in this process is children's innate social orientation.

Evolutionary psychology; Evolution-based psychology   School of thought that focuses on the function of a particular behavior pattern during evolution, in the context of explaining human actions.

Exercise play   Non-functional practice in performing different actions; see *constructive play*, *group play*, and *symbolic play*.

Experiment   Method to test a hypothesis on specific causal relationships or connections. One or several conditions are systematically altered, and the effect is recorded. As many conditions as possible are kept constant in order not to affect the outcome, increasing the probability that the results are solely related to the conditions being studied.

Exploration   According to Bowlby, a behavioral system whose function is to provide information about the environment and enable the individual to better adapt to it; activated by unfamiliar and/or complex objects; deactivated once the objects have been examined and become familiar to the individual; see *attachment* and *secure base*.

Exploratory behavior   According to Bowlby, exploratory behavior consists of three elements: an *orienting response*, movement in the direction of the object, and physical exploration of the object by moving it and experimenting with it; see *attachment*.

Extension (of a concept)   All actual and possible exemplars encompassed by a concept.

Externalizing disorder   Negative emotions directed at others; often expressed in the form of antisocial and aggressive behavior.

Fetal period   Ninth week of pregnancy until birth.

Gender constancy   The ability to understand that an individual's gender is linked to certain biological characteristics and remains the same, regardless of clothing and the like.

Gender difference; Sex difference   Characteristic, ability or behavior pattern that differs between the two sexes.

Gender identity   Sense of belonging to a particular gender; according to Kohlberg, the ability to distinguish between male and female.

Gender role; Sex role   Expectations about the actions or behavior of boys, girls, men and women in a particular society under different circumstances.

Gender stereotype   Generalized and often erroneous view of the behavior and characteristics of boys, girls, men and women.

Generalize   To perceive and react in the same way to events that are similar in some respects.

Gesture   Distinct movement primarily used as a means of communication and interpreted consistently within a social system.

Group play   Play in which several children interact; see *associated group play*, *collaborative play*, *constructive play*, *exercise play*, and *symbolic play*.

Hierarchical structure (of concepts)   Organization of objects or concepts into categories and subcategories that are part of larger categories.

Horizontal relation   Relationship in which both parties share an equal amount of knowledge and social power; see *vertical relation*.

Identification   Process characterized by a tendency to mimic behavior and assume someone else's points of view.

Identity   An individual's sense of who he or she is, as well as of affiliation with larger and smaller social groups and communities.

Imitation   The deliberate execution of an action to create a correspondence between what oneself does and what someone else does.

Imprinting   A form of rapid learning that takes place during a short and sensitive period immediately after birth; ducklings, for example, will follow the first person, animal or object they see move within a period of 48 hours after hatching.

Incidence   The appearance of new occurrences of a trait, disease or similar in a particular *population* during a particular time span, often expressed as the number of incidences per 1,000 individuals per year; see *prevalence*.

Individual differences   Variation in skills and characteristics between the individuals in a *population*; see *atypical development* and *typical development*.

Individualistic culture; individualistic society   Society where values emphasize on the uniqueness of each individual.

Infancy   The first year of life.

Inhibition   Shyness and withdrawal from social challenges.

Integration (in development)   Coordination; progress toward greater organization and a more complex structure.

Intellectual disability; Learning disability; Mental retardation Significant problems learning and adjusting that affect most areas of functioning; graded mild (IQ 70–50), moderate (IQ 49–35), severe (IQ 34–20) and profound (IQ below 20); in clinical contexts, a significant reduction in social adjustment is an additional criterion.

Interaction effect An influence by one or several other factors.

Internalization Process whereby external processes are reconstructed to become internal processes, such as when children independently adopt problem-solving strategies they have previously used in interaction with others, or adopt the attitudes, characteristics and standards of others as their own.

Internalizing disorder Negative emotions directed at oneself, anxiety, depression; often involving a negative self-image, shyness and seclusion; see *externalizing disorder*.

Intersubjectivity The consciously shared subjective experience of an event or phenomenon by two or more individuals simultaneously.

Joint attention Two or more individuals share a common focus of attention, while at the same time being aware that the same focus of attention is shared by the other person(s).

Learned helplessness The experience of lacking self-determination and the ability to affect one's environment as a result of having experienced situations in which one felt little control.

Learning Relatively permanent change in understanding and behavior as the result of experience; see *development* and *maturation*.

Learning disorder Significant problems developing skills in a specific area of knowledge, such as language impairment, reading/writing disorders (*dyslexia*) and difficulties with math (dyscalculia); often referred to as specific learning disorder as opposed to general learning disability; see *intellectual disability*.

Logical constructivism Psychological tradition that includes Piaget's theory and the theories of others that build on it; its main principle is that children actively construct their own understanding of the outside world, and that *perception* and *cognition* are affected by logical and conceptually driven processes.

Longitudinal study Research method that involves the observation of the same individuals at various age levels.

Maturation Developmental change caused by genetically determined regulating mechanisms that are relatively independent of the individual's specific experiences; see *development* and *learning*.

Mental age   See *age score*.

Mental disorder   Behavioral or psychological pattern that occurs in an individual and leads to clinically significant distress or impairment in one or more important areas of functioning.

Mentalizing   The interpretation of one's own and others' behavior as an expression of mental states, desires, feelings, perceptions, etc.; according to Fonagy, a process that includes all thoughts about relationships, human interactions and psychological processes in humans.

Metaphor   A type of *analogy*; meaning expressed illustratively or figuratively.

Mind understanding   Understanding that other people have internal states, such as knowledge, feelings and plans, that may be different from one's own and may affect their actions.

Moral dilemma   Situation involving a conflict between two or more solutions that may violate an individual's perception of what is right and wrong.

Moral reasoning   Reasoning about real or hypothetical moral dilemmas.

Neglected children (sociometry)   Children who are neither accepted nor rejected by their peers; few features distinguish them from other children, but they have less interaction with others, and little attention is paid to them; they typically show little aggressiveness and seem to try to avoid aggression to a somewhat greater degree than other children, but do not appear overly anxious or withdrawn; see *controversial children, neutral children, popular children* and *unpopular children*.

Neutral children (sociometry)   Children who do not fall into a particular group when their popularity is evaluated by their peers, i.e. who are neither *popular, unpopular* or *controversial*, but who at the same time are not *neglected children*.

Object (in psychodynamic theory)   Mental representation of a person or an object that is the goal of a drive, or through which a drive can achieve its goal.

Object permanence   Understanding that an object continues to exist even though it cannot be perceived by the senses.

Open aggression   A form of *hostile aggression*; actions whose purpose is to harm another person physically; seen *relational aggression*.

Parallel play   Play in which several children play side by side with similar objects or in a similar way, but without interacting.

Parenting style   General description of how parents raise their children.

Perception Knowledge gained through the senses; discernment, selection and processing of sensory input.

Personality An individual's characteristic tendency to feel, think and act in specific ways.

Personality traits Summary description of an individual's *personality*.

Popular children (sociometry) Children who are actively accepted by other children. Often they are physically strong with an attractive appearance, but their willingness to share, ability to cooperate and other social skills are equally important for their acceptance and popularity among peers; see *controversial children*, *neglected children*, *neutral children* and *unpopular children*.

Population (in statistics) The sum total of individuals, objects, events and the like included in a study. Also used to describe a group of individuals with a common measurable attribute, such as children in a certain school grade or young people in cities.

Pretend play Form of *symbolic play* that involves make-believe actions.

Prevalence Relative presence of for example traits, diseases and syndromes in a particular population at a certain time; see *incidence*.

Primary intersubjectivity According to Trevarthen, younger infants' perception of how they affect others, and the fact that others are aware of them; see *secondary intersubjectivity*.

Prosocial behavior Behavior intended to help others and share objects or other benefits without advantage to the individual itself; see *antisocial behavior*.

Protection (in development) Conditions that reduce the negative effects of *vulnerability* and *risk*.

Prototype Typical exemplar of a concept.

Psychoanalytic psychology; psychoanalytic theory Psychological theories based on Freud's theory and psychotherapeutic method (psychoanalysis); founded on the principle that an individual's thoughts and actions are determined by drives and impulses and their internal, often *unconscious*, regulation through interaction between the different parts of the human psyche; both *personality* and mental problems of children and adults are explained on the basis of unconscious processes and conflicts rooted in early childhood; see *ego* and *psychodynamic theory*.

Psychodynamic psychology; psychodynamic theory Tradition that emphasizes the importance of feelings and needs for an individual's thoughts and actions; describes *personality* and its development based on the assumption that the human psyche involves mental forces that frequently are in conflict with each other, and have an important basis in early childhood; *psychoanalysis* belongs to this tradition.

Psychopathology   Mental problems and disorders that make everyday functioning difficult.

Psychosocial moratorium   According to Erikson, a period in which adolescents have not yet decided on a future career or role in society, and find themselves between the safety of childhood and the independence of adult life (*autonomy*).

Punishment   In behavioral psychology, any event that reduces the probability of repeating an action under similar circumstances.

Recognition   The process of experiencing something in the moment that has been experienced before, such as when children consciously or nonconsciously show that they have seen a particular image before.

Reference group   Group that forms the basis for an individual's values, norms, attitudes and behaviors.

Relational aggression   A form of *hostile aggression*; actions whose main intent is to damage the relationship between two people, for example by speaking ill of them; see *open aggression*.

Representation (mental)   An individual's mental storage of understanding and knowledge about the world.

Resilience   Attributes that lead to a positive development under difficult childhood conditions, such as children who are biologically or socially at *risk* of aberrant or delayed development; see *vulnerability*.

Retrospective study   Study in which an individual is asked about earlier events.

Risk   Increased likelihood of a negative developmental outcome; may be linked to biological and environmental factors.

Role   Expectations of certain action patterns and behaviors associated with an individual by virtue of their function or position in society, for example as a girl, teenager or boy scout.

Role-play   Form of *pretend play* in which the participants make-believe they are another person, an animal or a human-like figure.

Rough-and-tumble play   A type of *exercise play* in which children run after each other, push, tickle, play-fight and similar.

Scaffold   In *social constructivism*, the external regulation, help and support provided by adults or more experienced peers to children, adapted to their level and allowing them to transcend their independent coping skills and develop new skills and knowledge; see *zone of proximal development*.

Schema   Mental *representation* that emerges when actions are generalized by means of repetition and transformed through mental processing, thus shaping the individual's perception of the environment.

School age   Age 6–12.

Script (cognition)   Generalized mental *representation* of a sequence of events that recur within the context of a specific situation; provides among other things the basis for an individual's expectations of how to behave in different situations, such as at school or at a restaurant.

Secondary intersubjectivity   According to Trevarthen, the *joint attention* of children and adults on something outside themselves, as well as their awareness of each other's attention.

Secure base   Describes the function of caregivers when they give younger children the opportunity for controlled *exploration* of objects and environments that can elicit fear, and to seek refuge when they become apprehensive; see *attachment*.

Segregation (education)   Special educational alternative outside the ordinary preschool group or school class a child is part of.

Self   Personal awareness, perception or evaluation of oneself.

Self as knower   The *I*, the subject that perceives its own existence and presence in the world; see *self as known*.

Self as known   The *me*, the entire complex of characteristics an individual thinks of when reflecting on their own person; see *self as knower*.

Self-concept   Awareness of having specific and independent traits; see *self as known*.

Self-disclosure   Communicating personal information about oneself to others; typical in *adolescence*.

Self-efficacy   The experience of acting and having control over one's own life; belief in one's own ability to deal with different situations and events.

Self-evaluation; Self-esteem   The assessment of one's own characteristics in relation to an inner standard that includes how and who one wishes to be; can also refer to questionnaires, surveys and the like about a person's characteristics.

Self-image   Positive or negative perception of oneself and one's own characteristics.

Self-referential emotion; Self-conscious emotions; Second-ary emotions Emotion associated with an individual's self-evaluation in relation to a standard based on personal emotional experiences and information provided by others; includes pride, shame, embarrassment, guilt and envy.

Self-regulation The ability to monitor and adapt one's own thoughts, feelings, reactions and actions in order to cope with the requirements, challenges and opportunities of the environment and be able to achieve one's goals; also referred to as self-control.

Sensitive period Limited period of time when an individual is particularly susceptible to specific forms of positive or negative stimulation and experience; if the stimulation or experience does not take place during the given time period, the individual will still be able to take advantage of, or be impaired by, similar types of stimulation or experience later in life, but to a lesser extent; see *critical period*.

Sensitivity (of a caregiver) Ability to understand a child's con-dition, respond quickly and adequately to the child's *signals* and behavior, and provide challenges the child is able to master.

Sensorimotor stage According to Piaget, the first of four stages in cognitive development, lasting until the age of 2.

Sex See *gender*.

Sex chromosomes Chromosomal pair that determines the sex of an individual and differs between males (XY) and females (XX).

Shaping (of behavior) Step-by-step *reinforcement* of behavior in such a way that it gradually changes and increasingly resembles desired behavior; part of *operant conditioning*.

Sign language Visual-manual language, primarily using move-ments of the arms, hands and fingers, supported by body move-ments, mouth movements and facial gestures.

Signals (in early development) Infant actions and expressions used by adults as an indication of the infant's interests, preferences and general well-being.

Sociability (temperament) Interest and enjoyment in being in the company of other people.

Social referencing Using other people's emotional reactions to evaluate uncertain situations; see *emotion regulation*.

Social selection Selectivity in choice of friends and social relations.

Socioeconomic status (SES) Assessment of an individual's eco-nomic and social status in society; for children, usually based on information about the parents' education and occupation.

Stability (in development)   Describes the constancy of an individual's position in relation to peers with respect to a particular characteristic; the fact that individual differences in the execution of a skill are constant from one developmental stage to another.

Stage (in development)   Delimited period of time in which thoughts, feelings and behavior are organized in a way that is qualitatively different from the preceding or following periods.

Stereotype   General and often erroneous view of the characteristics of a group of individuals, for example *gender stereotype*.

Strange Situation   Standardized situation to assess the quality of attachment between an adult and a child aged 1–2 years; see *attachment*.

Symbolic play   Play in which children take on the role of a person or an animal, and connect objects with a function unlike the one they usually have, performing a make-believe activity; see *constructive play*, *exercise play*, and *group play*.

Syndrome   Set of attributes and behavioral characteristics that regularly occur together.

Temperament   A biologically determined pattern of emotional reactivity and regulation unique to an individual; includes the degree of *emotionality*, *irritability* and *activity level*, and reactions to and ability to cope with emotional situations, new impressions and changes; see, *difficult temperament*.

Test   Measurement instrument; a collection of questions or tasks that provide a basis for assessing an individual's performance relative to peers or a specific set of criteria.

Toddlerhood   Age 1–3.

Transactional model   Developmental model based on mutual interaction between an individual and the environment over time: the environment changes the individual, the individual changes the environment, which in turn changes the individual, and so on.

Typical development   Course of development that characterizes the majority of a *population*; see *atypical development* and *individual differences*.

Unpopular children (sociometry)   Children who are actively rejected by other children; some children in this group appear particularly aggressive and hostile, others are socially withdrawn and often submissive, while others yet are immature and childish compared with their peers; see *controversial children*, *neglected children*, *neutral children* and *popular children*.

Vertical relation   Relationship in which one part has more knowledge and social power than the other, such as parent–child; see *horizontal relation*.

Vulnerability   An individual's susceptibility to be adversely affected by particular conditions or circumstances in the environment; see *resilience* and *risk*.

Williams syndrome   Genetic syndrome characterized by heart defects, distinctive facial features, a short stature, developmental delays in the fetal stage and later, problems thriving during *infancy*, mild or moderate *learning disabilities*, good language abilities compared with other skills, and trusting behavior toward other people.

Working model (in social relations)   Mental representation of an early relationship that forms the basis for expectations about the nature of social relationships, such as a caregiver's inclination to provide emotional support and be devoted and reliable.

Zone of proximal development   Children's mastery of skills in collaboration with more competent individuals within a specific area of knowledge or expertise, as opposed to self-mastery; see *scaffold*.

Bibliography

à Beckett, C., Lynch, S., & Pike, D. (2017). Playing with theory. In S. Lynch, D. Pike & C. à Beckett (Eds), *Multidisciplinary perspectives on play from birth and beyond* (pp. 1–22). Singapore: Springer.

Abecassis, M., Hartup, W. W., Haselager, G. J. T., Scholte, R. H. J., & van Lieshout, C. F. M. (2002). Mutual antipathies and their significance in middle childhood and adolescence. *Child Development, 73*, 1543–1556.

Abrams, D. (1989). Differential association: Social development in gender identity and intergroup relations during adolescence. In S. M. Skevington & D. Baker (Eds), *The social identity of women* (pp. 59–83). London: Sage.

Adams, G. R., & Marshall, S. K. (1996). A developmental social psychology of identity: Understanding the person-in-context. *Journal of Adolescence, 19*, 429–442.

Ainsworth, M. D. S. (1963). The development of infant–mother interaction among the Ganda. In B. M. Foss (Ed.), *Determinants of infant behavior, Volume 2* (pp. 67–104). New York, NY: Wiley.

Ainsworth, M. D. S. (1967). *Infancy in Uganda: Infancy and the growth of love.* Baltimore, MD: Johns Hopkins University Press.

Ainsworth, M. D. S. (1983). Patterns of infant–mother attachment as related to maternal care. In D. Magnusson & V. Allen (Eds), *Human development: An interactional perspective* (pp. 35–55). London: Academic Press.

Ainsworth, M. D. S., & Bowlby, J. (1991). An ethological account of personality development. *American Psychologist, 46*, 433–441.

Ainsworth, M. D. S., Bell, S. M., & Stayton, D. J. (1972). Individual differences in strange-situation behavior of one-year-olds. In H. R. Schaffer (Ed.), *The origin of human social relations* (pp. 17–57). London: Academic Press.

Ainsworth, M. D. S., Blehar, M. C., Waters, E., & Wahl, S. (1978). *Patterns of attachment.* Hillsdale, NJ: Erlbaum.

Aitken, M., VanderLaan, D. P., Wasserman, L., Stojanovski, S., & Zucker, K. J. (2016). Self-harm and suicidality in children referred for gender dysphoria. *Journal of the American Academy of Child and Adolescent Psychiatry, 55*, 513–520.

Alesi, M., Rappo, G., & Pepi, A. (2014). Depression, anxiety at school and self-esteem in children with learning disabilities. *Journal of Psychological Abnormalities in Children*, *3*, 125.

Allen, J. P., & Tan, J. S. (2016). The multiple facets of attachment in adolescence. In J. Cassidy & P. R. Shaver (Eds), *Handbook of attachment: Theory, research and clinical applications, Third edition* (pp. 399–415). New York, NY: Guilford Press.

Almås, I., Cappelen, A. W., Sørensen, E. Ø., & Tungodden, B. (2010). Fairness and the development of inequality acceptance. *Science*, *328*, 1176–1178.

Almqvist, A.-L., & Duvander, A.-Z. (2014). Changes in gender equality? Swedish fathers' parental leave, division of childcare and housework. *Journal of Family Studies*, *20*, 19–27

Alsaker, F. D., & Flammer, A. (1999). *The adolescent experience*. London: Lawrence Erlbaum.

Amaral, A. C. S., & Ferreira, M. E. C. (2017). Body dissatisfaction and associated factors among Brazilian adolescents: A longitudinal study. *Body Image*, *22*, 32–38.

American Academy of Child and Adolescent Psychiatry (2015). Screen time and children. Downloaded from www.aacap.org/AACAP/Families_and_Youth/Facts_for_Families/FFF-Guide/Children-And-Watching-TV-054.aspx.

American Academy of Pediatrics (2011). Media use by children younger than 2 years. *Pediatrics*, *128*, 1040–1045.

American Psychiatric Association (2013). *Diagnostic and statistical manual of mental disorders, Fifth edition (DSM-5)*. Washington, DC: American Psychiatric Association.

Amianto, F., Northoff, G., Daga, G. A., Fassino, S., & Tasca, G. A. (2016). Is anorexia nervosa a disorder of the self? A psychological approach. *Frontiers in Psychology*, 7, 849.

Ammaniti, M., van IJzendoorn, M. H., Speranza, A. M., & Tambelli, R. (2000). Internal working models of attachment during late childhood and early adolescence: An exploration of stability and change. *Attachment and Human Development*, *2*, 328–346.

Amsel, E., & Smalley, J. D. (2000). Beyond really and truly: Children's counter-factual thinking about pretend and possible worlds. In P. Mitchell & K. J. Riggs (Eds), *Children's reasoning and the mind* (pp. 121–147). Hove, UK: Psychology Press.

Anderson, C. A. (2004). An update on the effects of violent video games. *Journal of Adolescence*, *27*, 113–122.

Anderson, C. A., Bushman, B. J., Donnerstein, E., Hummer, T. A., & Warburton, W. (2015). SPSSI research summary on media violence. *Analyses of Social Issues and Public Policy*, *15*, 4–19.

Anderson, C. A., Shibuya, A., Ihori, N., Swing, E. L., Bushman, B. J., Sakamoto, A., & Saleem, M. (2010). Violent video game effects on aggression, empathy, and prosocial behavior in Eastern and Western countries. *Psychological Bulletin*, *136*, 151–173.

Anderson, D. R., & Kirkorian, H. L. (2015). Media and cognitive development. In R. M. Lerner, L. S. Liben & U. Müller (Eds), *Handbook of child psychology and developmental science, Seventh edition, Volume 2: Cognitive processes* (pp. 949–994). Hoboken, NJ: Wiley.

Anderson, D. R., & Pempek, T. A. (2005). Television and very young children. *American Behavioral Scientist, 48*, 505–522.

Archer, J. (1992). Childhood gender roles: Social context and organisation. In H. McGurk (Ed.), *Childhood social development: Contemporary perspectives* (pp. 31–61). Hove, UK: Erlbaum.

Arnett, J. J. (2001). Conceptions of the transition to adulthood: Perspectives from adolescence to midlife. *Journal of Adult Development, 8*, 133–143.

Arnett, J. J. (2006). Emerging adulthood: Understanding the new way of coming of age. *Emerging Adults in America: Coming of Age in the 21st Century, 22*, 3–19.

Arnett, J. J. (2015). *Emerging adulthood: The winding road from the late teens through the twenties, Second edition.* New York, NY: Oxford University Press.

Arnett, J. J., Žukauskienė, R., & Sugimura, K. (2014). The new life stage of emerging adulthood at ages 18–29 years: Implications for mental health. *The Lancet Psychiatry, 1*, 569–576.

Asher, S. R., & McDonald, K. (2009). The behavioral basis of acceptance, rejection, and perceived popularity. In K. K. Rubin, W. Bukowski & B. Laursen (Eds), *The handbook of peer interactions, relationships, and groups* (pp. 232–248). New York, NY: Guilford Press.

Atkinson, L., Chisholm, V. C., Scott, B., Goldberg, S., Vaughn, B. E., Blackwell, J., Dickens, S., & Tam, F. (1999). Maternal sensitivity, child functional level, and attachment in Down syndrome. *Monographs of the Society for Research in Child Development, 64*, 45–66.

Attwood, T. (1998). *Asperger's syndrome: A guide for parents and professionals.* London: Jessica Kingsley.

Axline, V. M. (1964). *Dibs: In search of self.* New York, NY: Ballantine.

Bagwell, C. L., & Schmidt, M. E. (2011). The friendship quality of overtly and relationally victimized children. *Merrill-Palmer Quarterly, 57*, 158–185.

Baltes, P. B., Lindenberger, U., & Staudinger, U. M. (2006). Lifespan theory in developmental psychology. In W. Damon & R. M. Lerner (Eds), *Handbook of child psychology, Sixth edition, Volume 1: Theoretical models of human development* (pp. 569–664). New York, NY: Wiley.

Bandura, A. (1994). Social cognitive theory of mass communication. In J. Bryant & R. Zillmann (Eds), *Media effects: Advances in theory and research* (pp. 61–90). Hillsdale, NJ: Erlbaum.

Bandura, A. (1997). *Self-efficacy: The exercise of control.* New York, NY: W. H. Freeman.

Bandura, A. (2008). Toward an agentic theory of the self. In H. Marsh, R. G. Craven & D. M. McInerney (Eds), *Advances in self research, Volume 3.*

Self-processes, learning, and enabling human potential (pp. 15–49). Charlotte, NC: Information Age Publishing.

Banse, R., Gawronski, B., Rebetez, C., Gutt, H., & Morton, J. B. (2010). The development of spontaneous gender stereotyping in childhood: Relations to stereotype knowledge and stereotype flexibility. *Developmental Science, 13,* 298–306.

Barlow, J., Schrader-McMillan, A., Axford, N., Wrigley, Z., Sonthalia, S., Wilkinson, T., Rawsthorn, M., Toft, A., & Coad, J. (2016). Attachment and attachment-related outcomes in preschool children–a review of recent evidence. *Child and Adolescent Mental Health, 21,* 11–20.

Barr, R., & Linebarger, D. N. (2017). *Media exposure during infancy and early childhood.* Cham, Switzerland: Springer.

Barr, R., Danziger, C., Hilliard, M. E., Andolina, C., & Ruskis, J. (2010). Amount, content and context of infant media exposure: A parental questionnaire and diary analysis. *International Journal of Early Years Education, 18,* 107–122.

Barron, C. M. (2014). "I had no credit to ring you back": Children's strategies of negotiation and resistance to parental surveillance via mobile phones. *Surveillance and Society, 12,* 401–413.

Barton, E. E. (2015). Teaching generalized pretend play and related behaviors to young children with disabilities. *Exceptional Children, 81,* 489–506.

Bat-Chava, Y. (2000). Diversity of deaf identities. *American Annals of the Deaf, 145,* 420–428.

Batorowicz, B., Stadskleiv, K., von Tetzchner, S., & Missiuna, C. (2016). Children who use communication aids instructing peer and adult partners during play-based activity. *Augmentative and Alternative Communication, 32,* 105–119.

Baumeister, R. F. (1993). Self-presentation: Motivational, cognitive, and interpersonal patterns. In G. L. Van Heck, P. Bonaiuto, I. J. Deary & W. Nowack (Eds), *Personality psychology in Europe, Volume 4* (pp. 257–279). Tilburg, NL: Tilburg University Press.

Baumeister, R. F. (2005). Rethinking self-esteem: Why non-profits should stop promoting self-esteem and start endorsing self-control. *Stanford Social Innovation Review, 3,* 34–41.

Baumeister, R. F., Smart, L., & Boden, J. M. (1996). Relation of threatened egotism to violence and aggression: The dark side of high self-esteem. *Psychological Review, 103,* 5–33.

Baumeister, R. F., Campbell, J. D., Krueger, J. I., & Vohs, K. D. (2003). Does high self-esteem cause better performance, interpersonal success, happiness, or healthier lifestyles? *Psychological Science in the Public Interest, 4,* 1–44.

Bavelier, D., Green, C. S., & Dye, M. W. G. (2010). Children, wired: For better and for worse. *Neuron, 67,* 692–701.

Becker, A. E., Fay, K. E., Agnew-Blais, J., Khan, A. N., Striegel-Moore, R. H., & Gilman, S. E. (2011). Social network media exposure and adolescent eating pathology in Fiji. *The British Journal of Psychiatry, 198,* 43–50.

Becker, I., Ravens-Sieberer, U., Ottová-Jordan, V., & Schulte-Markwort, M. (2017). Prevalence of adolescent gender experiences and gender expression in Germany. *Journal of Adolescent Health, 61,* 83–90.

Belsky, J. (2001). Developmental risks (still) associated with early child care. *Journal of Child Psychology and Psychiatry, 42,* 845–859.

Belsky, J. (2005). Attachment theory and research in ecological perspective. In K. E. Grossman, K. Grossman & E. Waters (Eds), *Attachment from infancy to adulthood: The major longitudinal studies* (pp. 71–97). New York, NY: Guilford Press.

Belsky, J. (2008). War, trauma and children's development: Observations from a modern evolutionary perspective. *International Journal of Behavioral Development, 32,* 260–271.

Bem, S. L. (1981). Gender schema theory: A cognitive account of sex typing. *Psychological Review, 88,* 354–364.

Bem, S. L. (1989). Genital knowledge and gender constancy in preschool children. *Child Development, 60,* 649–662.

Bem, S. L., Martyna, W., & Watson, C. (1976). Sex typing and androgyny: Further explorations of the expressive domain. *Journal of Personality and Social Psychology, 34,* 1016–1023.

Berndt, T. J. (1979). Developmental changes in conformity to peers and parents. *Developmental Psychology, 15,* 608–616.

Berndt, T. J. (1996). Exploring the effects of friendship quality on social development. In W. M. Bukowski, A. F. Newcomb & W. W. Hartup (Eds), *The company they keep: Friendship in childhood and adolescence* (pp. 346–365). Cambridge: Cambridge University Press.

Berndt, T. J. (2002). Friendship, quality and social development. *Current Directions in Psychological Science, 11,* 7–10.

Berndt, T. J., & Hanna, N. A. (1995). Intimacy and self-disclosure in friendships. In K. J. Rotenberg (Ed.), *Disclosure processes in children and adolescents* (pp. 57–77). Cambridge: Cambridge University Press.

Berndt, T. J., & Murphy, L. M. (2002). Influences of friends and friendships: Myths, truths, and research recommendations. *Advances in Child Development and Behavior, 30,* 275–310.

Berndt, T. J., Hawkins, J. A., & Hoyle, S. G. (1986). Changes in friendship during a school year: Effects on children's and adolescents' impressions of friendship and sharing with friends. *Child Development, 57,* 1284–1297.

Bernier, A., & Meins, E. (2008). A threshold approach to understanding the origins of attachment disorganization. *Developmental Psychology, 44,* 969–982.

Berti, A. E. (2005). Children's understanding of politics. In M. Barrett & E. Buchanan-Barrow (Eds), *Children's understanding of society* (pp. 69–103). New York, NY: Psychology Press.

Berti, A. E., & Bombi, A. S. (1988). *The child's construction of economics.* Cambridge: Cambridge University Press.

Best, D. L. (2010). Gender. In M. H. Bornstein (Ed.), *Hand-book of cultural developmental science* (pp. 209–222). New York, NY: Psychology Press.

Best, D. L., Williams, J. E., Cloud, J. M., Davis, S. W., Robertson, L. S., Edwards, J. R., et al. (1977). Development of sex-trait stereotypes among young children in the United States, England, and Ireland. *Child Development, 48*, 1375–1384.

Bhana, D. (2016). *Gender and childhood sexuality in primary school*. Singapore: Springer.

Bierman, K. L. (2004). *Peer rejection: Developmental processes and intervention strategies*. New York, NY: Guilford Press.

Bigler, R. S., & Liben, L. S. (2007). Developmental intergroup theory: Explaining and reducing children's social stereotyping and prejudice. *Current Directions in Psychological Science, 16*, 162–166.

Bishop, M., Hobson, R. P., & Lee, A. (2005). Symbolic play in congenitally blind children. *Development and Psychopathology, 17*, 447–465.

Blinka, L., Škařupová, K., Ševčíková, A., Wölfling, K., Müller, K. W., & Dreier, M. (2015). Excessive internet use in European adolescents: What determines differences in severity? *International Journal of Public Health, 60*, 249–256.

Blom, I., & Bergman, A. (2013). Observing development: A comparative view of attachment theory and separation–individuation theory. In J. E. Bettmann & D. D. Friedman (Eds), *Attachment-based clinical work with children and adolescents* (pp. 9–43). New York, NY: Springer.

Blum, H. P. (2004). Separation-individuation theory and attachment theory. *Journal of the American Psychoanalytic Association, 52*, 535–553.

Boden, J. M., Fergusson, D. M., & Horwood, L. J. (2008). Does adolescent self-esteem predict later life outcomes? A test of the causal role of self-esteem. *Development and Psychopathology, 20*, 319–339.

Bodrova, E., & Leong, D. J. (2015). Vygotskian and post-Vygotskian views on children's play. *American Journal of Play, 7*, 371–388.

Bohn-Gettler, C. M., Pellegrini, A. D., Dupuis, D., Hickey, M., Hou, Y., Roseth, C., & Solberg, D. (2010). A longitudinal study of preschool children's (homo sapiens) sex segregation. *Journal of Comparative Psychology, 124*, 219–228.

Boldt, L. J., Kochanska, G., Yoon, J. E., & Koenig Nordling, J. (2014). Children's attachment to both parents from toddler age to middle childhood: Links to adaptive and maladaptive outcomes. *Attachment and Human Development, 6*, 211–229.

Borge, A. I. H., Rutter, M., Côtè, S., & Tremblay, R. E. (2004). Early childcare effects on physical aggression: Differentiating social selection and social causation. *Journal of Child Psychology and Psychiatry, 45*, 367–376.

Bos, H., & Sandfort, T. (2015). Gender nonconformity, sexual orientation, and Dutch adolescents' relationship with peers. *Archives of Sexual Behavior, 44*, 1269–1279.

Bouffard, T., & Vezeau, C. (1998). The developing self-system and self-regulation of primary school children. In M. D. Ferrari & R. J. Sternberg

(Eds), *Self-awareness: Its nature and development* (pp. 246–272). New York, NY: Guilford Press.

Bowker, J. C., Nelson, L. J., Markovic, A., & Luster, S. (2014). Social withdrawal during adolescence and emerging adulthood. In R. J. Coplan & J. C. Bowker (Eds), *The handbook of solitude: Psychological perspectives on social isolation, social withdrawal, and being alone* (pp. 167–183). Chichester, UK: Wiley.

Bowlby, J. (1958). The nature of the child's tie to his mother. *The International Journal of Psycho-Analysis, 39,* 350.

Bowlby, J. (1969). *Attachment and loss, Volume 1. Attachment.* Harmonsworth, UK: Penguin.

Bowlby, J. (1973). *Attachment and loss, Volume 2. Separation: Anxiety and anger.* Harmondsworth, UK: Penguin.

Bowlby, J. (1980). *Attachment and Loss: Volume 3. Loss: Sadness and depression.* New York, NY: Basic Books.

Bowlby, J. (1982). Attachment and loss: Retrospect and prospect. *American Journal of Orthopsychiatry, 52,* 664–678.

Boyette, A. H. (2016). Children's play and culture learning in an egalitarian foraging society. *Child Development, 87,* 759–769.

Brandt, M. J. (2011). Sexism and gender inequality across 57 societies. *Psychological Science, 22,* 1413–1418.

Bretherton, I. (1990). Communication patterns, internal working models, and the intergenerational transmission of attachment relationships. *Infant Mental Health Journal, 11,* 237–252.

Brody, G. H. (1998). Sibling relationship quality: Its causes and consequences. *Annual Review of Psychology, 49,* 1–24.

Brody, L., & Hall, J. (1993). Gender and emotion. In M. Lewis & J. Haviland (Eds), *Handbook of emotions* (pp. 447–460). New York, NY: Guilford Press.

Brown, B. B., Bakken, J. P., Ameringer, S. W., & Mahon, S. D. (2008). A comprehensive conceptualization of the peer influence process in adolescence. In M. J. Prinstein & K. Dodge (Eds), *Understanding peer influence in children and adolescents* (pp. 17–44). New York, NY: Guilford Press.

Brown, C. S., & Stone, E. A. (2016). Gender stereotypes and discrimination: How sexism impacts development. *Advances in Child Development and Behavior, 50,* 105–133.

Brown, J. R., & Dunn, J. (1992). Talk with your mother or your sibling? Developmental changes in early family conversations about feelings. *Child Development, 63,* 336–349.

Brumariu, L. E., & Kerns, K. A. (2010). Parent–child attachment and internalizing symptoms in childhood and adolescence: A review of empirical findings and future directions. *Development and Psychopathology, 22,* 177–203.

Brummelman, E., & Thomaes, S. (2017). How children construct views of themselves: A social-developmental perspective. *Child Development, 88,* 1763–1773.

Brummelman, E., Thomaes, S., & Sedikides, C. (2016). Separating narcissism from self-esteem. *Current Directions in Psychological Science, 25,* 8–13.

Brummelman, E., Nelemans, S. A., Thomaes, S., & Orobio de Castro, B. (2017). When parents' praise inflates, children's self-esteem deflates. *Child Development*, *88*, 1799–1809.

Brummelman, E., Thomaes, S., Nelemans, S. A., De Castro, B. O., Overbeek, G., & Bushman, B. J. (2015). Origins of narcissism in children. *Proceedings of the National Academy of Sciences*, *112 (12)*, 3659–3662.

Bruner, J. S., & Kalmar, D. A. (1998). Narrative and meta-narrative in the construction of self. In M. D. Ferrari & R. J. Sternberg (Eds), *Self-awareness: Its nature and development* (pp. 308–331). New York, NY: Guilford Press.

Bryant-Waugh, R., & Watkins, B. (2015). Feeding and eating disorders. In A. Thapar, D. S. Pine, F. S. Leckman, S. Scott, M. J. Snowling & E. Taylor (Eds), *Rutter's child and adolescent psychiatry, Sixth edition* (pp. 1016–1034). Oxford: Wiley.

Buchanan-Barrow, E. (2005). Children's understanding of the school. In M. Barrett & E. Buchanan-Barrow (Eds), *Children's understanding of society* (pp. 17–42). Hove, UK: Psychology Press.

Buhrmester, D., & Furman, W. (1990). Perceptions of sibling relationships during middle childhood and adolescence. *Child Development*, *61*, 1387–1398.

Buhrmester, D., & Prager, K. (1995). Patterns and functions of self disclosure during childhood and adolescence. In K. J. Rotenberg (Ed.), *Disclosure processes in children and adolescents* (pp. 10–56). Cambridge: Cambridge University Press.

Bukowski, W. M., & Adams, R. (2005). Peer relationships and psychopathology: Markers, moderators, mediators, mechanisms, and meanings. *Journal of Clinical Child and Adolescent Psychology*, *34*, 3–10.

Bukowski, W. M., Motzoi, C., & Meyer, F. (2009). Friendship as process, function, and outcome. In K. H. Rubin, W. M. Bukowski & B. Laursen (Eds), *Handbook of peer interactions, relationships, and groups* (pp. 217–231). New York, NY: Guilford Press.

Buller, D. J. (2005). Evolutionary psychology: The emperor's new paradigm. *Trends in Cognitive Science*, *9*, 277–283.

Buller, D. J. (2008). Four fallacies of pop evolutionary psychology. *Scientific American*, *300*, 74–81.

Burghardt, G. M. (2005). *The genesis of animal play: Testing the limits*. Cambridge, MA: MIT Press.

Burriss, K. G., & Tsao. L.-L. (2002). Review of research: How much do we know about the importance of play in child development? *Childhood Education*, *78*, 230–233.

Bushman, B. J., & Anderson, C. A. (2015). Understanding causality in the effects of media violence. *American Behavioral Scientist*, *59*, 1807–1821.

Bushman, B. J., & Baumeister, R. F. (1998). Threatened egotism, narcissism, self-esteem, and direct and displaced aggression: Does self-love or self-hate lead to violence? *Journal of Personality and Social Psychology*, *75*, 219–229.

Buss, D. M. (2009). How can evolutionary psychology successfully explain personality and individual differences? *Perspectives on Psychological Science*, *4*, 359–366.

Bussey, K., & Bandura, A. (1992). Self-regulatory mechanisms governing gender development. *Child Development, 63*, 1236–1250.

Bussey, K., & Bandura, A. (1999). Social cognitive theory of gender development and differentiation. *Psychological Review, 106*, 676–713.

Byrne, J. G., O'Connor, T. G., Marvin, R. S., & Whelan, W. F. (2005). Practitioner review: The contribution of attachment theory to child custody assessments. *Journal of Child Psychology and Psychiatry, 46*, 115–127.

Cairns, R. B., Leung, M. C., Buchanan, L., & Cairns, B. D. (1995). Friendships and social networks in childhood and adolescence: Fluidity, reliability, and interrelations. *Child Development, 66*, 1330–1345.

Cairns, R. B., Cairns, B. D., Neckerman, H. J., Gest, S. D., & Garièpy, J.-L. (1988). Social networks and aggressive behavior: Peer support or peer rejection? *Developmental Psychology, 24*, 815–823.

Calvert, S. L. (2015). Children and digital media. In M. H. Bornstein, T. Leventhal & R. M. Lerner (Eds), *Hand book of child psychology and developmental science, Seventh edition, Volume 4: Ecological settings and processes in developmental systems* (pp. 375–415). Hoboken, NJ: Wiley.

Campos, J. J., Anderson, D. I., Barbu-Roth, M. A., Hubbard, E. M., Hertenstein, M. J., & Witherington, D. (2000). Travel broadens the mind. *Infancy, 1*, 149–219.

Cantor, J., & Wilson, B. J. (2003). Media and violence: Intervention strategies for reducing aggression. *Media Psychology, 5*, 363–403.

Card, N. (2010). Antipathetic relationships in child and adolescent development: A meta-analytic review and recommendations for an emerging area of study. *Developmental Psychology, 46*, 516–529.

Carlson, K. S., & Gjerde, P. F. (2009). Preschool personality antecedents of narcissism in adolescence and young adulthood: A 20-year longitudinal study. *Journal of Research in Personality, 43*, 570–578.

Carr, A. (2016). *The handbook of child and adolescent clinical psychology: A contextual approach*. Hove, UK: Routledge.

Casper, D. M., & Card, N. A. (2010). "We were best friends, but . . .": Two studies of antipathetic relationships emerging from broken friendships. *Journal of Adolescent Research, 25*, 499–526

Celeste, M. (2006). Play behaviors and social interactions of a child who is blind: In theory and practice. *Journal of Visual Impairment and Blindness, 100*, 75–90.

Chandler, F., & Dissanayake, C. (2014). An investigation of the security of caregiver attachment during middle childhood in children with high-functioning autistic disorder. *Autism, 18*, 485–492.

Chang, Y. C., Shire, S. Y., Shih, W., Gelfand, C., & Kasari, C. (2016). Preschool deployment of evidence-based social communication intervention: JASPER in the classroom. *Journal of Autism and Developmental Disorders, 46*, 2211–2223.

Chen, X., French, D., & Schneider. B. H. (2006). Culture and peer relationships. In X. Chen, D. C. French & B. H. Schneider (Eds), *Peer relationships in a cultural context* (pp. 3–20). Cambridge: Cambridge University Press.

Cheong, S. K., Lang, C. P., Hemphill, S. A., & Johnston, L. M. (2016). What constitutes self-concept for children with CP? A Delphi consensus survey. *Journal of Developmental and Physical Disabilities, 28*, 333–346.

Cherney, I. D., & London, K. (2006). Gender-linked differences in the toys, television shows, computer games, and outdoor activities of 5- to 13-year-old children. *Sex Roles, 54*, 717–726

Chib, A., Malik, S., Aricat, R. G., & Kadir, S. Z. (2014). Migrant mothering and mobile phones: Negotiations of transnational identity. *Mobile Media and Communication, 2*, 73–93.

Christakis, D. A., & Zimmerman, F. J. (2007). Violent television viewing during preschool is associated with antisocial behavior during school age. *Pediatrics, 120*, 993–999.

Christakis, D. A., Gilkerson, J., Richards, J. A., Zimmerman, F. J., Garrison, M. M., Xu, D., Gray, S., & Yapanel, U. (2009). Audible television and decreased adult words, infant vocalizations, and conversational turns: A population-based study. *Archives of Pediatrics and Adolescent Medicine, 163*, 554–558.

Christie, J. F., & Johnson, E. P. (1987). Reconceptualizing constructive play: A review of the empirical literature. *Merrill-Palmer Quarterly, 33*, 439–452.

Chung, J. M., Hutteman, R., van Aken, M. A., & Denissen, J. J. (2017). High, low, and in between: Self-esteem development from middle childhood to young adulthood. *Journal of Research in Personality, 70*, 122–133.

Chupetlovska-Anastasova, A. (2014). *Longitudinal exploration of friendship patterns of children and early adolescents with and without Attention-Deficit/Hyperactivity Disorder.* Doctoral dissertation, University of Ottawa.

Cicirelli, V. G. (1996). Sibling relationships in middle and old age. In G.-H. Brody (Ed.), *Sibling relationships: Their causes and consequences* (pp. 47–73). Stamford, CT: Ablex.

Cillessen, A. H. N., & Rose, A. J. (2005). Understanding popularity in the peer system. *Current Directions in Psychological Science, 14*, 102–105.

Cillessen, A. H. N., van IJzendoorn, H. W., van Lieshout, C. F. M., & Hartup, W. W. (1992). Heterogeneity among peer-rejected boys: Subtypes and stabilities. *Child Development, 63*, 893–905.

Clark, S. E., & Symons, D. K. (2000). A longitudinal study of Q-sort attachment security and self-processes at age 5. *Infant and Child Development, 9*, 91–104.

Clarke, A., & Clarke, A. (2000). *Early experience and the life path.* London: Jessica Kingsley.

Clemans, K. H., DeRose, L. M., Graber, J. A., & Brooks-Gunn, J. (2010). Gender in adolescence: Applying a person-in-context approach to gender identity and roles. In J. C. Chrisler & D. R. McCreary (Eds), *Handbook of gender research in psychology* (pp. 527–558). New York, NY: Springer.

Cohen, D., & MacKeith, S. (1990). *The development of imagination*. London: Routledge.

Cohen, P., Kasen, S., Chen, H., Hartmark, C., & Gordon, K. (2003). Variations in patterns of developmental transmissions in the emerging adulthood period. *Developmental Psychology, 39*, 657–669.

Cohen-Bendahan, C. C. C., van de Beek, C., & Berenbaum, S. A. (2005). Prenatal sex hormone effects on child and adult sex-typed behavior: Methods and findings. *Neuroscience and Biobehavioral Reviews, 29*, 353–384.

Coleman, J. C. (1980). Friendship and the peer group in adolescence. In J. Adelson (Ed.), *Handbook of adolescent psychology* (pp. 408–431). New York, NY: Wiley.

Condry, J., & Condry, S. (1976). Sex differences: A study of the eye of the beholder. *Child Development, 47*, 812–819.

Connell, S. L., Lauricella, A. R., & Wartella, E. (2015). Parental co-use of media technology with their young children in the USA. *Journal of Children and Media, 9*, 5–21.

Connolly, J. A., & Doyle, A. B. (1984). Relation of social fantasy play to social competence in preschoolers. *Developmental Psychology, 20*, 797–806.

Cooley, C. H. (1902). *Human nature and the social order*. New York, NY: Charles Schribner's Sons.

Coplan, R. J., Ooi, L. L., & Nocita, G. (2015). When one is company and two is a crowd: Why some children prefer solitude. *Child Development Perspectives, 9*, 133–137.

Coplan, R. J., Ooi, L. L., Rose-Krasnor, L., & Nocita, G. (2014). "I want to play alone": Assessment and correlates of self-reported preference for solitary play in young children. *Infant and Child Development, 23*, 229–238.

Cordua, G. D., McGraw, K. O., & Drabman, R. S. (1979). Doctor or nurse: Children's perception of sextyped occupations. *Child Development, 50*, 590–593.

Côté, J. E. (2014). The dangerous myth of emerging adulthood: An evidence-based critique of a flawed developmental theory. *Applied Developmental Science, 18*, 177–188.

Côté, S. M., Boivin, M., Nagin, D. S., Japel, C., Xu, Q., Zoccolillo, M., Junger, M., & Tremblay, R. A. (2007). The role of maternal education and nonmaternal care services in the prevention of children's physical aggression problems. *Archives of General Psychiatry, 64*, 1305–1312.

Courage, M. L., Edison, S. C., & Howe, M. L. (2004). Variability in the early development of visual self-recognition. *Infant Behavior and Development, 27*, 509–532.

Cramer, P. (2017). Identity change between late adolescence and adulthood. *Personality and Individual Differences, 104*, 538–543.

Crick, N. R., & Dodge, K. A. (1994). A review and reformulation of social information-processing mechanisms in children's social adjustment. *Psychological Bulletin, 115*, 74–101.

Crick, N. R., & Dodge, K. A. (1996). Social information processing mechanisms on reactive and proactive aggression. *Child Development, 67*, 993–1002.

Crockenberg, S. B. (1981). Infant irritability, mother responsiveness, and social support influences on the security of infant mother attachment. *Child Development, 52*, 857–865.

Crockenberg, S. B., & Leerkes, E. (2000). Infant social and emotional development in family context. In C. H. Zeanah (Ed.), *Handbook of infant mental health, Second edition* (pp. 60–90). London: Guilford Press.

Crosnoe, R., & Benner, A. D. (2015). Children at school. In M. Bornstein, T. Leventhal & R. M. Lerner (Eds), *Handbook of child psychology and developmental science, Seventh edition. Volume 4. Ecological settings and processes* (pp. 268–304). London: Wiley.

Crowell, J. A., Fraley, R. C., & Shaver, P. R. (2008). Measurement of individual differences in adolescent and adult attachment. In J. Cassidy & P. R. Shaver (Eds), *Handbook of attachment: Theory, research, and clinical applications, Second edition* (pp. 599–634). New York, NY: Guilford Press.

Cummings, H. M., & Vandewater, E. A. (2007). Relation of adolescent video game play to time spent in other activities. *Archives of Pediatrics & Adolescent Medicine, 161*, 684–689.

Cushman, P. (1991). Ideology obscured. Political uses of the self in Daniel Stern's infant. *American Psychologist, 46*, 206–219.

Cuskelly, M. & Gunn, P. (2003). Sibling relationships of children with Down syndrome: Perspectives of mothers, fathers, and siblings. *American Journal on Mental Retardation, 108*, 234–244.

Cutting, A. L., & Dunn, J. (2006). Conversations with siblings and with friends: Links between relationship quality and social understanding. *British Journal of Developmental Psychology, 24*, 73–87.

Dale, N., & Edwards, L. (2015). Children with specific sensory impairments. In A. Thapar, D. S. Pine, J. F. Leckman, S. Scott, M. J. Snowling & E. Taylor (Eds), *Rutter's child and adolescent psychiatry, Sixth edition* (pp. 612–622). Chichester, UK: Wiley.

Dallas, E., Stevenson, J., & McGurk, H. (1993a). Cerebral palsied children's interactions with siblings: I. Influence of severity of disability, age and birth order. *Journal of Child Psychology and Psychiatry, 34*, 621–647.

Dallas, E., Stevenson, J., & McGurk, H. (1993b). Cerebral palsied children's interactions with siblings: II. Interactional structure. *Journal of Child Psychology and Psychiatry, 34*, 649–671.

Damon, W., & Hart, D. (1988). *Self-understanding in childhood and adolescence.* Cambridge: Cambridge University Press.

Davidson, C., O'Hare, A., Mactaggart, F., Green, J., Young, D., Gillberg, C., & Minnis, H. (2015). Social relationship difficulties in autism and reactive attachment disorder: Improving diagnostic validity through structured assessment. *Research in Developmental Disabilities, 40*, 63–72.

de França, D. X. (2016). From a sense of self to understanding relations between social groups. In J. Vala, S. Waldzus & M. M. Calheiros (Eds), *The social developmental construction of violence and intergroup conflict* (pp. 35–53). Cham, Switzerland: Springer.

De Schipper, J. C., Stolk, J., & Schuengel, C. (2006). Professional caretakers as attachment figures in day care centers for children with intellectual disability and behavior problems. *Research in Developmental Disabilities27*, 203–216.

de Wolff, M. S., & van Ijzendoorn, M. H. (1997). Sensitivity and attachment: A meta-analysis on parental antecedents of infant attachment. *Child Development, 68*, 571–591.

DeLoache, J. S., Chiong, C., Sherman, K., Islam, N., Vanderborght, M., Troseth G. L., Strouse, G. A., & O'Doherty, K. (2010). Do babies learn from baby media? *Psychological Science, 21*, 1570–1574.

Dennis, T. A., Cole, P. M., Zahn-Waxler, C., & Mizuta, I. (2002). Self in context: Autonomy and relatedness in Japanese and U.S. mother–preschooler dyads. *Child Development, 73*, 1803–1817.

Derlega, V. J., & Grzelak, J. (1979). Appropriateness of self-disclosure. In G. J. Chelune (Ed.), *Self-disclosure: Origins, patterns, and implications of openness in interpersonal relationships* (pp. 151–176). San Francisco: Jossey-Bass.

Derluyn, I., & Broekaert, E. (2007). Different perspectives on emotional and behavioural problems in unaccompanied refugee children and adolescents. *Ethnicity and Health, 12*, 141–162.

DeRosier, M., Kupersmidt, J. B., & Patterson, C. J. (1994). Children's academic and behavioral adjustment as a function of the chronicity and proximity of peer rejection. *Child Development, 65*, 1799–1813.

Dew, A., Balandin, S., & Llewellyn, G. (2008). The psychosocial impact on siblings of people with lifelong physical disability: A review of the literature. *Journal of Developmental and Physical Disabilities, 20*, 485–507.

Dishion, T. J., & Piehler, T. F. (2009). Deviant by design: Peer contagion in development, interventions and schools. In K. H. Rubin, W. Bukowski & B. Laursen (Eds), *Handbook of peer interactions, relationships, and groups* (pp. 589–602). New York, NY: Guilford Press.

Dishion, T. J., Andrews, D. W., & Crosby, L. (1995). Antisocial boys and their friends in early adolescence: Relationship characteristics, quality, and interactional process. *Child Development, 66*, 139–151.

Dodge, K. A., Schlundt, D. G., Schocken, I., & Degulach, J. D. (1983). Social competence and children's social status: The role of peer group entry strategies. *Merrill-Palmer Quarterly, 29*, 309–336.

Dolgin, K. G., & Kim, S. (1994). Adolescents' disclosure to best and good friends: The effects of gender and topic intimacy. *Social Development, 3*, 146–157.

Dollard, J., & Miller, N. (1950). *Personality and psychotherapy: An analysis in terms of learning, thinking, and culture.* New York, NY: McGraw-Hill.

Donnellan, M. B., Trzesniewski, K. H., & Robins, R. W. (2011). Self-esteem: Enduring issues and controversies. In T. Chamorro-Premuzic, S. von Stumm &

A. Furnham (Eds), *The Wiley-Blackwell handbook of individual differences* (pp. 718–746). New York, NY: Wiley-Blackwell.

Dozier, M., & Rutter, M. (2008). Challenges to the development of attachment relationships faced by young children in foster and adoptive care. In J. Cassidy & P. R. Shaver (Eds), *Handbook of attachment: Theory, research, and clinical applications, Second edition* (pp. 698–717). New York, NY: Guilford Press.

Drijvers, P., Ball, L., Barzel, B., Heid, M. K., Cao, Y., & Maschietto, M. (Eds) (2016). *Uses of technology in lower secondary mathematics education*. Cham, Switzerland: Springer.

Dubowitz, H., Thompson, R., Proctor, L., Metzger, R., Black, M. M., English, D., Poole, G., & Magder, L. (2016). Adversity, maltreatment, and resilience in young children. *Academic Pediatrics, 16*, 233–239.

Dunn, J. (1988). *The beginnings of social understanding*. Cambridge, MA: Harvard University Press.

Dunn, J. (1993). *Young children's close relationships: Beyond attachment*. Thousand Oaks, CA: Sage.

Dunn, J. (1996). Brothers and sisters in middle childhood and early adolescence: Continuity and change in individual differences. In G. H. Brody (Ed.), *Sibling relationships: Their causes and consequences* (pp. 31–46). Stamford, CO: Ablex.

Dunn, J. (1999). Siblings, friends, and the development of social understanding. In W. A. Collins & B. Laursen (Eds), *Relationships as developmental contexts* (pp. 263–279). Mahwah, NJ: Erlbaum.

Dunn, J. (2004). *Children's friendships: The beginnings of intimacy*. Oxford: Blackwell.

Eden, K., Wylie, K., & Watson, E. (2012). Gender dysphoria: Recognition and assessment. *Advances in Psychiatric Treatment, 18*, 2–11.

Eder, R. A., & Mangelsdorf, S. C. (1997). The emotional basis of early personality development: Implications for the emergent self-concept. In R. Hogan, J. A. Johnson & S. Brigga (Eds), *Handbook of personality psychology* (pp. 209–240). London: Academic Press.

Egeland, B. R., Carlson, E., & Sroufe, L. A. (1993). Resilience as process. *Development and Psychopathology, 5*, 517–528.

Eggins, H. (Ed.) (2017). *The changing role of women in higher education*. Dordrecht, the Netherlands: Springer.

Ehrensaft, D. (2017). Gender nonconforming youth: Current perspectives. *Adolescent Health, Medicine and Therapeutics, 8*, 57–67.

Eisenberg, N., Cumberland, A., Guthrie, I. K., Murphy, B. C., & Shepard, S. A. (2005). Age changes in prosocial responding and moral reasoning in adolescence and early adulthood. *Journal of Research on Adolescence, 15*, 235–260.

Eisenberg, N., Vaughan, J., & Hofer, C. (2009). Temperament, self-regulation, and peer social competence. In K. H. Rubin, W. M. Bukowski & B. Laursen (Eds), *Handbook of peer interactions, relationships, and groups* (pp. 473–489). New York, NY: Guilford Press.

Eisenberg-Berg, N., Murray, E., & Hite, T. (1982). Children's reasoning regarding sex typed toy choices. *Child Development, 53*, 81–86.

Eivers, A. R., Brendgen, M. R., Vitaro, F., & Borge, A. I. H. (2012). Links between children's prosocial and antisocial behaviour and their nominated friends in early childhood. *Early Childhood Research Quarterly, 27*, 137–146.

Elicker, J., Englund, M., & Sroufe, L. A. (1992). Predicting peer competence and peer relationships in childhood from early parent child relationships. In R. D. Parke & G. W. Ladd (Eds), *Family peer relationships: Modes of linkage* (pp. 77–106). Hillsdale, NJ: Erlbaum.

Ellis, S., Rogoff, B., & Cromer, C. C. (1981). Age segregation in children's social interactions. *Developmental Psychology, 17*, 399–407.

Emler, N. (1992). Childhood origins of beliefs about institutional authority. *New Directions for Child Development, 56*, 65–78.

Emler, N., & Dickinson, J. (2005). Children's understanding of social class and occupational groupings. In M. Barrett & E. Buchanan-Barrow (Eds), *Children's understanding of society* (pp. 169–198). Hove, UK: Psychology Press.

Erikson, E. H. (1968). *Identity: Youth and crisis and the life cycle.* London: Norton.

Evans, E. H., Tovée, M. J., Boothroyd, L. G., & Drewett, R. F. (2013). Body dissatisfaction and disordered eating attitudes in 7-to 11-year-old girls: Testing a sociocultural model. *Body Image, 10*, 8–15.

Evans, E. H., Adamson, A. J., Basterfield, L., Le Couteur, A., Reilly, J. K., Reilly, J. J., & Parkinson, K. N. (2017). Risk factors for eating disorder symptoms at 12 years of age: A 6-year longitudinal cohort study. *Appetite, 108*, 12–20.

Ewing Lee, E. A., & Troop-Gordon, W. (2011). Peer socialization of masculinity and femininity: Differential effects of overt and relational forms of peer victimization. *British Journal of Developmental Psychology, 29*, 197–213.

Ex, C. T. G. M., Janssens, J. M. A. M., & Korzilius, H. P. L. M. (2002). Young females' images of motherhood in relation to television viewing. *Journal of Communication, 52*, 955–971.

Eydal, G. B., Gíslason, I. V., Rostgaard, T., Brandth, B., Duvander, A. Z., & Lammi-Taskula, J. (2015). Trends in parental leave in the Nordic countries: Has the forward march of gender equality halted? *Community, Work and Family, 18*, 167–181.

Fagot, B. I. (1985). Beyond the reinforcement principle: Another step toward understanding sex role development. *Developmental Psychology, 21*, 1097–1104.

Fairchild, S. R. (2006). Understanding attachment: Reliability and validity of selected attachment measures for preschoolers and children. *Child and Adolescent Social Work Journal, 23*, 235–261.

Faircloth, B. S., & Hamm, J. V. (2011). The dynamic reality of adolescent peer networks and sense of belonging. *Merrill-Palmer Quarterly, 57*, 48–72.

Farley, A., López, B., & Saunders, G. (2010). Self-conceptualisation in autism: Knowing oneself versus knowing self-through-other. *Autism, 14*, 519–530.

Fauconnier, G., & Turner, M. (2002). *The way we think: Conceptual blending and the mind's hidden complexities.* New York, NY: Basic Books.

Favaro, A., Caregaro, L., Tenconi, E., Bosello, R., & Santonastaso, P. (2009). Time trends in age at onset of anorexia nervosa and bulimia nervosa. *Journal of Clinical Psychiatry, 16)*, 1715–1721.

Fenson, L., & Schell, R. E. (1985). The origins of exploratory play. *Early Child Development and Care, 19*, 3–24.

Ferrari, M. (1998). Being and becoming self-aware. In M. D. Ferrari & R. J. Sternberg (Eds), *Self-awareness: Its nature and development* (pp. 387–422). New York, NY: Guilford Press.

Feshbach, S. (1961). The stimulating versus cathartic effects of vicarious aggressive activity. *Journal of Abnormal and Social Psychology, 63*, 381–385.

Fine, C., & Rush, E. (2018). "Why does all the girls have to buy pink stuff?" The ethics and science of the gendered toy marketing debate. *Journal of Business Ethics, 159*, 769–784.

Fingerman, K. L., & Yahirun, J. J. (2015). Emerging adulthood in the context of family. In J. J. Arnett (Ed.), *The Oxford handbook of emerging adulthood* (pp. 163–176). New York, NY: Oxford University Press.

Fink, E., Begeer, S., Peterson, C. C., Slaughter, V., & Rosnay, M. (2015). Friendlessness and theory of mind: A prospective longitudinal study. *British Journal of Developmental Psychology, 33*, 1–17.

Fivush, R., & Buckner, J. (1997). The self as socially constructed: A commentary. In U. Neisser & D. A. Jopling (Eds), *The conceptual self in context: Culture, experience, self-understanding* (pp. 176–181). Cambridge: Cambridge University Press.

Fivush, R., Habermas, T., Waters, T. E., & Zaman, W. (2011). The making of autobiographical memory: Intersections of culture, narratives and identity. *International Journal of Psychology, 46*, 321–345.

Fletcher, E. N., Whitaker, R. C., Marino, A. J., & Anderson, S. E. (2014). Screen time at home and school among low-income children attending Head Start. *Child Indicators Research, 7*, 421–436.

Fletcher, R., May, C., St George, J., Morgan, P. J., & Lubans, D. R. (2011). Fathers' perceptions of rough-and-tumble play: Implications for early childhood services. *Australasian Journal of Early Childhood, 36*, 131–138.

Fletcher, R., St George, J., & Freeman, E. (2013). Rough and tumble play quality: Theoretical foundations for a new measure of father–child interaction. *Early Child Development and Care, 183*, 746–759.

Fogel, A. (1979). Peer vs. mother directed behavior in 1-to 3-month-old infants. *Infant Behavior and Development, 2*, 215–226.

Fonagy, P., Gergely, G., Jurist, E., & Target. (2002). *Affect regulation, mentalization and the development of the self*. New York, NY: Other Press.

Fonagy, P., Gergely, G., & Target, M. (2007). The parent – infant dyad and the construction of the subjective self. *Journal of Child Psychology and Psychiatry, 48* (3–4), 288–328.

Foster, D., Davies, S., & Steele, H. (2003). The evacuation of British children during World War II: A preliminary investigation into the long-term psychological effects. *Aging and Mental Health, 7*, 398–408.

Fox, N. A., Kimmerly, N. L., & Schafer, W. D. (1991). Attachment to mother/
attachment to father: A meta-analysis. *Child Development, 62,* 210–225.

Fraiberg, S. (1977). *Insights from the blind.* New York, NY: Basic Books.

Fraley, R. C., & Tancredy, C. M. (2012). Twin and sibling attachment in a
nationally representative sample. *Personality and Social Psychology Bulletin, 38,*
308–316.

Frost, J. L. (2012). The changing culture of play. *International Journal of Play, 1,*
117–130.

Funk, J. B., Baldacci, H. B., Pasold, T., & Baumgardner, J. (2004). Violence
exposure in real-life, video games, television, movies, and the internet: Is there
desensitization? *Journal of Adolescence, 27,* 23–39.

Furman, W., & Rose, A. J. (2015). Friendships, romantic relationships, and peer
relationships. In R. M. Lerner, M. E. Lamb & C. G. Coll (Eds), *Handbook of
child psychology and developmental science, Seventh edition, Volume 3: Social and
emotional development* (pp. 1–43). Hoboken, NJ: Wiley.

Furth, H. G. (1980). *The world of grown-ups. Children's conceptions of society.* Amsterdam, NL: Elsevier.

Furth, H. G., & Kane, S. R. (1992). Children constructing society: A new perspective on children at play. In H. McGurk (Ed.), *Childhood social development:
Contemporary perspectives* (pp. 149–173). Hillsdale, NJ: Erlbaum.

Gass, K., Jenkins, J., & Dunn, J. (2007). Are sibling relationships protective?
A longitudinal study. *Journal of Child Psychology and Psychiatry, 48,* 167–175.

Gender Identity Research and Education Society (GIRES) (2006). Atypical gender development—A review. *International Journal of Transgenderism, 9,* 29–44,

Gentile, D. A. (2009). Pathological video-game use among youth ages 8 to 18:
A national study. *Psychological Science, 20,* 594–602.

Gentile, D. A. (2011). The multiple dimensions of video game effects. *Child
Development Perspectives, 5,* 75–81.

Gentile, D. A., & Gentile, J. R. (2008). Violent video games as exemplary teachers: A conceptual analysis. *Journal of Youth and Adolescence, 37,* 127–141.

Gentile, D. A., Mathieson, L. C., & Crick, N. R. (2011b). Media violence associations with the form and function of aggression among elementary school
children. *Social Development, 20,* 213–232.

Gentile, D. A., Anderson, C. A., Yukawa, S., Ihori, N., Saleem, M., Ming, L. K.,
Shibuya, A., Liau, A. K., Bushman, B. J., Rowell Huesmann, L., & Sakamoto, A.
(2009). The effects of prosocial video games on prosocial behaviors: International evidence from correlational, longitudinal, and experimental studies.
Personality and Social Psychology Bulletin, 35, 752–763.

Gentile, D. A., Choo, H., Liau, A., Sim, T., & Li, D. (2011a). Pathological
video game use among youths: A two-year longitudinal study. *Pediatrics, 127,*
e319–e329.

George, C., & Solomon, J. (2008). The caregiving system: A behavioral systems approach to parenting. In J. Cassidy & P. R. Shaver (Eds), *Handbook of*

attachment: Theory, research, and clinical applications, Second edition (pp. 833–856). New York, NY: Guilford Press.

George, T. P., & Hartmann, D. P. (1996). Friendship networks of unpopular, average, and popular children. *Child Development, 67,* 2301–2316.

Gergen, K. J. (2002). The challenge of absent presence. In J. E. Katz & M. Aakhus (Eds), *Perpetual contact: Mobile communication, private talk, public performance* (pp. 227–241). Cambridge: Cambridge University Press.

Gettys, L. D., & Cann, A. (1981). Children's perceptions of occupational sex stereotypes. *Sex Roles, 7,* 301–308.

Ginsberg, K. R., & American Academy of Pediatrics. (2007). Committee on Communications, Committee on Psychological Aspects of Child and Family Health. The importance of play in promoting healthy child development and maintaining strong parent–child bonds. *Pediatrics, 119,* 182–911.

Giumetti, G. W., & Kowalski, R. M. (2016). Cyberbullying matters: Examining the incremental impact of cyber-bullying on outcomes over and above traditional bullying in North America. In R. Navarro, S. Yubero & E. Larranaga (Eds), *Cyberbullying across the globe: Gender, family and mental health* (pp. 117–130). Cham, Switzerland: Springer.

Gjerde, P. F. (2014). An evaluation of ethnicity research in developmental psychology: Critiques and recommendations. *Human Development, 57,* 176–205.

Glenn, N. M., Knight, C. J., Holt, N. L., & Spence, J. C. (2013). Meanings of play among children. *Childhood, 20,* 185–199.

Goldberg, A. E., Kashy, D. A., & Smith, J. Z. (2012). Gender-typed play behavior in early childhood: Adopted children with lesbian, gay, and heterosexual parents. *Sex roles, 67,* 503–515.

Goldsmith, H. H., & Alansky, J. A. (1987). Maternal and infant temperamental predictors of attachment: A meta-analytic review. *Journal of Consulting and Clinical Psychology, 55,* 805–816.

Goldstein, J. H. (1994). Sex differences in toy play and use of video games. In J. H. Goldstein (Ed.), *Toys, play and child development* (pp. 110–129). Cambridge: Cambridge University Press.

Golombok, S., & Fivush, R. (1994). *Gender development.* Cambridge: Cambridge University Press.

Golombok, S., Rust, J., Zervoulis, K., Golding, J., & Hines, M. (2012). Continuity in sex-typed behavior from preschool to adolescence: A longitudinal population study of boys and girls aged 3–13 years. *Archives of Sexual Behavior, 41,* 591–597.

Golombok, S., Rust, J., Zervoulis, K., Croudace, T., Golding, J., & Hines, M. (2008). Developmental trajectories of sex-typed behavior in boys and girls: A longitudinal general population study of children aged 2.5–8 years. *Child Development, 79,* 1583–1593.

Göncü, A., Mistry, J., & Mosier, C. (2000). Cultural variations in the play of toddlers. *International Journal of Behavioral Development, 24,* 321–329.

Goods, K. S., Ishijima, E., Chang, Y. C., & Kasari, C. (2013). Preschool based JASPER intervention in minimally verbal children with autism: Pilot RCT. *Journal of Autism and Developmental Disorders, 43* (5), 1050–1056.

Gosso, Y., Morais, M., & Otta, E. (2007). Pretend play of Brazilian children: A window into different cultural worlds. *Journal of Cross-Cultural Psychology, 38,* 539–558.

Gottman, J., & Mettetal, G. (1986). Speculations about social and affective development: Friendship and acquaintanceship through adolescence. In J. M. Gottman & J. G. Parker (Eds), *Conversations of friends: Speculations on affective development* (pp. 192–240). Cambridge: Cambridge University Press.

Graham, N., Truman, J., & Holgate, H. (2014). An exploratory study: Expanding the concept of play for children with severe cerebral palsy. *British Journal of Occupational Therapy, 77,* 358–365.

Greitemeyer, T., & Mügge, D. O. (2014). Video games do affect social outcomes: A meta-analytic review of the effects of violent and prosocial video game play. *Personality and Social Psychology Bulletin, 40,* 578–589.

Groh, A. M., Narayan, A. J., Bakermans-Kranenburg, M. J., Roisman, G. I., Vaughn, B. E., Fearon, R. M., & van IJzendoorn, M. H. (2017). Attachment and temperament in the early life course: A meta-analytic review. *Child Development, 88,* 770–795.

Guernsey, L. (2017). Who's by their side? Questions of context deepen the research on children and media: Commentary on Chapter 1. In R. Barr & D. Nichols Linebarger (Eds), *Media exposure during infancy and early childhood* (pp. 25–32). Cham, Switzerland: Springer.

Gulbrandsen, L. M. (1998). *I barns dagligliv.* Oslo, NO: Universitetsforlaget.

Gunter, B., & McAleer, J. (1997). *Children and television: The one-eyed monster, Second edition.* London: Routledge.

Guralnick, M. J., Neville, B., Hammond, M. A., & Connor, R. T. (2007). The friendships of young children with developmental delays: A longitudinal analysis. *Journal of Applied Developmental Psychology, 28,* 64–79.

Gurian, M. (2011). *Boys and girls learn differently! A guide for teachers and parents, Second edition.* San Francisco, CA: Jossey-Bass.

Habermas, T., & Köber, C. (2015). Autobiographical reasoning in life narratives buffers the effect of biographical disruptions on the sense of self-continuity. *Memory, 23,* 664–674.

Habermas, T., & Reese, E. (2015). Getting a life takes time: The development of the life story in adolescence, its precursors and consequences. *Human Development, 58,* 172–201.

Hafen, C. A., Laursen, B., Burk, W. J., Kerr, M., & Stattin, H. (2011). Homophily in stable and unstable adolescent friendships: Similarity breeds constancy. *Personality and Individual Differences, 51,* 607–612.

Hafen, C. A., Laursen, B., Nurmi, J. E., & Salmela-Aro, K. (2013). Bullies, victims, and antipathy: The feeling is mutual. *Journal of Abnormal Child Psychology, 41,* 801–809.

Hale, L., & Guan, S. (2015). Screen time and sleep among school-aged children and adolescents: A systematic literature review. *Sleep Medicine Reviews, 21,* 50–58.

Halim, M. L. D., Bryant, D., & Zucker, K. J. (2016). Early gender development in children and links with mental and physical health. In M. R. Korin (Ed.), *Health promotion for children and adolescents* (pp. 191–213). New York, NY: Springer.

Halim, M. L. D., & Ruble, D. (2010). Gender identity and stereotyping in early and middle childhood. In J. C. Chrisler & D. R. McCreary (Eds), *Handbook of gender research in psychology* (pp. 495–525). New York, NY: Springer.

Halim, M. L. D., Ruble, D. N., Tamis-LeMonda, C. S., Shrout, P. E., & Amodio, D. M. (2017). Gender attitudes in early childhood: Behavioral consequences and cognitive antecedents. *Child Development, 88,* 882–899.

Halpern, H. P., & Perry-Jenkins, M. (2016). Parents' gender ideology and gendered behavior as predictors of children's gender-role attitudes: A longitudinal exploration. *Sex roles, 74,* 527–542.

Hames, A. (2008). Siblings' understanding of learning disability: A longitudinal study. *Journal of Applied Research in Intellectual Disabilities, 21,* 491–501.

Hammack, P. L. (2015). Theoretical foundations of identity. In K. C. McLean & M. Syed, (Eds). *The Oxford handbook of identity development* (pp. 11–30). Oxford, UK: Oxford University Press.

Hammack, P. L., & Toolis, E. E. (2015). Putting the social into personal identity: The master narrative as root metaphor for psychological and developmental science. *Human Development, 58,* 350–364.

Hardy, C. L., Bukowski, W. M., & Sippola, L. K. (2002). Stability and change in peer relationships during the transition to middle level school. *Journal of Early Adolescence, 22,* 117–142.

Harkness, S., & Super, C. M. (1985). The cultural context of gender segregation in children's peer groups. *Child Development, 56,* 219–224.

Harlow, H. F. (1959). Love in infant monkeys. *Scientific American, 200,* 68–74.

Harrop, C., Green, J., Hudry, K., & PACT Consortium. (2017). Play complexity and toy engagement in preschoolers with autism spectrum disorder: Do girls and boys differ? *Autism, 21,* 37–50.

Harter, S. (1987). The determinants and mediation role of global self-worth in children. In N. Eisenberg (Ed.), *Contemporary issues in developmental psychology* (pp. 219–242). New York, NY: Wiley.

Harter, S. (2006). The self. In W. Damon, R. M. Lerner & N. Eisenberg (Eds), *Handbook of child psychology, Volume 3: Social, emotional, and personality development* (pp. 505–570). New York, NY: Wiley.

Hartup, W. W. (1992). Friendships and their developmental significance. In H. McGurk (Ed.), *Childhood social development: Contemporary perspectives* (pp. 175–205). Hillsdale, NJ: Erlbaum.

Hartup, W. W. (1999). Peer experience and its developmental significance. M. Bennett (Ed.), *Developmental psychology: Achievements and prospects* (pp. 106–125). London: Psychology Press.

Hartup, W. W., & Stevens, N. (1997). Friendship and adaptation in the life course. *Psychological Bulletin, 121*, 355–370.

Haselager, G. J. T., Hartup, W. W., van Lieshout, C. F. M., & Riksen-Walraven, M. A. (1998). Similarities between friends and nonfriends in middle childhood. *Child Development, 69*, 1198–1208.

Hastings, E. C., Karas, T. L., Winsler, A., Way, E., Madigan, A., & Tyler, S. (2009). Young children's video/computer game use: Relations with school performance and behavior. *Issues in Mental Health Nursing, 30*, 638–649.

Hatano, N., & Takahashi, J. (2005). The development of societal cognition: A commentary. In M. Barrett & E. Buchanan-Barrow (Eds), *Children's understanding of society* (pp. 287–304). Hove, UK: Psychology Press.

Haugh, S. S., Hoffman, C. D., & Cowan, G. (1980). The eye of the very young beholder: Sex typing of infants by young children. *Child Development, 51*, 598–600.

Haughton, C., Aiken, M., & Cheevers, C. (2015). Cyber Babies: The impact of emerging technology on the developing infant. *Psychology Research, 5*, 504–518.

Hay, D. F. (2009). The roots and branches of human altruism. *British Journal of Psychology, 100*, 473–479.

Hazan, C., & Shaver, P. R. (1994). Attachment as an organizational framework for research on close relationships. *Psychological Inquiry, 5*, 1–22.

Hedegaard, M. (2005). Strategies for dealing with conflicts in value positions between home and school: Influences on ethnic minority students' development of motives and identity. *Culture and Psychology, 11*, 187–205.

Helwig, C. C., & Turiel, E. (2002). Civil liberties, autonomy, and democracy: Children's perspectives. *International Journal of Law and Psychiatry, 25*, 253–270.

Hess, E. H. (1972). "Imprinting" in a natural laboratory. *Scientific American, 227*, 24–31.

Hestenes, L. L., & Carroll, D. E. (2000). The play interactions of young children with and without disabilities: Individual and environmental influences. *Early Childhood Research Quarterly, 15*, 229–246.

Hewlett, B. S. (1991). *Intimate fathers*. Ann Arbor, MI: University of Michigan Press.

Hewlett, B. S. (Ed.) (1992). *Father-child relations: Cultural and biosocial contexts*. New York, NY: Aldine de Gruyter.

Hewlett, B. S. (2000). Culture, history, and sex. *Marriage and Family Review, 29*, 59–73,

Hilliard, L. J., & Liben, L. S. (2010). Differing levels of gender salience in preschool classrooms: Effects on children's gender attitudes and intergroup bias. *Child Development, 81*, 1787–1798.

Hinde, R. A. (1992). Human social development: An ethological/relationship perspective. In H. McGurk (Ed.), *Childhood social development: Contemporary perspectives* (pp. 13–29). Hove, UK: Lawrence Erlbaum.

Hinde, R. A. (2005). Ethology and attachment theory. In K. Grossman, E. Waters & K. Grossman (Eds), *Attachment from infancy to adulthood: The major longitudinal studies* (pp. 1–12). New York; NY: Guilford Press.

Hinde, R. A., Titmus, G., Easton, D., & Tamplin, A. (1985). Incidence of "friendship" and behavior toward strong associates versus nonassociates in pre-schoolers. *Child Development, 56,* 234–245.

Hines, M. (2015). Gendered development. In R. M. Lerner, M. E. Lamb & C. G. Coll (Eds), *Handbook of child psychology and developmental science, Seventh edition, Volume 3: Social and emotional development* (pp. 842–887). Hoboken, NJ: Wiley.

Hines, M., Golombok, S., Rust, J., Johnston, K. J., Golding, J., & Parents and Children Study Team. (2002). Testosterone during pregnancy and gender role behavior of preschool children: A longitudinal, population study. *Child Development, 73,* 1678–1687.

Hines, M., Pasterski, V., Spencer, D., Neufeld, S., Patalay, P., Hindmarsh, P. C., Hughes, I. A., & Acerini, C. L. (2016). Prenatal androgen exposure alters girls' responses to information indicating gender-appropriate behaviour. *Philosophical Transactions of the Royal Society B: Biological Sciences, 371 (1688),* 20150125.

Hirsh-Pasek, K., Zosh, J. M., Golinkoff, R. M., Gray, J. H., Robb, M. B., & Kaufman, J. (2015). Putting education in "educational" apps: Lessons from the science of learning. *Psychological Science in the Public Interest, 16,* 3–34.

Houshyar, S., Gold, A., & deVries, M. (2013). Resiliency in maltreated children. In S. Goldstein, & R. B. Brooks (Eds), *Handbook of resilience in children* (pp. 161–179). New York, NY: Springer.

Howe, N., Aquan-Assee, J., & Bukowski, W. M. (1995). Self disclosure and the sibling relationship: What did Romulus tell Remus? In K. J. Rotenberg (Ed.), *Disclosure processes in children and adolescents* (pp. 78–99). Cambridge: Cambridge University Press.

Howe, N., Della Porta, S., Recchia, H., & Ross, H. (2016). "Because if you don't put the top on, it will spill": A longitudinal study of sibling teaching in early childhood. *Developmental Psychology, 52,* 1832.

Howe, N., & Recchia, H. (2014). Sibling relations and their impact on children's development. In M. Boivin (Ed.), *Encyclopedia of early childhood development, December 2014 edition* (pp. 17–24).

Howe, N., Rosciszewska, J., & Persram, R. J. (2018). "I'm an ogre so I'm very hungry!" "I'm assistant ogre": The social function of sibling imitation in early childhood. *Infant and Child Development, 27,* e2040.

Howes, C. (1996). The earliest friendships. In W. M. Bukowski, A. F. Newcomb & W. W. Hartup (Eds), *The company they keep: Friendship in childhood and adolescence* (pp. 66–86). Cambridge: Cambridge University Press.

Howes, C. (2009). Friendship in early childhood. In K. H. Rubin, W. M. Bulowski & B. Laursen (Eds), *The handbook of peer interactions, relationship and group* (pp. 180–194). New York, NY: Guilford Press.

Howes, C., & Matheson, C. C. (1992). Sequences in the development of competent play with peers: Social and social pretend play. *Developmental Psychology*, *28*, 961–974.

Huang, H. Y. (2016). Examining the beneficial effects of individual's self-disclosure on the social network site. *Computers in Human Behavior*, *57*, 122–132.

Huesmann, L. R. (2007). The impact of electronic media violence: Scientific theory and research. *Journal of Adolescent Health*, *41*, S6–S13.

Huesmann, L. R. (2010). Nailing the coffin shut on doubts that violent video games stimulate aggression: Comment on Anderson et al. (2010). *Psychological Bulletin*, *136*, 179–181.

Huesmann, L. R., Moise T. J., Podolski, C. L., & Eron, L. D. (2003). Longitudinal relations between children's exposure to TV violence and their aggressive and violent behavior in young adulthood: 1977–1992. *Developmental Psychology*, *39*, 201–221.

Hunter, S. B., Barber, B. K., Olsen, J. A., McNeely, C. A., & Bose, K. (2011). Adolescents' self-disclosure to parents across cultures: Who discloses and why. *Journal of Adolescent Research*, *26*, 447–478.

Huston, A. C., & Wright, J. C. (1998). Mass media and children's development. In W. Damon, I. E. Siegel & K. A. Renninger (Eds), *Handbook of child psychology, Fifth edition, Volume 4: Child psychology in practice* (pp. 999–1058). New York, NY: Wiley.

Hymel, S., Bowker, A., & Woody, E. (1993). Aggressive versus withdrawn unpopular children: Variations in peer and self-perceptions in multiple domains. *Child Development*, *64*, 879–896.

Hymel, S., Rubin, K. H., Rowden, L., & Le Mare, L. (1990). Children's peer relationships: Longitudinal prediction of internalizing and externalizing problems from middle to late childhood. *Child Development*, *61*, 2004–2021.

Ishikawa, F., & Hay, D. F. (2006). Triadic interaction among newly acquainted 2-year-old. *Social Development*, *15*, 145–168.

Jago, R., Zahra, J., Edwards, M. J., Kesten, J. M., Solomon-Moore, E., Thompson, J. L., & Sebire, S. J. (2016). Managing the screen-viewing behaviours of children aged 5–6 years: A qualitative analysis of parental strategies. *BMJ Open*, *6*, e010355.

Jahoda, G. (1984). The development of thinking about socio-economic systems. In H. Tajfel (Ed.), *The social dimension*, Volume 1 (pp. 69–88). Cambridge: Cambridge University Press.

James, W. (1890). *The principles of psychology*. New York, NY: Holt.

Janssen, C. G. C., Schuengel, C., & Stolk, J. (2002). Understanding challenging behaviour in people with severe and profound intellectual disability: A stress-attachment model. *Journal of Intellectual Disability Research*, *46*, 445–453.

Jarrold, C., Boucher, J., & Smith, P. K. (1996). Generativity deficits in pretend play in autism. *British Journal of Developmental Psychology*, *14*, 275–300.

Jarvis, P., Newman, S., & Swiniarski, L. (2014). On "becoming social": The importance of collaborative free play in childhood. *International Journal of Play*, *3*, 53–68.

Johansson, A., & Götestam, K. G. (2004). Internet addiction: Characteristics of a questionnaire and prevalence in Norwegian youth (12–18 years). *Scandinavian Journal of Psychology, 45*, 223–229.

John, A., Halliburton, A., & Humphrey, J. (2013). Child–mother and child–father play interaction patterns with preschoolers. *Early Child Development and Care, 183*, 483–497.

Johnson, J. E., Ershler, J., & Lawton, J. T. (1982). Intellective correlates of preschoolers' spontaneous play. *The Journal of General Psychology, 106*, 115–122.

Kaare, B. H., Brandtzæg, P. B., Heim, J., & Endestad T. (2007). In the borderland between family orientation and peer culture: The use of communication technologies among Norwegian tweens. *New Media Society, 9*, 603–624.

Kagan, J. (1982). The construct of difficult temperament: A reply to Thomas, Chess, and Korn. *Merrill-Palmer Quarterly, 28*, 21–24.

Kagan, J. (1991). The theoretical utility of constructs of self. *Developmental Review, 11*, 244–250.

Kagan, J. (1998a). *Three seductive ideas*. Cambridge, MA: Harvard University Press.

Kagan, J. (1998b). Is there a self in infancy? In M. D. Ferrari & R. J. Sternberg (Eds), *Self-awareness: Its nature and development* (pp. 137–147). New York, NY: Guilford Press.

Kagan, J., Kearsley, R. B., & Zelazo, P. R. (1978). *Infancy: Its place in human development*. Cambridge, MA: Harvard University Press.

Kanz, K. M. (2016). Mediated and moderated effects of violent media consumption on youth violence. *European Journal of Criminology, 13*, 149–168.

Karpov, Y. V. (2005). *The neo-Vygotskian approach to child development*. Cambridge: Cambridge University Press.

Karu, M., & Tremblay, D. G. (2017). Fathers on parental leave: An analysis of rights and take-up in 29 countries. *Community, Work and Family, 21*, 344–362.

Kasari, C., Chang, Y. C., & Patterson, S. (2013). Pretending to play or playing to pretend: The case of autism. *American Journal of Play, 6*, 124–135.

Kay, C., & Green, J. (2013). Reactive attachment disorder following early maltreatment: Systematic evidence beyond the institution. *Journal of Abnormal Child Psychology, 41*, 571–581.

Kazemeini, T., & Pajoheshgar, M. (2013). Children's play in the context of culture: Parental ethnotheories. *Journal of Science and Today's World, 2*, 265–281.

Keijsers, L., Branje, S. J., VanderValk, I. E., & Meeus, W. (2010). Reciprocal effects between parental solicitation, parental control, adolescent disclosure, and adolescent delinquency. *Journal of Research on Adolescence, 20*, 88–113.

Keller, H., Kaertner, J., Yovsi, R., Borke, J., & Kleis, A. (2005). Parenting styles and the development of the categorical self: A longitudinal study on mirror self-recognition in Cameroonian Nso and German families. *International Journal of Behavioral Development, 29*, 496–504.

Keller, H., Yovsi, R., Borke, J., Kärtner, J., Jensen, H., & Papaligoura, Z. (2004). Developmental consequences of early parenting experiences: Self-recognition and self-regulation in three cultural communities. *Child Development, 75,* 1745–1760.

Kelly, J. B., & Lamb, M. E. (2000). Using child development research to make appropriate custody and access decisions for young children. *Family Court Review, 38,* 297–311.

Kennair, L. E. O., Nordeide, J., Andreassen, S., Strønen, J., & Pallesen, S. (2011). Sex differences in jealousy: A study from Norway. *Nordic Psychology, 63,* 20–34.

Kerns, K. A., Aspelmeier, J. E., Gentzler, A. L., & Grabill, C. M. (2001). Parent–child attachment and monitoring in middle childhood. *Journal of Family Psychology, 15,* 69–81.

Kerns, K. A., & Brumariu, L. E. (2014). Is insecure parent–child attachment a risk factor for the development of anxiety in childhood or adolescence? *Child Development Perspectives, 8,* 12–17.

Kerns, K. A., & Brumariu, L. E. (2016). Attachment in middle childhood. In J. Cassidy & P. R. Shaver (Eds), *Handbook of attachment: Theory, research and clinical applications, Third edition* (pp. 349–365). New York, NY: Guilford Press.

Kerr, L., & Cossar, J. (2014). Attachment interventions with foster and adoptive parents: A systematic review. *Child Abuse Review, 23,* 426–439.

Kildare, C. A., & Middlemiss, W. (2017). Impact of parents' mobile device use on parent-child interaction: A literature review. *Computers in Human Behavior, 75,* 579–593.

Killen, M., Rutland, A., & Jampol, N. S. (2009) Social exclusion in childhood and adolescence. In K. H. Rubin, W. M. Bulowski & B. Laursen (Eds), *The handbook of peer interactions, relationship and group* (pp. 249–266). New York, NY: Guilford Press.

Killen, M., Rutland, A., & Yip, T. (2016). Equity and justice in developmental science: Discrimination, social exclusion, and intergroup attitudes. *Child Development, 87,* 1317–1336.

Kim, J.-Y., McHale, S. M., Wayne Osgood, D., & Crouter, A. C. (2006). Longitudinal course and family correlates of sibling relationships from childhood through adolescence. *Child Development, 77,* 1746–1761.

Kirkorian, H. L., Wartella, E. A., & Anderson, D. R. (2008). Media and young children's learning. *The Future of Children, 18,* 39–61.

Klein, D. N., Bufferd, S. J., Dyson, M. W., & Danzig, A. P. (2014). Personality pathology. In M. Lewis & K. D. Rudolph (Eds), *Handbook of developmental psychopathology* (pp. 703–719). Boston, MA: Springer.

Klump, K. L. (2014). Developmental trajectories of disordered eating: Genetic and biological risk during puberty. In M. Lewis & K. D. Rudolph (Eds), *Handbook of developmental psychopathology, Third edition* (pp. 621–629). New York, NY: Springer.

Kobak, R., & Madsen, S. (2008). Disruptions in attachment bonds: Implications for theory, research, and clinical intervention. In J. Cassidy & P. R. Shaver

(Eds), *Handbook of attachment: Theory, research, and clinical applications, Second edition* (pp. 23–47). New York, NY: Guilford Press.

Kochanska, G., & Kim, S. (2013). Early attachment organization with both parents and future behavior problems: From infancy to middle childhood. *Child Development, 84*, 283–296.

Koh, J. B. K., & Wang, Q. (2012). Self-development. *Wiley Interdisciplinary Reviews: Cognitive Science, 3*, 513–524.

Kohlberg, L. (1966). Moral education in schools: A developmental review. *School Review, 74*, 1–30.

Koolstra, C. M., & Van Der Voort, T. H. (1996). Longitudinal effects of television on children's leisure-time reading: A test of three explanatory models. *Human Communication Research, 23*, 4–35.

Kowert, R., Vogelgesang, J., Festl, R., & Quandt, T. (2015). Psychosocial causes and consequences of online video game play. *Computers in Human Behavior, 45*, 51–58.

Krahé, B. (2016). Violent media effects on aggression: A commentary from a cross-cultural perspective. *Analyses of Social Issues and Public Policy, 16*, 439–442.

Krahé, B., Möller, I., Huesmann, R., Kirwil, L., Felber, J., & Berger, A. (2011). Desensitization to media violence: Links with habitual media violence exposure, aggressive cognitions, and aggressive behaviors. *Journal of Personality and Social Psychology, 100*, 630–646.

Kramer, L. (2014). Learning emotional understanding and emotion regulation through sibling interaction. *Early Education and Development, 25*, 160–184.

Kroger, J. (2004). *Identity in adolescence: The balance between self and other, Third edition.* London: Routledge.

Kucirkova, N., & Littleton, K. (2016) *The digital reading habits of children: A National survey of parents' perceptions of and practices in relation to children's reading for pleasure with print and digital books.* Book Trust. Available from: www. booktrust.org.uk/news-and-blogs/news/1371.

Kuebli, J., & Fivush, R. (1992). Gender differences in parent–child conversations about past emotions. *Sex Roles, 27*, 683–698.

Kupersmidt, J. B., Burchinal, M., & Patterson, C. J. (1995). Developmental patterns of childhood peer relations as predictors of externalizing behavior problems. *Development and Psychopathology, 7*, 825–843.

Kupersmidt, J. B., & Coie, J. D. (1990). Preadolescent peer status, aggression, and social adjustment as predictors of self-reported behavior problems in preadolescence. *Child Development, 61*, 1350–1362.

Lackaye, T., Margalit, M., Ziv, O., & Ziman, T. (2006). Comparisons of self-efficacy, mood, effort, and hope between students with learning disabilities and their non-LD-matched peers. *Learning Disabilities Research and Practice, 21*, 111–121.

Ladd, G. W. (1990). Having friends, keeping friends, making friends and being liked by peers in the classroom: Predictors of children's early school adjustment? *Child Development, 61*, 1081–1090.

Ladd, G. W., & Hart, C. H. (1992). Creating informal play opportunities: Are parents' and preschoolers' initiations related to the children's competence with peers? *Developmental Psychology, 28,* 1179–1187.

Lakoff, G., & Johnson, M. H. (1980). *Metaphors we live by.* Chicago, IL: Chicago University Press.

Lam, C. B., & McHale, S. M. (2015). Time use as cause and consequence of youth development. *Child Development Perspectives, 9,* 20–25.

Lam, Y. G., & Yeung, S. S. S. (2012). Cognitive deficits and symbolic play in preschoolers with autism. *Research in Autism Spectrum Disorders, 6,* 560–564.

Lamb, M. E., Easterbrooks, M. A., & Holden, G. W. (1980). Reinforcement and punishment among preschoolers: Characteristics, effects, and correlates. *Child Development,* 1230–1236.

Largo, R. H., & Howard, J. A. (1979a). Developmental progression in play behavior of children between nine and thirty months, I: Spontaneous play and language development. *Developmental Medicine and Child Neurology, 21,* 492–503.

Largo, R. H., & Howard, J. A. (1979b). Developmental progression in play behavior of children between nine and thirty months: II. Spontaneous play and imitations. *Developmental Medicine and Child Neurology, 21,* 299–310.

Larson, R. W. (1990). The solitary side of life: An examination of the time people spend alone from childhood to old age. *Developmental Review, 10,* 155–183.

Larson, R. W., & Verma, S. (1999). How children and adolescents spend time across the world: Work, play, and developmental opportunities. *Psychological Bulletin, 125,* 701–736.

Lauricella, A. R., Blackwell, C. K., & Wartella, E. (2017). The "new" technology environment: The role of content and context on learning and development from mobile media. In R. Barr & D. Nichols Linebarger (Eds), *Media exposure during infancy and early childhood* (pp. 1–23). Cham, Switzerland: Springer.

Lauricella, A. R., Cingel, D. P., Blackwell, C., Wartella, E., & Conway, A. (2014). The mobile generation: Youth and adolescent ownership and use of new media. *Communication Research Reports, 31,* 357–364.

Laursen, B., & Pursell, G. (2009). Conflict in peer relationships. In K. H. Rubin, W. M. Bulowski & B. Laursen (Eds), *The handbook of peer interactions, relationship and group* (pp. 267–286). New York, NY: Guilford Press.

Lawler, J. M., Hostinar, C. E., Mliner, S. B., & Gunnar, M. R. (2014). Disinhibited social engagement in postinstitutionalized children: Differentiating normal from atypical behavior. *Development and Psychopathology, 26,* 451–464.

Layton, T., Chuang, M. C., & Hao, G. (2014). Play behaviors in Chinese toddlers with Down syndrome. *Journal of Psychological Abnormalities in Children, 3,* 131.

Leahy, R. L. (1983). The development of the conception of social class. In R. L. Leahy (Ed.), *The child's construction of social inequality* (pp. 79–107). London: Academic Press.

Lecce, S., Pagnin, A., & Pinto, G. (2009). Agreement in children's evaluations of their relationships with siblings and friends. *European Journal of Developmental Psychology*, *6*, 153–169.

Lenhart, A., Purcell, K., Smith, A., & Zickuhr, K. (2010). *Social media and mobile Internet use among teens and young adults*. Washington, DC: Pew Internet and American Life Project.

Letourneau, N., Tryphonopoulos, P., Giesbrecht, G., Dennis, C. L., Bhogal, S., & Watson, B. (2015). Narrative and meta-analytic review of interventions aiming to improve maternal–child attachment security. *Infant Mental Health Journal*, *36*, 366–387.

Levert-Levitt, E., & Sagi-Schwartz, A. (2015). Integrated attachment theory. In J. D. Wright (Ed.), *International encyclopedia of the social and behavioral sciences, Second edition*, Volume *12* (pp. 228–234). Amsterdam, NL: Elsevier.

Levine, L. E. (1983). Mine: Self definitions in two-year-old boys. *Developmental Psychology*, *19*, 544–549.

Lewin, K. (1935). *A dynamic theory of personality*. New York, NY: McGraw-Hill.

Lewis, M. (1991). Ways of knowing: Objective self-awareness or consciousness. *Developmental Review*, *11*, 231–243.

Lewis, M. (1997). The development of a self. Comments on the paper of Neisser. *Annals New York Academy of Sciences*, *818*, 279–283.

Lewis, M. (2011). Problems in the study of infant emotional development. *Emotion Review*, *3*, 131–137.

Lewis, M., & Brooks-Gunn, J. (1979). *Social cognition and the acquisition of self*. New York, NY: Plenum Press.

Lewis, M., Young, G., Brooks, J., & Michalson, L. (1975). The beginning of friendship. In M. Lewis & L. Rosenblum (Eds), *Friendship and peer relations* (pp. 27–66). New York, NY: Wiley.

Lewis, V., Norgate, S., Collis, G., & Reynolds, R. (2000). The consequences of visual impairment for children's symbolic and functional play. *British Journal of Developmental Psychology*, *18*, 449–464.

Liben, L. S. (2014). The individual ↔ context nexus in developmental intergroup theory: Within and beyond the ivory tower. *Research in Human Development*, *11*, 273–290.

Liben, L. S., & Bigler, R. S. (2008). Developmental gender differentiation: Pathways in conforming and nonconforming outcomes. *Journal of Gay and Lesbian Mental Health*, *12*, 95–119.

Lickliter, R., & Honeycutt, H. (2003). Developmental dynamics: Towards a biologically plausible evolutionary psychology. *Psychological Bulletin*, *129*, 819–835.

Lifter, K., Foster-Sanda, S., Arzamarski, C., Briesch, J., & McClure, E. (2011). Overview of play: Its uses and importance in early intervention/early childhood special education. *Infants and Young Children*, *24*, 225–245.

Lillard, A. S. (2001). Pretend play as Twin Earth. *Developmental Review*, *21*, 1–33.

Lillard, A. S. (2015). The development of play. In L. S. Liben & U. Mueller (Eds), *Handbook of child psychology and developmental science, Seventh edition, Volume 2: Cognitive processes* (pp. 425–468). New York, NY: Wiley.

Lillard, A. S., Lerner, M. D., Hopkins, E. J., Dore, R. A., Smith, E. D., & Palmquist, C. M. (2013). The impact of pretend play on children's development: A review of the evidence. *Psychological Bulletin, 139*, 1–34.

Linebarger, D. L., & Walker, D. (2005). Infants' and toddlers' television viewing and language outcomes. *American Behavioral Scientist, 48*, 624–645.

Ling, R., & Haddon, L. (2008). Children, youth and the mobile phone. In K. Dortner & L. Livingstone (Eds), *International handbook of children, media and culture* (pp. 137–151). London: Sage.

Liu, D., & Brown, B. B. (2014). Self-disclosure on social networking sites, positive feedback, and social capital among Chinese college students. *Computers in Human Behavior, 38*, 213–219.

LoBue, V., & DeLoache, J. S. (2011). Pretty in pink: The early development of gender-stereotyped colour preferences. *British Journal of Developmental Psychology, 29*, 656–667.

Locke, J., Shih, W., Kretzmann, M., & Kasari, C. (2016). Examining playground engagement between elementary school children with and without autism spectrum disorder. *Autism, 20*, 653–662.

Lorenz, K. (1935). Der Kumpan in der Umvelt des Vogels. *Journal für Ornithologie, 83*, 137–213 & 289–413.

Lowell, A., Renk, K., & Adgate, A. H. (2014). The role of attachment in the relationship between child maltreatment and later emotional and behavioral functioning. *Child Abuse and Neglect, 38*, 1436–1449.

Lu, L. (2008). The individual-oriented and social-oriented Chinese bicultural self: Testing the theory. *The Journal of Social Psychology, 148*, 347–374.

Luckey, A. J., & Fabes, R. A. (2005). Understanding nonsocial play in early childhood. *Early Childhood Education Journal, 33*, 67–72.

Ma, L., & Lillard, A. S. (2006). Where is the real cheese? Young children's ability to discriminate between real and pretend acts. *Child Development, 77*, 1762–1777.

Maccoby, E. E. (1990). Gender and relations: A developmental account. *American Psychologist, 45*, 513–520.

Maccoby, E. E. (1998). *The two sexes: Growing up apart, coming together.* Cambridge, MA: Harvard University Press.

Maccoby, E. E. (2000). Perspectives on gender development. *International Journal of Behavioral Development, 24*, 398–406.

Maccoby, E. E. (2002). Gender and group process: A developmental perspective. *Current Directions in Psychological Science, 11*, 54–58.

Maccoby, E. E., & Jacklin, C. N. (1987). Gender segregation in childhood. *Advances in Child Development and Behavior, 20*, 239–288.

Maciel, J. A., & Knudson-Martin, C. (2014). Don't end up in the fields: Identity construction among Mexican adolescent immigrants, their parents, and socio-contextual processes. *Journal of Marital and Family Therapy, 40*, 484–497.

Madigan, S., Atkinson, L., Laurin, K., & Benoit, D. (2013). Attachment and internalizing behavior in early childhood: A meta-analysis. *Developmental Psychology, 49*, 672–689.

Mahler, M. S., Pine, F., & Bergman, A. (1975). *The psychological birth of the human infant symbiosis and individuation*. New York, NY: Basic Books.

Main, M., & Weston, D. R. (1981). The quality of the toddler's relationship to mother and father: Relation to conflict behavior and readiness to establish new relationships. *Child Development, 52*, 932–940.

Mangelsdorf, S., Gunnar, M., Kestenbaum, M., Lang, S., & Andreas, D. (1990). Infant proneness-to-distress temperament, maternal personality, and mother–infant attachment: Associations and goodness of fit. *Child Development, 61*, 820–831.

Markus, H. R., & Kitayama, S. (2010). Cultures and selves: A cycle of mutual constitution. *Perspectives on Psychological Science, 5*, 420–430.

Markus, H. R., Mullally, P. R., & Kitayama, S. (1997). Selfways: Diversity in modes of cultural participation. In U. Neisser & D. A. Jopling (Eds), *The conceptual self in context: Culture, experience, self-understanding* (pp. 13–61). Cambridge: Cambridge University Press.

Marsh, H. W., & O'Mara, A. (2008). Reciprocal effects between academic self-concept, self-esteem, achievement, and attainment over seven adolescent years: Unidimensional and multidimensional perspectives of self-concept. *Personality and Social Psychology Bulletin, 34*, 542–552.

Martin, C. L., & Fabes, R. A. (2001). The stability and consequences of young children's same-sex peer interactions. *Developmental Psychology, 37*, 431–446.

Martin, C. L., Fabes, R. A., & Hanish, L. D. (2014). Gendered-peer relationships in educational contexts. *Advances in Child Development and Behavior, 47*, 151–187.

Martin, C. L., & Ruble, D. N. (2009). Patterns of gender development. *Annual Review of Psychology, 61*, 353–381.

Martin, C. L., Ruble, D. N., & Szkrybalo, J. (2002). Cognitive theories of early gender development. *Psychological Bulletin, 128*, 903–933.

Martins, N., & Jensen, R. E. (2014). The relationship between "teen mom" reality programming and teenagers' beliefs about teen parenthood. *Mass Communication and Society, 17*, 830–852.

Martinsen, H., & Nærland, T. (2009). *Sosial utvikling i førskolealder. Vennskap, konflikter & kommunikasjon i barnehagen*. Oslo, NO: Gyldendal Akademisk.

Martinsen, H., Nærland, T., & Vereijken, B. (2010). Observation-based descriptions of social status in the pre-school. *Early Child Development and Care, 180*, 1231–1241.

Marvin, R. S., & Britner, P. (2008). Normative development: The ontogeny of attachment. In J. Cassidy & P. R. Shaver (Eds), *Handbook of attachment: Theory, research, and clinical applications, Second edition* (pp. 269–294). New York, NY: Guilford Press.

Marvin, R. S., Britner, P., & Russell, B. S. (2016). Normative development: The ontogeny of attachment in childhood. In J. Cassidy & P. R. Shaver (Eds), *Handbook of attachment: Theory, research, and clinical applications* (pp. 273–290). New York, NY: Guilford Press.

Masten, A. S. (2016). Resilience in developing systems: The promise of integrated approaches. *European Journal of Developmental Psychology, 13,* 297–312

Masur, E. F., Flynn, V., & Olson, J. (2015). The presence of background television during young children's play in American homes. *Journal of Children and Media, 9,* 349–367.

Mathur, R., & Berndt, T. J. (2006). Relations of friends' activities to friendship quality. *Journal of Early Adolescence, 26,* 365–388.

Mayseless, O. (2005). Ontogeny of attachment in middle childhood: Conceptualization of normative changes. In K. A. Kerns & R. A. Richardson (Eds), *Attachment in middle childhood* (pp. 1–23). New York, NY: Guilford Press.

McAdams, D. P. (2013). The psychological self as actor, agent, and author. *Perspectives on Psychological Science, 8,* 272–295.

McAdams, D. P., & Cox, K. S. (2010). Self and identity across the life span. In R. Lerner, A. Freund & M. Lamb (Eds), *Handbook of life span development,* Volume 2 (pp. 158–207). New York, NY: Wiley.

McChesney, G., & Toseeb, U. (2018). Happiness, self–esteem, and prosociality in children with and without autism spectrum disorder: Evidence from a UK population cohort study. *Autism Research, 11,* 1011–1023.

McDaniel, B. T., & Radesky, J. S. (2018). Technoference: Parent distraction with technology and associations with child behavior problems. *Child Development, 89,* 100–109.

McDonald, K. L., Dashiell-Aje, E., Menzer, M. M., Rubin, K. H., Oh, W., & Bowker, J. C. (2013). Contributions of racial and sociobehavioral homophily to friendship stability and quality among same-race and cross-race friends. *The Journal of Early Adolescence, 33,* 897–919.

McGuire, S., Manke, B., Eftekhari, A., & Dunn, J. (2000). Children's perceptions of sibling conflict during middle childhood: Issues and sibling (dis)similarity. *Social Development, 9,* 173–190.

McGuire, S., McHale, S. M., & Updegraff, K. (1996). Children's perception of the sibling relationship in middle childhood: Connections within and between family relationships. *Personal Relationships, 3,* 229–239.

McGuire, S., & Shanahan, L. (2010). Sibling experiences in diverse family contexts. *Child Development Perspectives, 4,* 72–79.

McHale, S. M., Updegraff, K. A., & Whiteman, S. D. (2012). Sibling relationships and influences in childhood and adolescence. *Journal of Marriage and Family, 74,* 913–930.

McHale, S. M., Shanahan, L., Updegraff, K. A., Crouter, A. C., & Booth, A. (2004). Developmental and individual differences in girls' sex-typed activities in middle childhood and adolescence. *Child Development, 75*, 1575–1593.

McLean, K. C., & Syed, M. (2015). Personal, master, and alternative narratives: An integrative framework for understanding identity development in context. *Human Development, 58*, 318–349.

McLean, K. C., Syed, M., & Shucard, H. (2016). Bringing identity content to the fore: Links to identity development processes. *Emerging Adulthood, 4*, 356–364.

Meehan, C. L., Hagen, E. H., & Hewlett, B. S. (2017). Persistence in infant care patterns among Aka foragers. In V. Reyes-García & A. A. Pyhälä (Eds), *Hunter-gatherers in a changing world* (pp. 213–232). Cham, Switzerland: Springer.

Meeus, W. (2011). The study of adolescent identity formation 2000–2010: A review of longitudinal research. *Journal of Research on Adolescence, 21*, 75–94.

Meltzer, A., & Kramer, J. (2016). Siblinghood through disability studies perspectives: Diversifying discourse and knowledge about siblings with and without disabilities. *Disability and Society, 31*, 17–32.

Mertala,. P., Karikoski, H., Tähtinen, L., & Sarenius, V.-M. (2016). The value of toys: 6–8-year-old children's toy preferences and the functional analysis of popular toys. *International Journal of Play, 5*, 11–27.

Messias, E., Castro, J., Saini, A., Usman, M., & Peeples, D. (2011). Sadness, suicide, and their association with video game and Internet overuse among teens: Results from the Youth Risk Behavior Survey 2007 and 2009. *Suicide and Life-Threatening Behavior, 41*, 307–315.

Meyer-Bahlburg, H. F. L. (2005). Gender identity outcome in female-raised 46XY persons with penile agenesis, cloacal exstrophy of the bladder, or penile ablation. *Archives of Sexual Behavior, 34*, 423–438.

Meyer-Bahlburg, H. F. L., Dolezal, C., Baker, S. W., Ehrhardt, A. A., & New, M. I. (2006). Gender development in women with congenital adrenal hyperplasia as a function of disorder severity. *Archives of Sexual Behavior, 35*, 667–684.

Mikulincer, M., & Shaver, P. R. (2008). Adult attachment and affect regulation. In J. Cassidy & P. R. Shaver (Eds), *Handbook of attachment: Theory, research, and clinical applications, Second edition* (pp. 503–531). New York, NY: Guilford Press.

Miller, C. F., Lurye, L. E., Zosuls, K. M., & Ruble, D. N. (2009). Accessibility of gender stereotype domains: Developmental and gender differences in children. *Sex roles, 60*, 870–881.

Mistry, R. S., Brown, C. S., White, E. S., Chow, K. A., & Gillen-O'Neel, C. (2015). Elementary school children's reasoning about social class: A mixed-methods study. *Child Development, 86*, 1653–1671.

Mitchison, D., & Mond, J. (2015). Epidemiology of eating disorders, eating disordered behaviour, and body image disturbance in males: A narrative review. *Journal of Eating Disorders, 3*, 20.

Miyahara, M., & Piek, J. (2006). Self-esteem of children and adolescents with physical disabilities: Quantitative evidence from meta-analysis. *Journal of Developmental and Physical Disabilities, 18*, 219–234.

Moksnes, U. K., Bradley Eilertsen, M. E., & Lazarewicz, M. (2016). The association between stress, self-esteem and depressive symptoms in adolescents. *Scandinavian Journal of Psychology, 57*, 22–29.

Money, J. (1975). Ablatio penis: Normal male infant sex-reassigned as a girl. *Archives of Sexual Behavior, 4*, 65–71.

Money, J., & Ehrhardt, A. A. (1972). *Man and woman, boy and girl: Differentiation and dimorphism of gender identity from conception to maturity*. Oxford: Johns Hopkins University Press.

Montessori, M. (1910). *The advanced method*. Harlow, UK: Longmans.

Moore, C., & Lemmon, K. (Eds). (2001). *The self in time*. London: Lawrence Erlbaum.

Morelli, G., Rogoff, B., & Angelillo, C. (2003). Cultural variation in young children's access to work or involvement in specialised child-focused activities. *International Journal of Behavioral Development, 27*, 264–274.

Morrison, T. L., Goodlin-Jones, B. L., & Urquiza, A. J. (1997). Attachment and the representation of intimate relationships in adulthood. *Journal of Psychology, 131*, 57–71.

Moser, F., & Hannover, B. (2014). How gender fair are German schoolbooks in the twenty-first century? An analysis of language and illustrations in schoolbooks for mathematics and German. *European Journal of Psychology of Education, 29*, 387–407.

Mumford, S. (2012). Play therapy. In W. M. Klykylo & J. Kay (Eds), *Clinical child psychiatry, Third edition* (pp. 120–129). Oxford: Wiley.

Munroe, R. L., & Romney, A. K. (2006). Gender and age differences in same-sex aggregation and social behavior: A four-culture study. *Journal of Cross-Cultural Psychology, 37*, 3–19.

Nader-Grosbois, N. (2014). Self-perception, self-regulation and metacognition in adolescents with intellectual disability. *Research in Developmental Disabilities, 35*, 1334–1348.

Nathanson, A. I., & Rasmussen, E. E. (2011). TV viewing compared to book reading and toy playing reduces responsive maternal communication with toddlers and preschoolers. *Human Communication Research, 37*, 465–487.

Navarro, R., Yubero, S., & Larrañaga, E. (Eds) (2016). *Cyberbullying across the globe: Gender, family, and mental health*. Cham, Switzerland: Springer.

Negele, A., & Habermas, T. (2010). Self-continuity across developmental change in and of repeated life narratives. In K. C. McLean & M. Pasupathi (Eds), *Narrative development in adolescence: Creating the storied self* (pp. 1–22). New York, NY: Springer.

Neisser, U. (1997). Concepts and self-concepts. In U. Neisser & D. A. Jopling (Eds), *The conceptual self in context* (pp. 3–12). Cambridge: Cambridge University Press.

Nelson, K. (2007a). *Young minds in social worlds: Experience, meaning and memory*. Cambridge, MA: Harvard University Press.

Nelson, K. (2007b). Development of extended memory. *Journal of Physiology, 101*, 223–229.

Nelson, K. (2015). Making sense with private speech. *Cognitive Development, 36,* 171–179.

Nelson, K., & Fivush, R. (2004). The emergence of auto-biographical memory: A social cultural developmental theory. *Psychological Review, 11,* 486–511.

Nelson, L. J., & Barry, C. M. (2005). Distinguishing features of emerging adulthood: The role of self-classification as an adult. *Journal of Adolescent Research, 20,* 242–262.

Newcomb, A. F., & Bagwell, C. L. (1996). The developmental significance of children's friendship relations. In W. M. Bukowski, A. F. Newcomb & W. W. Hartup (Eds), *The company they keep: Friendship in childhood and adolescence* (pp. 289–321). Cambridge: Cambridge University Press.

Newman, B. M., Lohman, B. J., & Newman, P. R. (2007). Peer group membership and a sense of belonging: Their relationship to adolescent behavior problems. *Adolescence, 42,* 241–263.

Newman, L. K., & Steel, Z. (2008). The child asylum seeker: Psychological and developmental impact of immigration detention. *Child and Adolescent Psychiatric Clinics, 17,* 665–683.

Nicolopoulou, A. (1993). Play, cognitive development, and the social world: Piaget, Vygotsky, and beyond. *Human Development, 36,* 1–23.

Nielsen, M., Simcock, G., & Jenkins, L. (2008). The effect of social engagement on 24-month-olds' imitation from live and televised models. *Developmental Science, 11,* 722–731.

Nievar, M. A., & Becker, B. J. (2008). Sensitivity as a privileged predictor of attachment: A second perspective on de Wolff and van IJzendoorn's meta-analysis. *Social Development, 17,* 102–114.

Noller, P. (2005). Sibling relationships in adolescence: Learn ing and growing together. *Personal Relationships, 12,* 1–22.

Nordenström, A., Servin, A., Bohlin, G., Larsson, A., & Wedell, A. (2002). Sex-typed toy play behavior correlates with the degree of prenatal androgen exposure assessed by CYP21 genotype in girls with congenital adrenal hyperplasia. *The Journal of Clinical Endocrinology and Metabolism, 87,* 5119–5124.

Novak, G., & Peláez, M. (2004). *Child and adolescent development: A behavioral systems approach.* London: Sage.

O'Brien, M., & Huston, A. C. (1985). Development of sex-typed play behavior in toddlers. *Developmental Psychology, 21,* 866–871.

O'Brien, M., & Wall, K. (Eds) (2017). *Comparative perspectives on work-life balance and gender equality: Fathers on leave alone.* Cham, Switzerland: Springer.

O'Byrne, C., & Muldoon, O. (2017). Stigma, self-perception and social comparisons in young people with an intellectual disability. *Irish Educational Studies, 36,* 307–322.

O'Connell, B., & Bretherton, I. (1984). Toddlers' play alone and with mother: The role of maternal guidance. In I. Bretherton (Ed.), *Symbolic play: The development of social understanding* (pp. 337–368). London: Academic Press.

O'Connor, K. J., & Braverman, L. M. (Eds) (1997). *Play therapy theory and practice: A comparative presentation.* New York, UK: Wiley.

O'Connor, M., Sanson, A., Hawkins, M. T., Letcher, P., Toumbourou, J. W., Smart, D., Vassallo, S., & Olsson, C. A. (2011). Predictors of positive development in emerging adulthood. *Journal of Youth and Adolescence, 40*, 860–874.

O'Keeffe, G. S. (2016). Social media: Challenges and concerns for families. *Pediatric Clinics, 63*, 841–849.

Olds, T., Ridley, K., & Dollman, J. (2006). Screenieboppers and extreme screenies: The place of screen time in the time budgets of 10–13 year-old Australian children. *Australian and New Zealand Journal of Public Health, 30*, 137–142.

Ontai, L. L., & Thompson, R. A. (2008). Attachment, parent–child discourse and theory-of-mind development. *Social Development, 17*, 47–60.

Orue, I., Bushman, B. J., Calvete, E., Thomaes, S., de Castro, B. O., & Hutteman, R. (2011). "Monkey see, Monkey do, Monkey hurt": Longitudinal effects of exposure to violence on children's aggressive behavior. *Social Psychological and Personality Science, 2*, 432–437.

Østvik, J., Ytterhus, B., & Balandin, S. (2017). "So, how does one define a friendship? ": Identifying friendship among students using AAC in inclusive education settings. *European Journal of Special Needs Education, 33*, 334–348.

Otto, H., Potinius, I., & Keller, H. (2014). Cultural differences in stranger–child interactions: A comparison between German middle-class and Cameroonian Nso stranger–infant dyads. *Journal of Cross-Cultural Psychology, 45*, 322–334.

Owen, A. M., Hampshire, A., Grahn, J. A., Stenton, R., Dajani, S., Burns, A. S., Howard, R. J., & Ballard, C. G. (2010). Putting brain training to the test. *Nature, 465 (7299)*, 775–779.

Padilla-Walker, L. M., Coyne, S. M., & Collier, K. M. (2016). Longitudinal relations between parental media monitoring and adolescent aggression, prosocial behavior, and externalizing problems. *Journal of Adolescence, 46*, 86–97.

Palagi, E., Burghardt, G. M., Smuts, B., Cordoni, G., Dall'Olio, S., Fouts, H. N., Řeháková-Petrů, M., Siviy, S. M., & Pellis, S. M. (2016). Rough-and-tumble play as a window on animal communication. *Biological Reviews, 91*, 311–327.

Papacek, A. M., Chai, Z., & Green, K. B. (2016). Play and social interaction strategies for young children with autism spectrum disorder in inclusive preschool settings. *Young Exceptional Children, 19*, 3–17.

Parker, J. G., & Asher, S. R. (1993). Friendship and friendship quality in middle childhood: Links with peer group acceptance and feelings of loneliness and social dissatisfaction. *Developmental Psychology, 29*, 611–621.

Parten, M. B. (1932). Social participation among preschool children. *Journal of Abnormal and Social Psychology, 27*, 243–269.

Pasupathi, M., McLean, K. C., & Weeks, T. (2009). To tell or not to tell: Disclosure and the narrative self. *Journal of Personality, 77*, 89–124.

Patchin, J. W., & Hinduja, S. (2010). Cyberbullying and self-esteem. *Journal of School Health, 80*, 614–621.

Pauletti, R. E., Menon, M., Menon, M., Tobin, D. D., & Perry, D. G. (2012). Narcissism and adjustment in preadolescence. *Child Development, 83 (3)*, 831–837.

Pedersen, S., Vitaro, F., Barker, E. D., & Borge, A. I. H. (2007). The timing of middle-childhood peer rejection and friendship: Linking early behaviour to early-adolescent adjustment. *Child Development, 78*, 1037–1051.

Pellegrini, A. D. (2011). The development and function of locomotor play. In A. Pellegrini (Ed.), *The Oxford hand-book of the development of play* (pp. 172–184). New York, NY: Oxford University Press.

Pellegrini, A. D. (2013). Play. In P. D. Zelazo (Ed.), *Oxford handbook of developmental psychology, Volume 2: Self and other* (pp. 276–298). New York, NY: Oxford University Press.

Pellegrini, A. D., & Smith, P. K. (1998). Physical activity play: The nature and function of a neglected aspect of play. *Child Development, 69*, 577–598.

Pellegrini, A. D., Dupuis, D., & Smith, P. K. (2007). Play in evolution and development. *Developmental Review, 27*, 261–276.

Pempek, T. A., Kirkorian, H. L., & Anderson, D. R. (2014). The effects of background television on the quantity and quality of child-directed speech by parents. *Journal of Children and Media, 8*, 211–222.

Perry, E., & Flood, A. (2016). Autism spectrum disorder and attachment: A clinician's perspective. In H. K. Fletcher, A. Flood & D. J. Hare (Eds), *Attachment in intellectual and developmental disability: A clinician's guide to practice and research* (pp. 79–103). Oxford: Wiley.

Petalas, M. A., Hastings, R. P., Nash, S., & Duff, S. (2015). Typicality and subtle difference in sibling relationships: Experiences of adolescents with autism. *Journal of Child and Family Studies, 24*, 38–49.

Petrina, N., Carter, M., & Stephenson, J. (2014). The nature of friendship in children with autism spectrum disorders: A systematic review. *Research in Autism Spectrum Disorders, 8*, 111–126.

Pfeifer, L. I., Pacciulio, A. M., Santos, C. A. D., Santos, J. L. D., & Stagnitti, K. E. (2011). Pretend play of children with cerebral palsy. *Physical and Occupational Therapy in Pediatrics, 31*, 390–402.

Phinney, J. S. (1990). Ethnic identity in adolescents and adults: Review of research. *Child Development, 65*, 499–514.

Phinney, J. S. (1993). A three-stage model of ethnic identity development in adolescence. In M. E. Bernal & G. P. Knights (Eds), *Ethnic identity: Formation and transmission among Hispanics and other minorities* (pp. 61–79). Albany, NY: State University of New York Press.

Piaget, J. (1951). *Play, dreams and imitation in childhood*. London: Heineman.

Pike, A., Coldwell, J., & Dunn, J. F. (2005). Sibling relationships in early/middle childhood: Links with individual adjustment. *Journal of Family Psychology, 19*, 523–532.

Pine, F. (2004). Mahler's concepts of "symbiosis" and separation-individuation: Revisited, reevaluated, refined. *Journal of the American Psychoanalytic Association, 52*, 511–533.

Plotnik, J., de Waal, F. B. M., & Reiss, D. (2006). Self-recognition in an Asian elephant. *Proceedings of the National Academy of Sciences of the United States of America, 103*, 17053–17057.

Plotnik, J. M., de Waal, F. B. M., Moore, D., & Reiss, D. (2010). Self-recognition in the Asian elephant and future directions for cognitive research with elephants in zoological settings. *Zoo Biology, 29,* 179–191.

Pope, A. W. (2003). Developmental risk associated with mutual dislike in elementary school children. *New Directions for Child and Adolescent Development, 102,* 89–110.

Potter, W. J. (1999). *On media violence.* London: Sage.

Poulin, F., & Chan, A. (2010). Friendship stability and change in childhood and adolescence. *Developmental Review, 30,* 257–272.

Povinelli, D. J., Landau, K. R., & Perilloux, H. K. (1996). Self-recognition in young children using delayed versus live feedback: Evidence for a developmental asynchrony. *Child Development, 67,* 1540–1554.

Powers, K. L., Brooks, P. J., Aldrich, N. J., Palladino, M. A., & Alfieri, L. (2013). Effects of video-game play on information processing: A meta-analytic investigation. *Psychonomic Bulletin and Review, 20,* 1055–1079.

Preisler, G. M. (1993). A descriptive study of blind children in nurseries with sighted children. *Child Care, Health and Development, 19,* 295–315.

Price, J. M. (1996). Friendships of maltreated children and adolescents: Contexts for expressing and modifying relationship history. In W. M. Bukowski, A. F. Newcomb & W. W. Hartup (Eds), *The company they keep: Friendship in childhood and adolescence* (pp. 262–285). Cambridge: Cambridge University Press.

Prinstein, M. J., & Dodge, K. A. (2008). *Understanding friendship in children and adolescents* New York, NY: Guilford Press.

Prot, S., Gentile, D. A., Anderson, C. A., Suzuki, K., Swing, E., Lim, K. M., Horiuchi, Y., Jelic, M., Krahé, B., Liuqing, W., et al. (2014). Long-term relations among prosocial-media use, empathy, and prosocial behavior. *Psychological Science, 25,* 358–368.

Quinn, T., & Gordon, C. (2011). The effects of cerebral palsy on early attachment: Perceptions of rural South African mothers. *Journal of Human Ecology, 36,* 191–197.

Raby, K. L., Cicchetti, D., Carlson, E. A., Egeland, B., & Andrew Collins, W. (2013). Genetic contributions to continuity and change in attachment security: A prospective, longitudinal investigation from infancy to young adulthood. *Journal of Child Psychology and Psychiatry, 54,* 1223–1230.

Raby, K. L., Steele, R. D., Carlson, E. A., & Sroufe, L. A. (2015). Continuities and changes in infant attachment patterns across two generations. *Attachment and Human Development, 17,* 414–428.

Raby, K. L., Yarger, H. A., Lind, T., Fraley, R. C., Leerkes, E., & Dozier, M. (2017). Attachment states of mind among internationally adoptive and foster parents. *Development and Psychopathology, 29,* 365–378.

Rambaran, J. A., Dijkstra, J. K., Munniksma, A., & Cillessen, A. H. (2015). The development of adolescents' friendships and antipathies: A longitudinal multivariate network test of balance theory. *Social Networks, 43,* 162–176.

Rankin, J. L., Lane, D. J., Gibbons, F. X., & Gerrard, M. (2004). Adolescent self-consciousness: Longitudinal age changes and gender differences in two cohorts. *Journal of Research on Adolescence*, *14*, 1–21.

Rasmussen, M., Meilstrup, C. R., Bendtsen, P., Pedersen, T. P., Nielsen, L., Madsen, K. R., & Holstein, B. E. (2015). Perceived problems with computer gaming and Internet use are associated with poorer social relations in adolescence. *International Journal of Public Health*, *60*, 179–188.

Redick, T. S., & Webster, S. B. (2014). Videogame interventions and spatial ability interactions. *Frontiers in Human Neuroscience*, *8*, 183.

Reed, G. M., Drescher, J., Krueger, R. B., Atalla, E., Cochran, S. D., First, M. B., Arango-de Montis, I., Parish, S. J., Cottler, S., Briken, P., & Saxena, S. (2016). Disorders related to sexuality and gender identity in the ICD-11: Revising the ICD-10 classification based on current scientific evidence, best clinical practices, and human rights considerations. *World Psychiatry*, *15*, 205–221.

Ribak, R. (2009). Remote control, umbilical cord and beyond: The mobile phone as a transitional object. *British Journal of Developmental Psychology*, *27*, 183–196.

Rice, M. L., Huston, A. C., Truglio, R., & Wright, J. C. (1990). Words from "Sesame Street": Learning vocabulary while viewing. *Developmental Psychology*, *26*, 421–428.

Rideout, V. (2012). *Social media, social life: How teens view their digital lives*. San Francisco, CA: Common Sense Media.

Rideout, V. (2013). *Zero to eight: Children's media use in America*. San Francisco, CA: Common Sense Media.

Rideout, V. (2014). *Learning at home: Families' educational media use in America*. New York, NY: Joan Ganz Cooney Center.

Rideout V. (2015). *The Common Sense Census: Media use by tweens and teens*. San Francisco, CA: Common Sense Media.

Rideout, V. (2016). Measuring time spent with media: The Common Sense census of media use by US 8-to 18-year-olds. *Journal of Children and Media*, *10*, 138–144.

Rideout, V., Foehr, U. G., & Roberts, D. F. (2010). *Generation M: Media in the lives of 8-to 18-year-olds*. Menlo Park, CA: Henry J. Kaiser Family Foundation.

Ristori, J., & Steensma, T. D. (2016). Gender dysphoria in childhood. *International Review of Psychiatry*, *28*, 13–20,

Rivas-Drake, D., Syed, M., Umaña-Taylor, A., Markstrom, C., French, S., Schwartz, S. J., & Lee, R. (2014). Feeling good, happy, and proud: A meta-analysis of positive ethnic–racial affect and adjustment. *Child Development*, *85*, 77–102.

Roberts, B. W., Walton, K. E., & Viechtbauer, W. (2006). Patterns of mean-level change in personality traits across the life course: A meta-analysis of longitudinal studies. *Psychological Bulletin*, *132*, 1–25.

Robertson, J., & Bowlby, J. (1952). Responses of young children to separation from their mothers. *Courrier Centre Internationale Enfance, 2*, 131–142.

Rochat, P. (2013). Self-conceptualizing in development. In P. D. Zelazo (Ed.), *Oxford handbook of developmental psychology, Volume 2: Self and other* (pp. 378–397). New York, NY: Oxford University Press.

Rodkin, P. C., Farmer, T. W., Pearl, R., & Acker, R. V. (2006). They're cool: Social status and peer group supports for aggressive boys and girls. *Social Development, 15*, 175–204.

Rodkin, P. C., Pearl, R., Farmer, T. W., & van Acker, R. (2003). Enemies in the gendered societies of middle childhood: Prevalence, stability, association with social status and aggression. *New Directions for Child and Adolescent Development, 102*, 73–88.

Rogoff, B. (2003). *The cultural nature of human development*. London: Oxford University Press.

Rohde, P., Stice, E., & Marti, C. N. (2015). Development and predictive effects of eating disorder risk factors during adolescence: Implications for prevention efforts. *International Journal of Eating Disorders, 48*, 187–198.

Rossetti, Z., & Keenan, J. (2018). The nature of friendship between students with and without severe disabilities. *Remedial and Special Education, 39*, 195–210.

Rotenberg, K. J. (1995). Moral development and children's differential disclosure to adults versus peers. In K. J. Rotenberg (Ed.), *Disclosure processes in children and adolescents* (pp. 135–147). Cambridge: Cambridge University Press.

Rubin, K. H., Bukowski, W., & Bowker, J. C. (2015). Children in peer groups. In R. M. Lerner, M. H. Bornstein & T. Leventhal (Eds), *Handbook of child psychology and developmental science, Volume 4: Ecological settings and processes* (pp. 175–222). New York, NY: Wiley.

Rubin, K. H., Bukowski, W., & Parker, J. G. (2006). Peer interactions, relationships and groups. In W. Damon & N. Eisenberg (Eds), *Handbook of child psychology, Sixth edition, Volume 3: Social, emotional, and personality development* (pp. 619–700). New York, NY: Wiley.

Rubin, K. H., Bowker, J. C., McDonald, K. L., & Menzer, M. (2013). Peer relationships in childhood. In P. D. Zelazo (Ed.), *The Oxford handbook of developmental psychology*, Volume 2 (pp. 242–275). New York, NY: Oxford University Press.

Rubin, K. H., Burgess, K. B., & Hastings, P. D. (2002). Stability and social-behavioral consequences of toddlers' inhibited temperament and parenting. *Child Development, 73*, 483–495.

Rubin, K. H., & Coplan, R. J. (Eds) (2010). *The development of shyness and social withdrawal*. New York, NY: Guilford Press.

Rubin, K. H., Lynch, D., Coplan, R. J., Rose-Kasnor, L., & Booth, C. L. (1994). "Birds of a feather . . .": Behavioral concordances and preferential personal attraction in children. *Child Development, 65*, 1778–1785.

Rubin, K. H., Stewart, S. L., & Coplan, R. J. (1995). Social withdrawal in childhood. Conceptual and empirical perspectives. *Advances in Clinical Child Psychology, 17*, 157–196.

Ruble, D. N. (1987). The acquisition of self-knowledge: A self-socialization perspective. In N. Eisenberg (Ed.), *Contemporary issues in developmental psychology* (pp. 243–270). New York, NY: Wiley.

Ruble, D. N., Martin, C. L., & Berenbaum, B. A. (2006). Gender development. In W. Damon, R. M. Lerner & N. Eisenberg (Eds), *Handbook of child psychology, Sixth edition, Volume 3: Social, emotional, and personality development* (pp. 858–932). New York, NY: Wiley.

Ruble, D. N., Taylor, L. J., Cyphers, L., Greulich, F. K., Lurye, L. E., & Shrout, P. E. (2007). The role of gender constancy in early gender development. *Child Development, 78,* 1121–1136.

Rudi, J., Dworkin, J., Walker, S., & Doty, J. (2015). Parents' use of information and communications technologies for family communication: Differences by age of children. *Information, Communication and Society, 18,* 78–93.

Rutgers, A. H., Bakermans-Kranenburg, M. J., van IJzendoorn, M. H., & Berckelaer-Onnes, I. A. (2004). Autism and attachment: A meta-analytic review. *Journal of Child Psychology and Psychiatry, 45,* 1123–1134.

Rutgers, A. H., van IJzendoorn, M. H., Bakermans-Kranenburg, M. J., Swinkels, S. H. N., van Daalen, E., Dietz, C., Naber, F. B. A., Buitelaar, J. K., & van Engeland, H. (2007). Autism, attachment and parenting: A comparison of children with autism spectrum disorder, mental retardation, language disorder, and non-clinical children. *Journal of Abnormal Child Psychology, 35,* 859–870.

Rutter, M. (2008). Institutional effects on children: Design issues and substantive findings. *Monographs of the Society for Research in Child Development, 73,* 271–278.

Rutter, M., Kreppner, J., & Sonuga-Barke, E. (2009). Emanuel Miller Lecture: Attachment insecurity, disinhibited attachment, and attachment disorders: Where do research findings leave the concepts? *Journal of Child Psychology and Psychiatry, 50,* 529–543.

Sagi-Schwartz, A., & Aviezer, O. (2005). Correlates of attachment to multiple caregiver in kibbutz children from birth to emerging adulthood: The Haifa longitudinal study. In K. E. Grossmann, K. Grossmann & E. Watters (Eds), *Attachment from infancy to adulthood: The major longitudinal studies* (pp. 165–197). New York, NY: Guilford Press.

Saunders, J. F., & Frazier, L. D. (2017). Body dissatisfaction in early adolescence: The coactive roles of cognitive and sociocultural factors. *Journal of Youth and Adolescence, 46,* 1246–1261.

Schaan, V. K., & Melzer, A. (2015). Parental mediation of children's television and video game use in Germany: Active and embedded in family processes. *Journal of Children and Media, 9,* 58–76.

Schaffer, H. R. (1996). *Social development.* Oxford: Blackwell.

Schaffer, H. R., & Emerson, P. E. (1964). The development of social attachment in infancy. *Monographs of the Society for Research in Child Development, 29,* 1–77.

Schneider, B. H. (2016). *Childhood friendships and peer relations: Friends and enemies, Second edition.* Abingdon, UK: Routledge.

Schneider, B. H., & Tessier, N. G. (2007). Close friendship as understood by socially withdrawn, anxious early adolescents. *Child Psychiatry and Human Development, 38*, 339–351.

Schulenberg, J. E., Sameroff, A. J., & Cicchetti, D. (2004). The transition to adulthood as a critical juncture in the course of psychopathology and mental health. *Development and Psychopathology, 16*, 799–806.

Schwartz, S. J. (2001). The evolution of Eriksonian and Neo-Eriksonian identity theory and research: A review and integration. *Identity, 1*, 7–58.

Seibert, A. C., & Kerns, K. A. (2009). Attachment figures in middle childhood. *International Journal of Behavioral Development, 33*, 347–355.

Seiffge-Krenke, I. (2015). Leaving home: Antecedents, consequences, and cultural patterns. In J. J. Arnett (Ed.), *The Oxford handbook of emerging adulthood* (pp. 177–189). New York, NY: Oxford University Press.

Seiffge-Krenke, I., & Haid, M. L. (2012). Identity development in German emerging adults: Not an easy task. *New Directions for Child and Adolescent Development, 138*, 35–59.

Selby, J. M., & Bradley, B. S. (2003). Infants in groups: A paradigm for the study of early social experience. *Human Development, 46*, 197–231.

Seligman, M., & Darling, R. B. (2007). *Ordinary families, special children: A systems approach to childhood disability, Third edition*. London: Guilford Press.

Seligman, M. E. P. (1975). *Helplessness: On depression, development, and death*. San Francisco, CA: Freeman.

Serbin, L. A., Moller, L. C., Gulko, J., Powlishta, K. K., & Colburne, K. A. (1994). The emergence of gender segregation in toddler playgroups. *New Directions for Child and Adolescent Development, 65*, 7–17.

Servin, A., Nordenström, A., Larsson, A., & Bohlin, G. (2003). Prenatal androgens and gender-typed behavior: A study of girls with mild and severe forms of congenital adrenal hyperplasia. *Developmental Psychology, 39*, 440–450.

Shapiro, L. A. S., & Margolin, G. (2014). Growing up wired: Social networking sites and adolescent psychosocial development. *Clinical Child and Family Psychology Review, 17*, 1–18.

Sheridan, M. D., Howard, J., & Alderson, D. (2011). *Play in early childhood: From birth to six*. Abingdon, UK: Routledge.

Sherman, L. J., Rice, K., & Cassidy, J. (2015). Infant capacities related to building internal working models of attachment figures: A theoretical and empirical review. *Developmental Review, 37*, 109–141.

Shifrin, D., Brown, A., Hill, D., Jana, L., & Flinn, S. K. (2015). *Growing up digital: Media research symposium*. Itasca, IL: American Academy of Pediatrics.

Shmukler, D. (1981). Mother–child interaction and its relationship to the predisposition to imaginative play. *Genetic Psychology Monographs, 104*, 215–235.

Shutts, K., Roben, C. K. P., & Spelke, E. S. (2013). Children's use of social categories in thinking about people and social relationships. *Journal of Cognition and Development, 14*, 35–62.

Sigelman, C. K. (2012). Rich man, poor man: Developmental differences in attributions and perceptions. *Journal of Experimental Child Psychology, 113*, 415–429.

Silverman, D. (2004). Early developmental issues reconsidered: Commentary on Pine's ideas on symbiosis. *Journal of the American Psychoanalytic Association, 53*, 239–251.

Simonelli, A., De Palo, F., Moretti, M., Baratter, P. M., & Porreca, A. (2014). The strange situation procedure: The role of the attachment patterns in the Italian culture. *American Journal of Applied Psychology, 3*, 47–56.

Singer, D. G., Golinkoff, R. M., & Hirsh-Pasek, K. (Eds) (2006). *Play=Learning: How play motivates and enhances children's cognitive and social-emotional growth*. New York, NY: Oxford University Press.

Singer, E. (2013). Play and playfulness, basic features of early childhood education. *European Early Childhood Education Research Journal, 21*, 172–184.

Skär, L., & Tamm, M. (2002). Disability and social network. A comparison between children and adolescents with and without restricted mobility. *Scandinavian Journal of Disability Research, 4*, 118–137.

Slade, A. (1987). A longitudinal study of maternal involvement and symbolic play during the toddler period. *Child Development, 58*, 367–375.

Smetana, J. G., Campione-Barr, N., & Metzger, A. (2006). Adolescent development in interpersonal and societal contexts. *Annual Review of Psychology, 57*, 255–284.

Smetana J. G., Villalobos M., Tasopoulos-Chan M., Gettman, D. C., & Campione-Barr, N. (2009). Early and middle adolescents' disclosure to parents about activities in different domains. *Journal of Adolescence, 32*, 693–713.

Smink, F. R., Van Hoeken, D., & Hoek, H. W. (2012). Epidemiology of eating disorders: Incidence, prevalence and mortality rates. *Current Psychiatry Reports, 14*, 406–414.

Smith, E. D., & Lillard, A. S. (2012). Play on: Retrospective reports of the persistence of pretend play into middle childhood. *Journal of Cognition and Development, 13*, 524–549.

Smith, P. K., & Simon, T. (1984). Object play, problem solving and creativity in children. In P. K. Smith (Ed.), *Play in animals and humans* (pp. 199–216). Oxford: Blackwell.

Smith, S. L., & Wilson, B. J. (2002). Children's comprehension of and fear reactions to television news. *Media Psychology, 4*, 1–26.

Smith, T. (Ed.) (2010). *Statement of good practice, Fourth edition*. Copenhagen, DK: Save the Children.

Smyke, A. T., Zeanah, C. H., Fox, N. A., Nelson, C. A., & Guthrie, D. (2010). Placement in foster care enhances quality of attachment among young institutionalized children. *Child Development, 81*, 212–223.

Snyder, T. D., de Brey, C., & Dillow, S. A. (2016). *Digest of Education Statistics 2015, 51st Edition*. Washington, DC: National Center for Education Statistics.

Soares, I., Belsky, J., Mesquita, A. R., Osório, A., & Sampaio, A. (2013). Why do only some institutionalized children become indiscriminately friendly?

Insights from the study of Williams Syndrome. *Child Development Perspectives, 7*, 187–192.

Solomon, J., & George, C. (2016). The measurement of attachment security and related constructs in infancy and early childhood. In J. Cassidy & P. R. Shaver (Eds), *Handbook of attachment, Third edition* (pp. 366–398). New York, NY: Guilford Press.

Spence, I., & Feng, J. (2010). Video games and spatial cognition. *Review of General Psychology, 14*, 92–104.

Sroufe, L. A., Egeland, B., & Carlson, E. (1999). One social world: The integrated development of parent–child and peer relationships. In W. A. Collins & B. Laursen (Eds), *Development during the transition to adolescence* (pp. 241–261). Hove, UK: Lawrence Erlbaum.

Sroufe, L. A., Egeland, B., Carlson, E., & Collins, W. A. (2005). *The development of the person: The Minnesota study of risk and adaptation from birth to adulthood*. New York, NY: Guilford Press.

Stadelmann, S., Grunewald, M., Gibbels, C., Jaeger, S., Matuschek, T., Weis, S., Klein, A. M., Hiemisch, A., von Klitzing, K., & Döhnert, M. (2017). Self-esteem of 8–14- year-old children with psychiatric disorders: Disorder- and gender-specific effects. *Child Psychiatry and Human Development, 48*, 40–52.

Steensma, T. D., Biemond, R., de Boer, F., & Cohen-Kettenis, P. T. (2011). Desisting and persisting gender dysphoria after childhood: A qualitative follow-up study. *Clinical Child Psychology and Psychiatry, 16*, 499–516.

Steensma, T. D., McGuire, J. K., Kreukels, B. P., Beekman, A. J., & Cohen-Kettenis, P. T. (2013). Factors associated with desistence and persistence of childhood gender dysphoria: A quantitative follow-up study. *Journal of the American Academy of Child and Adolescent Psychiatry, 52*, 582–590.

Stern, D. N. (1998). *The interpersonal world of the infant: A view from psychoanalysis and developmental psychology*. New York, NY: Karnac Books.

Stern, M., & Karraker, K. H. (1989). Sex stereotyping of infants: A review of gender labeling studies. *Sex Roles, 20*, 501–522.

Sterrett, K., Shire, S., & Kasari, C. (2017). Peer relationships among children with ASD: Interventions targeting social acceptance, friendships, and peer networks. *International Review of Research in Developmental Disabilities, 52*, 37–74.

Stevenson, H. W., & Lee, S. Y. (1990). Contents of achievement: A study of American, Chinese and Japanese children. *Monographs of the Society for Research in Child Development, 55*, 3–4.

Stevenson-Hinde, J. (2005). The interplay between attachment, temperament, and maternal style: A Madinglet perspective. In K. E. Grossmann, K. Grossmann & E. Waters (Eds), *Attachment from infancy to adulthood* (pp. 198–222). New York, NY: Guilford Press.

Stewart, R. B. (1983). Sibling attachment relationships: Child–infant interaction in the strange situation. *Developmental Psychology, 19*, 192–199.

Stocker, C., & Dunn, J. (1990). Sibling relationships in childhood: Links with friendship and peer relationships. *British Journal of Developmental Psychology, 8*, 227–244.

Strandell, H. (2014). Mobile phones in children's after-school centres: Stretching of place and control. *Mobilities*, *9*, 256–274.

Stromquist, N. P. (2007). The gender socialization process in schools: A cross-national comparison. Paper commissioned for the EFA Global Monitoring Report 2008, Education for All by 2015: Will we make it?

Su, R., Rounds, J., & Armstrong, P. I. (2009). Men and things, women and people: A meta-analysis of sex differences in interests. *Psychological Bulletin*, *135*, 859–884.

Suddendorf, T., & Collier-Baker, E. (2009). The evolution of primate visual self-recognition: Evidence of absence in lesser apes. *Proceedings of the Royal Society B: Biological Sciences*, *276*, 1671–1677.

Sun, C. R. (2017). An examination of the four-part theory of the Chinese self: The differentiation and relative importance of the different types of social-oriented self. *Frontiers in Psychology*, *8*, 1106.

Suomi, S. J. (2008). Attachment in rhesus monkeys. In J. Cassidy & P. R. Shaver (Eds), *Handbook of attachment, Second edition* (pp. 173–191). New York, NY: Guilford Press.

Sutton-Smith, B. (1986). *Toys as culture*. New York, NY: Gardner Press.

Sutton-Smith, B. (1994). Does play prepare the future? In J. H. Goldstein (Ed.), *Toys, play and child development* (pp. 131–146). Cambridge: Cambridge University Press.

Takahashi, K. (1990). Are the key assumptions of the "Strange Situation" procedure universal? A view from Japanese research. *Human Development*, *33*, 23–30.

Taumoepeau, M., & Reese, E. (2014). Understanding the self through siblings: Self-awareness mediates the sibling effect on social understanding. *Social Development*, *23*, 1–18.

Taylor, M., Carlson, S. M., Maring, B. L., Gerow, L., & Charley, C. M. (2004). The characteristics and correlates of fantasy in school-age children: Imaginary companions, impersonation, and social understanding. *Developmental Psychology*, *40*, 1173–1187.

Teti, D. M., Sakin, J. W., Kucera, E., Corns, K. M., & Eiden, R. D. (1996). And baby makes four: Predictors of attachment security among preschool age firstborns during the transition to siblinghood. *Child Development*, *67*, 579–596.

Theule, J., Germain, S. M., Cheung, K., Hurl, K. E., & Markel, C. (2016). Conduct disorder/oppositional defiant disorder and attachment: A meta-analysis. *Journal of Developmental and Life-Course Criminology*, *2*, 232–255.

Thomaes, S., Stegge, H., Bushman, B. J., Olthof, T., & Denissen, J. (2008). Development and validation of the Childhood Narcissism Scale. *Journal of Personality Assessment*, *90*, 382–391.

Thompson, R. A. (1998). Early sociopersonality development. In W. Damon & N. Eisenberg (Eds), *Handbook of child psychology, Fifth edition, Volume 3. Social, emotional, and personality development* (pp. 25–104). New York, NY: John Wiley.

Thompson, R. A. (2006). The development of the person: Social understanding, relationship, conscience, self. In W. Damon, R. M. Lerner & N. Eisenberg

(Eds), *Handbook of child psychology, Sixth edition, Volume 3: Social, emotional, and personality development* (pp. 24–98). New York, NY: Wiley.

Thompson, R. A. (2016). Early attachmnet and later development: Reframing the questions. In J. Cassidy & P. R. Shaver (Eds), *Handbook of attachment: Theory, research, and clinical applications, Third edition* (pp. 330–348). New York, NY: Guilford Press.

Thorne, B. (1986). Boys and girls together, but mostly apart. In W. W. Hartup & Z. Rubin (Eds), *Relationship and development* (pp. 167–184). Hillsdale, NJ: Lawrence Erlbaum.

Todd, B. K., Barry, J. A., & Thommessen, S. A. (2017). Preferences for "gender-typed" toys in boys and girls aged 9 to 32 months. *Infant and Child Development, 26,* e1986.

Toomey, R. B., Card, N. A., & Casper, D. M. (2014). Peers' perceptions of gender nonconformity: Associations with overt and relational peer victimization and aggression in early adolescence. *The Journal of Early Adolescence, 34,* 463–485.

Torney-Purta, J. (1992). Cognitive representations of the political system in adolescents: The continuum from prenovice to expert. *New Directions for Child Development, 56,* 11–25.

Tracy, J. L., Cheng, J. T., Robins, R. W., & Trzesniewski, K. H. (2009). Authentic and hubristic pride: The affective core of self-esteem and narcissism. *Self and Identity, 8,* 196–213.

Trautner, H. M. (1992). The development of sex typing in children: A longitudinal analysis. *German Journal of Psychology, 16,* 183–199.

Trautwein, U., Lüdtke, O., Köller, O., & Baumert, J. (2006). Self-esteem, academic self-concept, and achievement: How the learning environment moderates the dynamics of self-concept. *Journal of Personality and Social Psychology, 90,* 334–349.

Trawick-Smith, J. (1989). Play is not learning: A critical review of the literature. *Child and Youth Care Quarterly, 18,* 161–170.

Tremblay-Leveau, H., & Nadel, J. (1996). Exclusion in triads: Can it serve "meta-communicative" knowledge in 11- and 23-month-old children? *British Journal of Developmental Psychology, 14,* 145–158.

Trionfi, G., & Reese, E. (2009). A good story: Children with imaginary companions create richer narratives. *Child Development, 80,* 1301–1313.

Tzampazi, F., Kyridis, A., & Christodoulou, A. (2013). "What will I be when I grow up? " Children's preferred future occupations and their stereotypical views. *International Journal of Social Science Research, 1,* 19–38.

Umaña-Taylor, A. J., Quintana, S. M., Lee, R. M., Cross, W. E., Rivas-Drake, D., Schwartz, S. J., Syed, M., Yip, T., Seaton, E., & Ethnic and Racial Identity in the 21st Century Study Group (2014). Ethnic and racial identity during adolescence and into young adulthood: An integrated conceptualization. *Child Development, 85,* 21–39.

Valerio, M., Amodio, P., Zio, M. D., Vianello, A., & Zacchello, G. P. (1997). The use of television in 2- to 8- year-old children and the attitude of parents about such use. *Archives of Pediatric and Adolescence Medicine, 151,* 22–26.

Valkenburg, P. M., & Peter, J. (2007). Preadolescents' and adolescents' online communication and their closeness to friends. *Developmental Psychology, 43,* 267–277.

Valkenburg, P. M., & Peter, J. (2009). Social consequences of the Internet for adolescents: A decade of research. *Current Directions in Psychological Science, 18,* 1–5.

Valkenburg, P. M., Sumter, S. R., & Peter, J. (2011). Gender differences in online and offline self-disclosure in pre-adolescence and adolescence. *British Journal of Developmental Psychology, 29,* 253–269.

van Aken, M. A. G., van Lieshout, C. F. M., & Haselager, G. J. T. (1996). Adolescents' competence and the mutuality of their self-descriptions and descriptions of them provided by others. *Journal of Youth and Adolescence, 25,* 285–306.

Vandell, D. L. (2004). Early child care: The known and the unknown. *Merrill-Palmer Quarterly, 50,* 387–414.

Vandell, D. L., Wilson, K. S., & Buchanan, N. R. (1980). Peer interaction in the first year of life: An examination of its structure, content, and sensitivity to toys. *Child Development, 51,* 481–488.

van dem Boom, D. C. (1989). Neonatal irritability and the development of attachment. In G. A. Kohnstamm, J. E. Bates & M. K. Rothbart (Eds), *Temperament in childhood* (pp. 299–318). Chichester, UK: John Wiley.

van den Eijnden, R. J. J. M., Spijkerman, R., Vermulst, A. A., van Rooij, T. J., & Engels, R. C. M. E. (2010). Compulsive internet use among adolescents: Bidirectional parent-child relationships. *Abnormal Child Psychology, 38,* 77–89.

van den Eijnden, R. J. J. M., Vermulst, A. A., van Rooij, A., Scholte, R., & van de Mheen, D. (2011). Online and real life victimisation and adolescents' psychosocial problems: What is the cause and what is the consequence? *Psychology and Health, 26,* 204–205.

Vandewater, E., Bickham, D., Lee, J., Cummings, H., Wartella, E., & Rideout, V. (2005). When the television is always on: Heavy television exposure and young children's development. *American Behavioral Scientist, 48,* 562–577.

Vatne, T. M., Helmen, I. Ø., Bahr, D., Kanavin, Ø., & Nyhus, L. (2015). "She came out of mum's tummy the wrong way" (Mis)conceptions among siblings of children with rare disorders. *Journal of Genetic Counseling, 24,* 247–258.

Vaughn, B. E., Bost, K. K., & van IJzendoorn, M. H. (2008). Attachment and temperament: Additive and interactive influences on behavior, affect, and cognition during infancy and childhood. In J. Cassidy & P. R. Shaver (Eds), *Handbook of attachment: Theory, research, and clinical applications, Second edition* (pp. 192–216). New York, NY: Guilford Press.

Veiga, G., Ketelaar, L., De Leng, W., Cachucho, R., Kok, J. N., Knobbe, A., Neto, C., & Rieffe, C. (2017). Alone at the playground. *European Journal of Developmental Psychology, 14,* 44–61.

Velez, J. A., Greitemeyer, T., Whitaker, J. L., Ewoldsen, D. R., & Bushman, B. J. (2016). Violent video games and reciprocity: The attenuating effects of cooperative game play on subsequent aggression. *Communication Research, 43,* 447–467.

Venuti, P., De Falco, S., Esposito, G., & Bornstein, M. H. (2009). Mother–child play: Children with Down syndrome and typical development. *American Journal on Intellectual and Developmental Disabilities, 114,* 274–288.

Vignoles, V. L., Schwartz, S. J., & Luyckx, K. (2011). Introduction: Toward an integrative view of identity. In S. J. Schwartz, K. Luyckx & V. L. Vignoles (Eds), *Handbook of identity theory and research* (pp. 1–28). New York, NY: Springer.

Vittrup, B., Snider, S., Rose, K. K., & Rippy, J. (2016). Parental perceptions of the role of media and technology in their young children's lives. *Journal of Early Childhood Research, 14,* 43–54.

Vogel, D. A., Lake, M. A., Evans, S., & Karraker, K. H. (1991). Children's and adults' sex-stereotyped perceptions of infants. *Sex Roles, 24,* 605–616.

von Tetzchner, S. (2004). Early intervention and prevention of challenging behaviour in children with learning disabilities. *Perspectives in Education, 22,* 85–100.

Vygotsky, L. S. (1967). Play and its role in the mental development of the child. *Soviet Psychology, 5,* 6–18.

Wang, Q. (2014). The cultured self and remembering. In P. Bauer & R. Fivush (Eds), *The Wiley handbook on the development of children's memory* (pp. 605–625). Malden, MA: Wiley.

Wängqvist, M., & Frisén, A. (2016). Who am I online? Understanding the meaning of online contexts for identity development. *Adolescent Research Review, 1,* 139–151.

Wartella, E., Rideout, V., Lauricella, A. R., & Connell, S. L. (2013). *Parenting in the age of digital technology. A national survey.* Evanston, IL: Center on Media and Human Development. School of Communication. Northwestern University.

Wartella, E., Beaudoin-Ryan, L., Blackwell, C. K., Cingel, D. P., Hurwitz, L. B., & Lauricella, A. R. (2016). What kind of adults will our children become? The impact of growing up in a media-saturated world. *Journal of Children and Media, 10,* 13–20.

Washington, K. (2007). Research review: Sibling placement in foster care: A review of the evidence. *Child and Family Social Work, 12,* 426–433.

Waters, E. (1995). Appendix A: The Attachment Q-Set (Version 3.0). *Monographs of the Society for Research in Child Development, 60,* 234–246.

Way, N., & Rogers, O. (2015). "They say black men won't make it, but I know I'm gonna make it": Ethnic and racial identity development in the context of cultural stereotypes. In K. McLean & M. Syed (Eds), *The Oxford handbook of identity development* (pp. 269–282). Oxford: Oxford University Press.

Webb, S., & Rodgers, M. P. H. (2009). Vocabulary demands of television programs. *Language Learning, 59,* 335–366.

Webley, P. (2005). Children's understanding of economics. In M. Barrett & E. Buchanan-Barrow (Eds), *Children's understanding of society* (pp. 43–65). New York, NY: Psychology Press.

Weisberg, D. S. (2015). Pretend play. *Wiley interdisciplinary reviews: Cognitive Science, 6*, 249–261.

Wentzel, K. R. (2009). Peer relationships and motivation at school. In K. Rubin, W. Bukowski, & B. Laursen (Eds), *Handbook on peer relationships* (pp. 531–547). New York, NY: Guilford Press.

Werner, H. (1948). *Comparative psychology of mental development, Revised edition.* New York, NY: International Universities Press.

Wiedeman, A. M., Black, J. A., Dolle, A. L., Finney, E. J., & Coker, K. L. (2015). Factors influencing the impact of aggressive and violent media on children and adolescents. *Aggression and Violent Behavior, 25*, 191–198.

Wilson, B. J., Smith, S. L., Potter, W. J., Kunkel, D., Linz, D., Colvin, C. M., & Donnerstein, E. (2002). Violence in children's television programming: Assessing the risks. *Journal of Communication, 52*, 5–35.

Wilson, E. O. (1998). *Consilience: The unity of knowledge.* New York, NY: Knopf.

Winnicott, D. W. (1960). The theory of parent–infant relationship. *International Journal of Psycho-Analysis, 41*, 585–595.

Winnicott, D. W. (1971). *Playing and reality.* London: Routledge.

Wong, W. I., & Hines, M. (2015). Preferences for pink and blue: The development of color preferences as a distinct gender-typed behavior in toddlers. *Archives of Sexual Behavior, 44*, 1243–1254.

Wong-Lo, M., & Bullock, L. M. (2011). Digital aggression: Cyberworld meets school bullies. *Preventing School Failure: Alternative Education for Children and Youth, 55*, 64–70.

Woolley, H. (2013). Now being social: The barrier of designing outdoor play spaces for disabled children. *Children and Society, 27*, 448–458.

World Health Organization (WHO) (2018). *The international statistical classification of diseases and related health problems, ICD-11.* Geneve, Switzerland: World Health Organization.

Worrell, F. C. (2015). Racial and ethnic identity. In C. M. Rubie-Davies, J. M. Stephens & P. Watson (Eds), *Routledge international handbook of social psychology of the classroom* (pp. 111–120). Abingdon, UK: Routledge.

Wridt, P. J. (2004). An historical analysis of young people's use of public space, parks and playgrounds in New York City. *Children Youth and Environments, 14*, 86–106.

Wright, J. C., Huston, A. C., Murphy, K. C., Peters, M. S., Pinon, M., Scantlin, R., & Kotler, J. (2001). The relations of early television viewing to school readiness and vocabulary of children from low-income families: The early window project. *Child Development, 72*, 1347–1366.

Wyn, J. (2004). Becoming adult in the 2000s. *Family Matters, 68*, 6–12.

Yan, Z. (2018). Child and adolescent use of mobile phones: An unparalleled complex developmental phenomenon. *Child Development, 89*, 5–16.

Yu, M., & Baxter, J. (2016). Australian children's screen time and participation in extracurricular activities. In *The Longitudinal Study of Australian Children Annual Statistical Report 2015* (pp. 99–125). Melbourne: AIFS.

Zeanah, C. H., & Gleason, M. M. (2015). Annual research review: Attachment disorders in early childhood–clinical presentation, causes, correlates, and treatment. *Journal of Child Psychology and Psychiatry, 56,* 207–222.

Zeanah, C. H., & Smyke, A. T. (2015). Disorders of attachment and social engagement related to deprivation. In A. Thapar, D. S. Pine, J. F. Leckman, S. Scott, M. J. Snowling & E. Taylor (Eds), *Rutter's child and adolescent psychiatry, Sixth edition* (pp. 793–805). London: Wiley-Blackwell.

Zeanah, C. H., Scheeringa, M., Boris, N. W., Heller, S. S., Smyke, A. T., & Trapani, J. (2004). Reactive attachment disorder in maltreated toddlers. *Child Abuse and Neglect, 28,* 877–888.

Zeigler-Hill, V. (2011). The connections between self-esteem and psychopathology. *Journal of Contemporary Psychotherapy, 41,* 157–164.

Zimmer-Gembeck, M. J., Webb, H. J., Pepping, C. A., Swan, K., Merlo, O., Skinner, E. A., Avdagic, E., & Dunbar, M. (2017). Is parent–child attachment a correlate of children's emotion regulation and coping? *International Journal of Behavioral Development, 41,* 74–93.

Zimmerman, F., Christakis, D., & Meltzoff, A. (2007) Associations between media viewing and language development in children under age 2 years. *Journal of Pediatrics, 4,* 364–368.

Zosuls, K. M., Andrews, N. C., Martin, C. L., England, D. E., & Field, R. D. (2016). Developmental changes in the link between gender typicality and peer victimization and exclusion. *Sex Roles, 75,* 243–256.

Zosuls, K. M., Ruble, D. N., Tamis-LeMonda, C. S., Shrout, P. E., Bornstein, M. H., & Greulich, F. K. (2009). The acquisition of gender labels in infancy: Implications for gender-typed play. *Developmental Psychology, 45,* 688–701.

Zucker, K. J., & Seto, M. C. (2015). Gender dysphoria and paraphilic sexual disorders. In A. Thapar, D. S. Pine, F. S. Leckman, S. Scott, M. J. Snowling & E. Taylor (Eds), *Rutter's child and adolescent psychiatry, Sixth edition* (pp. 981–998). Oxford: Wiley.

Zucker, K. J., Wood, H., & VanderLaan, D. P. (2014). Models of psychopathology in children and adolescents with gender dysphoria. In B. P. C. Kreukels, T. D. Steensma & A. L. C. de Vries (Eds), *Gender dysphoria and disorders of sex development: Progress in care and knowledge* (pp. 171–192). New York, NY: Springer.

Index

Locators in *italics* refer to figures and those in **bold** to tables.

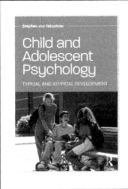

The **Topics from Child and Adolescent Psychology Series** is drawn from Stephen von Tetzchner's comprehensive textbook for all students of developmental psychology, *Child and Adolescent Psychology: Typical and Atypical Development*

Table of Contents

Praise for *Child and Adolescent Psychology: Typical and Atypical Development*

'An extensive overview of the field of developmental psychology. It illustrates how knowledge about typical and atypical development can be integrated and used to highlight fundamental processes of human growth and maturation.'

Dr. John Coleman, *PhD, OBE, UK*

'A broad panoply of understandings of development from a wide diversity of perspectives and disciplines, spanning all the key areas, and forming a comprehensive, detailed and extremely useful text for students and practitioners alike.'

Dr. Graham Music, *Consultant Psychotherapist,*
Tavistock Clinic London, UK

'An extraordinary blend of depth of scholarship with a lucid, and engaging, writing style. Its coverage is impressive . . . Both new and advanced students will love the coverage of this text.'

Professor Joseph Campos, *University of California, USA*

'Encyclopedic breadth combined with an unerring eye for the central research across developmental psychology, particularly for the period of its explosive growth since the 1960s. Both a text and a reference work, this will be the go-to resource for any teacher, researcher or student of the discipline for the foreseeable future.'

Professor Andy Lock, *University of Lisbon, Portugal*

It is accompanied by a companion website featuring chapter summaries, glossary, quizzes and instructor resources.

www.ingramcontent.com/pod-product-compliance
Ingram Content Group UK Ltd.
Pitfield, Milton Keynes, MK11 3LW, UK
UKHW020347010325
455677UK00020B/329